MW01252741

Titles include:

Leslie Elliott Armijo (*editor*)
FINANCIAL GLOBALIZATION AND DEMOCRACY IN EMERGING MARKETS

Eudine Barriteau
THE POLITICAL ECONOMY OF GENDER IN THE TWENTIETH-CENTURY
CARIBBEAN

Esteban R. Brenes and Jerry Haar (*editors*)
THE FUTURE OF ENTREPRENEURSHIP IN LATIN AMERICA

Gabriel G. Casaburi
DYNAMIC AGROINDUSTRIAL CLUSTERS
The Political Economy of Competitive Sectors in Argentina and Chile

Peter Clegg
THE CARIBBEAN BANANA TRADE
From Colonialism to Globalization

Matt Davies
INTERNATIONAL POLITICAL ECONOMY AND MASS COMMUNICATION IN
CHILE
National Intellectuals and Transnational Hegemony

Yvon Grenier
THE EMERGENCE OF INSURGENCY IN EL SALVADOR
Ideology and Political Will

Ivelaw L. Griffith (*editor*)
THE POLITICAL ECONOMY OF DRUGS IN THE CARIBBEAN

Jerry Haar and Anthony T. Bryan (*editors*)
CANADIAN–CARIBBEAN RELATIONS IN TRANSITION
Trade, Sustainable Development and Security

Tricia Juhn
NEGOTIATING PEACE IN EL SALVADOR
Civil–Military Relations and the Conspiracy to End the War

Richard G. Lipsey and Patricio Meller (*editors*)
WESTERN HEMISPHERE TRADE INTEGRATION
A Canadian–Latin American Dialogue

Gordon Mace, Andrew F. Cooper and Timothy M. Shaw (*editors*)
INTER-AMERICAN COOPERATION AT A CROSSROADS

Don Marshall
CARIBBEAN POLITICAL ECONOMY AT THE CROSSROADS
NAFTA and Regional Developmentalism

Juan Antonio Morales and Gary McMahon (*editors*)
ECONOMIC POLICY AND THE TRANSITION TO DEMOCRACY
The Latin American Experience

Manuela Nilsson and Jan Gustafsson (*editors*)
LATIN AMERICAN RESPONSES TO GLOBALIZATION IN THE 21st CENTURY

Leo Panitch and Martijn Konings (*editors*)
AMERICAN EMPIRE AND THE POLITICAL ECONOMY OF GLOBAL FINANCE

Eul-Soo Pang
THE INTERNATIONAL POLITICAL ECONOMY OF TRANSFORMATION IN
ARGENTINA, BRAZIL, AND CHILE SINCE 1960

Julia Sagebien and Nicole Marie Lindsay (*editors*)
GOVERNANCE ECOSYSTEMS
CSR in the Latin American Mining Sector

Henry Veltmeyer, James Petras and Steve Vieux
NEOLIBERALISM AND CLASS CONFLICT IN LATIN AMERICA
A Comparative Perspective on the Political Economy of Structural Adjustment

Henry Veltmeyer and James Petras
THE DYNAMICS OF SOCIAL CHANGE IN LATIN AMERICA

Christopher Wylde
LATIN AMERICA AFTER NEOLIBERALISM
Developmental Regimes in Post-Crisis States

International Political Economy Series
Series Standing Order ISBN 978–0–333–71708–0 hardcover
Series Standing Order ISBN 978–0–333–71110–1 paperback
(*outside North America only*)

You can receive future titles in this series as they are published by placing a
standing order. Please contact your bookseller or, in case of difficulty, write to us
at the address below with your name and address, the title of the series and one
of the ISBNs quoted above.

Customer Services Department, Macmillan Distribution Ltd, Houndmills,
Basingstoke, Hampshire RG21 6XS, England

Latin America After Neoliberalism

Developmental Regimes in Post-Crisis States

Christopher Wylde
Teaching Fellow, University of York, UK

First published 2012 by
PALGRAVE MACMILLAN

Palgrave Macmillan in the UK is an imprint of Macmillan Publishers Limited, registered in England, company number 785998, of Houndmills, Basingstoke, Hampshire RG21 6XS.

Palgrave Macmillan in the US is a division of St Martin's Press LLC, 175 Fifth Avenue, New York, NY 10010.

Palgrave Macmillan is the global academic imprint of the above companies and has companies and representatives throughout the world.

Palgrave® and Macmillan® are registered trademarks in the United States, the United Kingdom, Europe and other countries.

ISBN 978–0–230–30159–7

This book is printed on paper suitable for recycling and made from fully managed and sustained forest sources. Logging, pulping and manufacturing processes are expected to conform to the environmental regulations of the country of origin.

A catalogue record for this book is available from the British Library.

A catalog record for this book is available from the Library of Congress.

10   9   8   7   6   5   4   3   2   1
21   20   19   18   17   16   15   14   13   12

Printed and bound in the United States of America

For Carmen

Contents

List of Tables and Figures

Tables

Figures

Preface

This book is the product of two major field trips to Latin America, the first in 2007 and the second in 2011. While attempts have been made to cite specific interview evidence where possible, due to ethical considerations not all material has been directly cited. Nevertheless, this primary material has been triangulated and cross-referenced with the existing literature on the subject, which has proliferated in recent years. The book attempts to both complement and develop this corpus of literature. In terms of its case studies, the detailed analysis of Kirchner's Argentina and Lula's Brazil should provide up-to-date analysis of those regimes. In terms of its theoretical framework, not only will this help develop a more nuanced understanding of those case studies but also of the region as a whole. The relatively broad-brush approach that has been used for a wider regional analysis beyond that of the specific case studies of Argentina and Brazil has the advantage of facilitating an ability to discern broad trends, while at the same time it has the disadvantage of glossing over the nuance and rich contextual detail of specific country analysis. The theoretical framework also represents an attempt to move beyond traditional models of capital accumulation in the academic field of political economy, reviving a model first developed by T. J. Pempel of Cornell University and (re)working it into a Latin American context. I hope that this has facilitated both a new and (re)invigorated understanding of both the subject and the object of study, that is, of Latin America, and of the theory of the Developmental Regime itself. This could potentially open up new avenues of enquiry that will further our understanding of different models of political economy and thus of economic crisis and successful post-crisis development strategy – two questions whose efficacy is of both continued and heightened importance in today's world.

I would like to thank all those who contributed directly to this book through interviews, reading of drafts, and helpful comments along the way. Due to the large amount of help that I have received, these individuals are far too numerous to name individually. I would also like to thank my series editor, Tim Shaw, comments from anonymous reviewer(s), and the editorial team at Palgrave Macmillan for their efficiency and professionalism.

List of Acronyms

ABDI	Agência Brasileira de Desenvolvimento Industrial
ACC	Advanced Capitalist Country
ALBA	Alianza Bolivariana para los Pueblos de Nuestra América
BCB	Banco Central do Brasil
BRIC	Brazil, Russia, India, China
BRICS	Brazil, Russia, India, China, South Africa
CDES	Conselho de Desenvolvinedo Economi e Social
CEPAL	La Comisión Económica para América Latina
CCT	Conditional Cash Transfer
CGT	Confederación General de Trabajo
CTA	Confederación de Trabajadores Argentina
CPI	Consumer Price Index
CUT	Central Geral dos Trabalhadores
ECLA	Economic Commission for Latin America
ECLAC	Economic Commission for Latin America and the Caribbean
EMNC	Emerging Multinational Corporation
EOI	Export-Orientated Industrialisation
EU	European Union
FARC	Revolutionary Armed Forces of Colombia
FDI	Foreign Direct Investment
FHC	Fernando Henrique Cardoso
GDP	Gross Domestic Product
GFCF	Gross Fixed Capital Formation
GNI	Gross National Income
HDR	Human Development Report
IFI	International Financial Institution
IMF	International Monetary Fund

IR	International Relations
ISI	Import Substituting Industrialisation
LAC	Latin America and Caribbean
LDC	Less Developed Country
LOC	Left of Centre
MERCOSUR	Mercado Común Del Sur
NGO	Non-governmental Organisation
NIC	Newly Industrialised Country
NIE	New Institutional Economics
NTB	Non-tariff Barrier
PAC	Programa de Aceleração do Crescimento
PACTI	Plano de Ação em Ciência, Tecnologia e Inovação para o Desenvolvimento Nacional
PFI	Public Finance Initiative
PIG	Portugal, Ireland, Greece
PIIG	Portugal, Ireland, Italy, Greece
PIGS	Portugal, Ireland, Greece, Spain
PITCE	Política Industrial e de Comércio Exterior
PJ	Partido Justicialista
PRSP	Poverty Reduction Strategy Paper
PT	Partido Trabalhadores
PyME	Pequeño y Mediano Empresa
REER	Real Effective Exchange Rate
RER	Real Exchange Rate
SAP	Structural Adjustment Programme
SCRER	Stable and Competitive Real Exchange Rate
SMC	Social Market Capitalism
SME	Small and Medium Enterprise
SOE	State-owned Enterprise
TARP	Troubled Asset Relief Fund
TFP	Total Factor Productivity
TNC	Transnational Corporation

UK	United Kingdom
UNDP	United Nations Development Programme
US	United States
USA	United States of America
VISTA	Vietnam, Indonesia, South Africa, Turkey, Argentina
WDR	World Development Report
WTO	World Trade Organization

1
Introduction: The Political Economy of Development and Crisis

In an article in 2004 William Robinson wrote that in the early twenty-first century global capitalism was in crisis, based on the twin edifices of a structural crisis of overaccumulation and a subjective crisis of legitimacy (Robinson, 2004). The attacks on the twin towers in New York had given capitalist globalisation a 'new and terrifying coercive dimension' and the 'new war order' emerging from this was only going to aggravate the dimensions of this crisis (Robinson, 2004: 150). What Robinson could not have known in 2004 was that this perceived crisis in the periphery would be superseded by an even larger crisis of the neoliberal model of accumulation in the core in 2007 – tentatively labelled 'The Great Recession'.

In the summer of 2007 problems in the global financial architecture began to manifest themselves in the form of paralysis in global inter-bank credit markets. The full extent of this 'credit crunch' did not become apparent until the collapse of a number of key institutions in the global financial structure – the giant US mortgage banks Fannie May and Freddie Mac, the largest insurance company in the world AIG, and the bankruptcy of Lehman Brothers in September 2008. These collapses 'triggered a wave of bank insolvencies and rescues around the world, and rapidly led to a general collapse of business and consumer confidence' (Radice, 2011: 21). The fallout of these collapses led to governments stepping in to bailout institutions that were 'too big to fail', combined with provision of liquidity by central banks across the world through first dropping interest rates to at or near zero per cent and then through a programme of 'quantitative easing' (the creation of money through central banks buying government bonds with newly issued money). This policy was combined with attempts to remove 'toxic debt' from banks balance sheets through government purchase, the largest of which was the US government's US$700 billion Troubled Asset Relief Fund (TARP) (for a step-by-step chronology of the crisis, see Gamble, 2009: 23).

These measures prevented the total meltdown of the global economy, but did not prevent the arrival of a global recession. Sharp falls in output, investment, and employment were seen in the US and Europe through 2009. Across the rest of the world there was a more mixed picture. The banking systems in many less advanced economies were much less implicated in the over-lending and speculation that preceded the credit crunch (Radice, 2011: 22), but as demand from many Advanced Capitalist Countries (ACCs) collapsed as a result of recession, key sources of growth for these developing economies dried up.

At the time of writing this book (mid-2011) a tentative recovery is discernible at the global level. However, many of the ACCs are plagued by weak or anaemic growth, high levels of unemployment, large budget deficits, and huge debt/GDP ratios as a result of bailing out the financial sector. The post-crisis world order that will emerge is still unknown. What is known is that the developing world has weathered the storm much better than the ACCs of the core. After mild recession many returned to robust growth soon after, in contrast to the US and much of Europe. In Latin America, the core area of study in this book, many countries rebounded from recession in 2009 to record growth in 2010 that was broadly in line with trends present before the onset of the global crisis.

The contemporary debate that dominates the agenda in the ACCs concerns a dichotomy between retrenchments of the Anglo-Saxon model versus a reassertion of productive over financial capital in the global economy, a form of global (neo)Keynesianism pushed by reformist elements in the core. However, in the periphery, the debate is much wider, and the experimentation with alternative policy tool kits and models of capitalist accumulation more active. In Latin America the twenty-first century has seen the rise of a pink tide, characterised by left and left-of-centre regimes taking control of state apparatuses and engaging in different forms of capital accumulation and models of participation outside the dichotomy between neoliberalism and Social Market Capitalism (SMC). Latin America has often been a laboratory for experiments on the best method of organising an economy, 'but that laboratory has often been a battlefield' (Kingstone, 2011: 128). Rejection of the neoliberal model as a result of economic and legitimacy crises across the continent in the 1980s and 1990s paved the way for a revitalisation of key areas of development studies, such as the relationship between the state and the market – or the public and private spheres – the relationship between politics and economics, and the possibilities of national development in an era marked by the phenomena of globalisation.

The central thesis of this book is that this revitalisation and subsequent experiments in neodevelopmentalism represent a coherent form of political economy, which can be characterised within a Developmental Regime (Pempel, 1998, 1999) framework. Contrary to accounts that highlight the continuity of Argentine political economy with the corporatism and clientelism of its Peronist past, or the continuity of Brazilian political economy with the neoliberalism of Fernando Henrique Cardoso (hereafter FHC), this book suggests in Part I that Latin America has witnessed the rise of a new model of capital accumulation. In this context, this new approach faces concerted opposition not only in the world of politics and policy but also in academia. Neoclassical sectors suggest that the development results of these experiments can be disputed, especially in the longer term, while the radical left criticise the supposed continuity with old neoliberal policies (Boschi and Gaitán, 2009: 14). In Part II it examines this claim more closely with a detailed study of the rise of Left of Centre (LOC) regimes in Argentina and Brazil in post-crisis contexts. The new model of capital accumulation present in both these cases possesses elements of both continuity and change with previous forms of political economy within the region. What emerges is a new domestic configuration of state–market and state–society relationships, as well as how those relationships intersect with global capital.

These configurations can be characterised within a Developmental Regime framework, a model of political economy derived from Pempel (1998, 1999) that is outlined in detail in Chapter 3, and applied specifically to the post-crisis regimes present in Argentina in Chapter 5 and Brazil in Chapter 7. This framework can trace its intellectual heritage to the Developmental State literature, but departs from and builds upon it in important ways. While state–market relations can be seen to be very similar, state–society relations are qualitatively different from those present in the corpus of material present in the traditional Developmental State literature. In addition, in an era of globalisation, the role of international economic forces is fully integrated into the model in order to provide a complete understanding of all the pressures placed on the modern state.

Too often Latin America has been a country of extremes in terms of political economy, swinging from the left of Import Substituting

Industrialisation (ISI) to the right of the Washington Consensus in the twentieth century. The new Developmental Regime discourse recognises the importance of good governance and macroeconomic stability, while at the same time acknowledging the role of the state in terms of the promotion of development – although in a more limited sense than associated with the classical structuralist position (Pereira, 2010). Key to this new configuration is the role of international trade, given the context of globalisation. Therefore, a key discussion throughout this book will be the role of trade in forging this new development paradigm in terms of export promotion, diversification, and the thesis of 'decoupling' in the sense of Latin American states constructing a path to development independent of ACCs, something that in its economic history has been anathema.

The second argument that this book advances is that due to the robustness by which these economies have emerged from the latest crisis of capital accumulation the Developmental Regime demonstrates a viable alternative to both neoliberalism and SMC as a successful model for development and post-crisis political economy. This will be demonstrated by the strength that both Argentina and Brazil emerged from their respective crises, Argentina in 2001–2 and Brazil in 1998 and 2003. In addition, Part III will demonstrate how these new regimes have survived the exogenous shock of the global financial crisis that originated in the United States and spread quickly to other ACCs and then across the whole world as these countries entered recession. While both countries were no doubt impacted by the crisis, as was every country in the world, Argentina and Brazil (as well as Latin America more broadly) have emerged from the crisis stronger than most.

The role of crisis in providing both the political space and impetus for changes in models of capital accumulation provides the third thread; articulated specifically in Chapters 5 and 7 with regard to Argentina and Brazil respectively, and argued generally and theoretically in Chapter 9. These chapters will demonstrate that crisis in Argentina and Brazil facilitated the political impetus to stimulate new perspectives among political and business elites. Downturns frequently destroy equilibria, opening up space for alternative ideas and allowing new battles to be fought by their competing domestic and international advocates (MacIntyre, Pempel, and Ravenhill, 2008: 3). In particular, the crises in these countries led to a questioning of former models of capital accumulation, especially those models that dominated the years up to the crisis, namely neoliberalism. However, as the analysis of this book will demonstrate, change was not simply a return to old models of ISI and populism. Rather, a new model was articulated, one that possesses elements of continuity as well as change with both pre-crisis neoliberalism and more historical forms of political economy. In addition, this book will look at the dichotomy between international and domestic sources of change, or the 'foreign–domestic faultline' in crisis outcomes (Robertson, 2008a: 2). There are competing narratives on whether foreigners capitalise on crises in developing countries based on either the primacy of domestic or international processes (Robertson, 2008a: 2). It is a popular belief among polities, the media, and areas of academia that developing economies are often pushed towards undesirable structural change in the wake of economic crisis. This book will suggest that this stereotype need not necessarily be true, and will problematise the concept of undesirable change through detailed analysis of both Argentina and Brazil – showing that domestically driven change has led to highly successful post-crisis changes in their models of capital accumulation both in terms of economic and social recovery and resistance to future crises in the capitalist system. However, these domestically driven changes have been shaped and moulded by international constraints, that is, by the processes of contemporary globalisation. Furthermore, this domestically driven change has supplanted previous periods of post-crisis change in the region that were driven by international actors (the Latin American debt crisis of the 1980s representing the most obvious example).

Definitions

Before proceeding further a number of definitions of terms must first be offered. The definition of political economy in this book is the role and particular ensemble of policies/structures/institutions, as well as how they are regulated, within a specified economy, usually associated with a specific national economy although one can also talk of a global or an international economy. If standard economics is about what individuals do (Krugman, 1996: 2), then political economy is about social classes, states, and 'correlations of forces' (Palan, 2000: 9).

The definition of development is more problematic. Understandings of what development is, and development studies more broadly, are varied, multiple, and contentious (Kothari, 2005: 3). Furthermore, an opinion on what development is has implications for what development studies should be doing. Thomas (2004) outlines three major interpretations of development, and the subsequent implications for the discipline of development studies. The first views development as 'visions or measures of progressive change', and therefore development studies is about debating what is desirable or progressive for society, understanding human needs and measuring dimensions of poverty and 'development' (philosophy, psychology, economics, statistics etc.). The second view is that development is an 'historical change process' and therefore development studies is more about knowing about lives, livelihoods, social relations etc. in different parts of the world, and how they have changed. The third interpretation of development views it as a 'deliberate effort at progress', and is therefore concerned with types of development agency, concepts of trusteeship, accountability, and understanding the architecture of policy and governance both locally and globally (Thomas, 2004).

This book associates itself closest with the second view, that of development as a process of 'historical change'. The implications are that this book is interested in knowing about social relations in Latin America (Argentina and Brazil more specifically) and how they have changed. This is to be conducted in the context of debating and applying theories of social change at local and global levels in order to make sense of and understand any change that is quantitatively or qualitatively deduced.

A final definition that must be clarified is that of Latin America. There is no clear or set definition of this term within existing scholarship, with some including the Caribbean or Central America to those countries of South America. While this book clearly focuses on the two detailed case studies of Argentina and Brazil, the analysis also extends to other countries within the continent. This analysis is largely focused on other Southern Cone[1] countries (Chile, Uruguay, and Paraguay), although at times extends to other countries in the Americas where Spanish or Portuguese is spoken. Analysis of Caribbean economies does not form part of this book. This is largely a reflection of the geography by which leftist governments have been elected across the continent. Mexico as well cannot be drawn into the analysis of this book due to its geographical proximity to the US and the subsequent economic implications. Another exception to the general analysis would be Colombia, the only South American country that has not elected a leftist president since the start of the pink tide in 1998. A final important distinction to make would be between those countries where the political right has regained power since the global financial crisis, namely Chile, El Salvador, and Honduras – thus creating one group of countries that has seen a shift in power post-crisis (García-Sayán, 2009: 26).

The role of theory in analysis

The study of the political economy of development concerns transformations in the social system (Heymann et al., 2006: 33). Tracking such processes and representing them in a precise way not only requires detailed analysis of events and policies, but also effective interpretation. Therefore, the role of theory for the purposes of this book is to facilitate holistic analysis and interpretation of otherwise apparently disconnected series of events. Furthermore, theory allows analysis to move beyond spatially and temporally specific events and thus facilitates comparative reflections (in the context of the political economy of development) on patterns of production, consumption, and distribution. Such reflections produce heuristic devices that enrich any attempts to characterise specific Developmental Regimes.

The main approach and thrust of this book is therefore theoretical. The empirical focus on continuity and change in the post-crisis administrations of Néstor Kirchner 2003–7 and Lula's Brazil 2003–10 in Part II represents a starting point. Such analysis is important to facilitate complex understandings of the inter-relationship of important variables present in the character and make-up of post-crisis Argentina and Brazil. However, the application of meta-theory to such analysis facilitates deeper understanding, and allows the specific constellation of production, consumption, and distribution present to be placed in the broader context of both Latin America (Chapter 2) and the global economy (Chapter 8) more widely. There is therefore a symbiotic relationship present, with both the specific contexts of Argentina and Brazil, and the general consideration of meta-theoretical narratives being enriched by such an analysis. Furthermore, in applying such theoretical explanations to the administrations of Néstor Kirchner and Lula, further avenues of enquiry can be pursued in the field of comparative political economy. The contributions of this book to both the study of contemporary Argentina and Brazil specifically and Latin America more widely, and the broader study of meta-theory in the field of political economy of development, will be discussed further in the concluding chapter.

In this study of the political economy of development such heuristic devices must be drawn from the discipline of political economy as a whole. The dominant *economic* ideology of the early twentieth century sought to restrict both economic reality and economic thinking though a separation of politics from economics. Subsequent critiques of laissez-faire capitalism, most notably the birth of Keynesian economics, showed that the free market economy may not be able to achieve an optimal resource allocation at the full employment level of output, thus justifying the practice of active budgetary policy; this required that economics as a discipline (re)acknowledge the role of the state, thereby (re)opening the possibility of the study of *political* economy. In the quarter-century after World War II (the 'Golden Age of Capitalism') interventionist policies were highly successful across the world, and firmly established the state as an important and often leading actor in the functioning of the economy. In the ACCs this led to Keynesianism or SMC, and in the less developed countries (LDCs) to even more intervention due to the influence of dependency and structuralism. The collapse of the 'Golden Age' from the late 1960s onwards in the ACCs, and the 1980s in LDCs, paved the way for the monetarist critique of Keynesianism and later the rise of neoliberalism. The neoliberal revival represented a partial return to the nineteenth century laissez-faire tradition, supplemented by an emphasis on the limited transferability of knowledge and the role of entrepreneurship.

How should these shifts in the meanings and interpretations of political economy be accounted for? One way to do this is to 'treat this kind of genealogy of development discourse as a deconstruction of development, i.e. as part of a development critique' (Pieterse, 2000: 199). Thus, each development theory offers 'a *Gestalt* of development, a total picture from a particular angle, then the array of successive and rival development theories offers a kaleidoscopic view into the collective mirror' (Pieterse, 2000: 200). The main contours of development thinking can be mapped across different periods, and furthermore can be placed in the context of the pattern of hegemony in international relations and the structures of explanation prevalent at that time. Development thinking and policy, then, is a terrain of hegemony and counter-hegemony (Pieterse, 2000: 201).

The plan of the book

This introductory chapter has offered a general overview of the arguments that will be presented in detail in subsequent chapters. As well as clearly setting out definitions of key issues that will be used throughout the analysis of the book, it has provided a contribution on the role of theory in analysis. This is in order to demonstrate how this book intends to use theory to symbiotically inform both analysis of contemporary (international) political economy (especially in the context of post-crisis Latin America), as well as help further inform and develop theory itself so that more robust hermeneutical devices can be added to a researcher's tool kit for future research agendas.

Part I of the book will then begin with Chapter 2, offering a general interpretation of the rise of the so-called pink tide in Latin America in the twenty-first century. This interpretation will provide the necessary contextual background to begin an examination of existing meta-theoretical narratives in the political economy of development in order to help interpretation of this phenomenon, and therefore develop greater understanding. In the developed world, neoliberalism and SMC are the two dominant models offered. In the developing world, dependency and its subsequent reformulation (through several stages) into Developmental State theory or Developmental Regime theory are the most salient in terms of challenging the hegemonic discourse. Such a characterisation does not always line up so neatly however, as neoliberalism in particular has also been used extensively in terms of developing economies. This chapter will therefore offer a stylised account of these theories, which will underlie subsequent analysis throughout the book. Further analysis will then investigate how these different theoretical approaches to political economy manifest themselves in real development processes. This, in turn, will provide an extra layer of analysis to the case studies presented in Part II and, through a grounded theoretical approach, provide a deeper understanding of the processes of development present during these administrations.

This will be undertaken through an examination of three related dichotomies: the 'state–market' dichotomy, the 'national–international' dichotomy, and the 'state–society' dichotomy, in relation to each of the main bodies of theoretical thinking present in the field of political economy. These three 'developmental dichotomies' are appropriate due to the nature of contemporary world order in an era of globalisation. The state–market dichotomy encompasses an important debate present throughout the history of political economy about the nature of government intervention in the market, and therefore in the development process. This analysis is complemented by the state–society debate, which seeks to understand how domestic society interacts with the state in order to produce government policies that influence the developmental process. Finally the national–international dichotomy is important as it recognises the role and influence of international capital in the development process in an era of globalisation, influences that often interact with the other dichotomies to produce results that can only be understood when all three are considered jointly in the analysis. The chapter will suggest that traditional forms of political economy present in the history of Latin America are inadequate for capturing the exact nature of contemporary processes in the political economy of the pink tide. Therefore, theories of populism, dependency, (neo)liberalism, and SMC must all be rejected.

This rejection sets the stage for Chapter 3, which will construct an appropriate theory for understanding twenty-first century Latin American political economy. This meta-theoretical task will show that the Developmental Regime (Pempel, 1998, 1999), a reformulation of traditional Developmental State analyses, offers the best way forward for achieving this task. Due to the historical roots of this theory resting in Asia, and its use to first characterise the Asian Tiger Economies, lessons from this part of the world will be used to inform the analysis.

Having established an appropriate theoretical interpretation of the contemporary nature of Latin America's left turn, Part II of the book will look at this in much greater detail through country-level studies. Chapters 4 and 5 will analyse Argentina, laying out in detail the economic policies of the Kirchner administration (2003–7) in Chapter 4 and contextualising these within a broader political economy analysis in Chapter 5, concluding that greater analytical clarity is gained through the deployment of a Developmental Regime framework. Chapters 6 and 7 offer a similar exercise for Lula's Brazil (2003–10). In their totality, the case studies of Part II will form a more detailed and nuanced empirical basis for the assertions made in Part I – that there is such a thing as a pink tide in twenty-first century Latin American political economy, and that such a tide can be interpreted through a Developmental Regime framework.

Part III of the book then moves the debate forward to the wider regional and global implications of such conclusions. Chapter 8 will therefore begin with a stylised account of a series of economic global crises, moving from Mexico to Asia to Russia, then Brazil, again to Argentina and once again back to Brazil, then finally to the contemporary global financial crisis. After a direct analysis of the impacts of these events on the political economy of Argentina and Brazil compared to the ACCs the chapter will compare and contrast these thoughts, concluding that the Developmental Regime offers a viable development strategy for post-crisis states.

Chapter 9 will conclude the book by summarising the arguments presented in the context of continuity and change in a post-crisis political economy. The development of the main thesis of this book contains a number of important stages that will be explicitly addressed. Firstly, that there is such a phenomena as a rise of a pink tide in Latin America. Second, that such a rise can best be characterised within a Developmental Regime framework. Third, this framework demonstrates a more viable and robust alternative to other forms of post-crisis strategy (ones that revolve around neoliberalism or SMC for example) in facilitating renewed economic growth and development. This final conclusion will create a closing discussion in the book, which will examine the potential for the model developed to be used in the rest of the BRIC (and beyond the BRIC to perhaps the VISTA countries) in order to facilitate more sustained development vis-à-vis the ACCs, which are arguably entering a period of relative trans-Atlantic decline (along with Japan), mired in anaemic growth with economies orientated towards either Anglo-Saxon models, or Keynesian SMC models. Such an examination will facilitate identification of both limitations of the analysis and new avenues of enquiry, allowing for articulation of a future research agenda.

Part I
Comparative Theoretical Perspectives and Debates

2
The Rise of Developmentalism in Latin America: Beyond the Washington Consensus?

Contemporary literature on Latin America has often addressed the central theme of the rise of the so-called pink tide. This catch-all term has been used to characterise the rise of left or LOC regimes across the continent. Therefore, Latin Americanists now analyse regimes such as Lula (and Dilma Rousseff) in Brazil, the Kirchners in Argentina, Tabaré Vasquez in Uruaguay, Michelle Bachelet in Chile, Evo Morales in Bolivia, Hugo Chávez in Venezuela, Daniel Ortega in Nicaragua, Alan García in Peru, Lugo (the 'Red Bishop') in Paraguay, Mauricio Funes in El Salvador, and Rafael Correa in Ecuador. This is in stark contrast to earlier decades, where individuals such as Alberto Fujimori, Carlos Menem, Carlos Andrés Pérez, Gonzalo Sànchez de Lozada, and FHC ruled across Latin America. The criteria and content of this rise of the pink tide has been concerned with the nature and degree of state intervention, policies for reforming governance and democracy, the scale and content of welfare programmes, the degree of equality – especially in terms of income and wealth, and regional and international policy stances (Lievesley and Ludlam, 2009a: 5). Many of these left or LOC regimes mentioned previously have been experimenting in these areas in ways that represent radical or reformist deviations from neoliberalism, a form of political economy that dominated the continent in the 1980s and 1990s.

At the same time, this 'new left' has been less radical than the governments of the left in the earlier part of the twentieth century due to the fact that they have forgone a comprehensive, systematic assault on capitalist property relations (Weyland, 2010: 3). As Weyland (2010: 7) goes on to say, '[t]he radical position cuts the Gordian knot of economic and political constraints with the sword of revolutionary violence'. Instead, this book argues that the left and LOC governments of twenty-first century Latin America have chosen a more moderate path, sensitive to the constraints placed on it by both domestic society and an international system dominated by the interests of capital. It is therefore a mode of government that claims to build on the mistakes of both neoliberalism and twentieth-century socialism, seeking to increase state regulation and power but in a democratic manner that allocates resources more efficiently and does not stifle innovation or personal choice (Kenmore and Weeks, 2011: 267).

Leiva (2008) suggests that this alternative development path has been shaped by Latin American neostructuralism, first developed by CEPAL in 1990.[1] However, many journalistic reports, both right-wing accounts and also some left-wing analyses, 'over-romanticise developments' (Lievesley and Ludlam, 2009a: 5) and often present the pink tide as a homogenous force, with the whole Latin American continent uniformly shifting the political economy of the region to the left. Such accounts are mistaken, and the different movements across the continent represent a wide array of approaches and diversity of policy (Kingstone, 2011: 92–3). Therefore, the policy mix present in Bolivia, for example, demonstrates fundamental differences with that in Argentina. The radical policies of Venezuela stand in contrast to those Brazil. As a result, '[e]ven though all these cases can certainly be viewed as part and parcel of a general leftist turn in Latin America, there is little doubt that each country is a case of its own' (Tavolaro and Tavolaro, 2007: 426). Indeed, Lievesley and Ludlam (2009a: 3) remind us that this is natural: '[t]he left led governments have different ambitions and are subject to different political and economic constraints. Their presidential majorities may not be reproduced in their legislatures, nor among powerful provincial executives or mayoralties in great cities. Their histories are also different.'

Cardoso (2006) has challenged the regional nature of the pink tide concept, stressing the uniqueness of each national process in a way much similar to Tavolaro and Tavolaro and Lievesley and Ludlam. However, as Lynch (2007: 375) has pointed out: 'one can always emphasise the exceptionalism of national histories, but taken to the extreme, this methodological option would lead us to even reject the very existence of Latin America. The argument that focuses on national singularities ultimately seeks to deny the tendency. However ... there is no doubt that what we are witnessing is a trend that transcends national borders and that expresses a regional historical dynamic.' It is the purpose of the next section to outline the different attempts to characterise these trends that transcend national borders, and therefore characterise the pink tide. Such an exercise will provide the necessary contextual background to examine core meta-theoretical narratives in the political economy of development that may or may not help characterise this pink tide. In analysing these narratives, this chapter will reject each one in turn, thus paving the way for the articulation of an alternative meta-theory in Chapter 3 that this book contends is able to capture the essence of this leftist turn in contemporary Lain American political economy.

Contemporary themes in Latin American political economy

The 1980s and the 1990s was a story of rising democratisation in Latin America. However, at the same time, in the field of economics, the hegemony of neoliberalism led to the domination of the interests of capital in the national political economies of these 'new' democracies (Panizza, 2009; Tussie, 2009: 68). This created friction and tension. In the words of Lynch (2007: 374), '[t]here is a fundamental contradiction between a regime based on political equality such as democracy and an economy that only benefits a restricted sector of the population ... This tension deeply erodes the regime's material foundation and leads citizens to look for better alternatives for reconciling the economy with politics'. Therefore, the Washington Consensus model implemented across Latin America dictated a form of capitalism that concentrated income, reduced employment opportunities, limited business opportunities, and restricted social rights. In the context of rising levels of democracy this facilitated resistance, and 'less than two years after the financial crisis brought about by macroeconomic mismanagement by either Right or Centre-Right governments, leftist parties or candidates ... won the subsequent presidential elections in a range of countries' (Tussie, 2009: 71; see also Robinson, 2004: 137).

The question that becomes evident is why should this political process be considered as a left turn? Indeed, could it be described as left at all? Saad-Filho, Iamini, and Molinari (2007: 14) suggest that leaders such as Kirchner in Argentina and Lula in Brazil 'profess a critique of neoliberalism but ... in reality replicate the economic policies which they had previously vowed to abandon'. Furthermore, Arditi (2008: 59) suggests, '[u]nderstanding what the term stands for has become more difficult ever since mainstream socialist and LOC organisations started to adopt a market-friendly outlook and to phase out language of class warfare, national liberation, internationalism, strict Westphalian sovereignty, state ownership and so on'. Nevertheless, Lynch (2007: 374) argues that it is Leftist 'because it draws from what the left has meant (for the most part) in Latin America in the past century: An effort to establish democracy and social justice, and a better distribution of economic resources'. This is an analysis that Panizza (2005: 726) agrees with: '[m]atters of social justice and economic development have been at the core of LOC parties' identities in Latin America'. Therefore, 'the new consensus has incorporated a new agenda about the value of democracy for economic development, the strengthening of state institutions, the need for strategic state intervention, the importance of investment in health and education and a higher priority for social justice and the fight against poverty' (Panizza, 2005: 728). Thus, as Tussie (2009: 80) put it, 'Post-neoliberalism ... is the search for a new social contract and the emergence of a pragmatic belief in a role for coordinated state management'.

One manifestation of this new social contract has been in the policy area of social assistance. The myriad of programmes that have emerged from the continent – such as Bolsa Famila, Jefes y Jefas de Hogar, Chile Solidario, Bono de Desarrollo Humano, Red Solidaria, Red de Opportunidades, Bono Dignidad – signal a significant break with the past and therefore reflect a change in the development model of the region (Barrientos and Santibáñez, 2009: 3). The weight of social policy shifted towards social assistance that focused on poverty and vulnerability reduction based on a multidimensional and intergenerational understanding of poverty (Barrientos and Santibáñez, 2009: 13). This change in the structure of social protection thus represents an important element in the search for a new political settlement and social contract to work alongside the development model (Barrientos and Santibáñez, 2009: 26).

This shift in the social contract in Latin America has shaped the complementary characteristics of this pink tide: economic and social equity achieved through coordinated state management of the economy. Such a shift entailed the 'practical acceptance of some of the principles and policies originally associated with the so-called neoliberal model while attempting to make policies more compassionate and sensitive to the needs of the poor and excluded. Indeed, a more equitable social order requires a stable macroeconomic environment and internationally competitive economies (Panizza, 2005: 727). Therefore, to characterise and analyse the contemporary pink tide in Latin America it is necessary to account for transformations in the social make-up of the left, and realise that the practical programmatic moderation that has characterised the pink tide while in government has been the result of broader political and social change. The political right's dismantling of the institutions of Latin American ISI, first by military dictatorships and later by neo-liberal democracies, led to the shrinking of organised urban working classes. This combined with the general retreat of the state, which facilitated public sector job cuts and the rise of the 'new poor' middle classes. As a result, the left in Latin America introduced 'additional complications into [their] pursuit of the – always illusionary – "unity of the oppressed"' (Panizza, 2005: 725). Therefore, the left found itself transcending its traditional constituencies and adopting new policy directions and mixes in order to appeal to other sectors of society that included the middle classes and the business sector. Therefore, for Tussie (2009: 71) the pink tide is the result of the emergence of a new mindset of the left, based on 'social learning, adaptation, and contestation'. This is the product of both a positive and a negative consensus. The positive consensus is based on a belief to bring the state back in to the economy and development, the negative consensus derives from the critique of neoliberalism.

As well as new constituencies in the wake of social and structural change, the left in Latin America has also had to deal with the realities of globalisation, its characterisation fundamentally within the neoliberal paradigm, and the subsequent realisation that there is little room in the region for an anti-systemic model, 'and that instead the emphasis should be placed in making states, markets, and democracy work to better represent the people, promote development, address social demands and attack the root causes of discrimination and inequality' (Panizza, 2005: 730). Furthermore, leftist candidates or presidents not only must appeal to their new, wider and more heterogeneous constituencies, but also to the financial markets. Radical discourse can frighten international investors, and in an age of integrated capital markets create a run on the national currency and subsequent capital flight (see Part II of this book for detailed case studies of how this affected both Argentina and Brazil).

As a result of these factors the pink tide in Latin America has not been a uniform turn. It shows different characteristics according to the various national processes and different currents within this left-wing tendency (Lynch, 2007: 376). Due to recognition of these different national idiosyncrasies the literature on the pink tide in Latin America has usually adopted one of two approaches for classifying the regimes in the continent. The first has been to 'make the meaning of the left dependent on the evocative force of the term' (Arditi, 2008: 60) – that is, to examine series of policies, rhetoric, and patterns of behaviour. However, 'the fact that the referents are far from unequivocal can create all sorts of difficulties' (Arditi, 2008: 60). Therefore, a more popular choice has been to create typologies of different leftist regimes. Castañeda's (2006: 32) distinction between the 'good left' and the 'bad left' is probably the most well known. Castañeda's *Foreign Affairs* article 'pits the right, modern, democratic, accountable, sensible, and market-friendly left – which is virtually a clone of the one governing Chile – against the wrong, populist, authoritarian, corrupt, state-centred, and irresponsible one of Chàvez, Morales, López Obrador, Humala, Néstor Kirchner, and ... his wife Cristina Fernàndez de Kirchner' (Arditi, 2008: 60). Such a division represents a highly normative and reductionist exercise, in which new projects in Kirchner's Argentina or Humala's (and now perhaps Pérez's) Peru (the 'bad' left) are reduced to crude populism, and those in Bachelet's (and now Piñera's) Chile or Lula's (and now Rousseff's) Brazil (the 'good' left) are simple expressions of social democracy. Such expressions are not sufficiently sensitive to the nature of these specific regimes. Or, as Fortes (2009: 110) suggests, 'such Manichean schemes fall apart when applied to the complexities of contemporary Latin American reality'. Some have attempted to modify Castañeda's original dichotomy by redefining who or what counts as the 'bad' and 'good' left, or by adding shades of grey and expanding the number of lefts to three or more. However, this book contends that old categories such as populism or social democracy are simply inadequate hermeneutical devices for capturing the nature of the regional trends present in contemporary Latin America. This thesis will be developed throughout the book, with Part I outlining a model that is able to sufficiently capture both the pink tide as a whole, while remaining sufficiently flexible so as to be able to account for national differences. Part II will use the detailed case studies of Argentina and Brazil to provide an empirical base for this theoretical exercise, while Part III will offer wider regional and global implications of this analysis.

Other attempts categorising the pink tide exist that are not so embedded in normative frameworks. One such example is that of Kirby (2010b) who also identifies two groups: one encompasses Chile, Brazil, and Uruguay, and the other Venezuela, Bolivia, and Ecuador, with Argentina somewhere in between. Kirby acknowledges that this happens to fall into Castañeda's same categorisation, however he assures us that this is simply tangential. The grouping of Chile, Uruguay, and Brazil is due to the fact that they 'lack a clear comparative advantage that oil and natural gas offer the other group' (Kirby, 2010b). This has implications for the resulting nature of how each group interacts with international capital, which in turn shapes their domestic political economy. Those states that have large oil exports (Venezuela, Bolivia, and Ecuador) are largely independent of the market discipline that is imposed upon the others (Brazil, Chile, and Uruguay), due to the latter's need to insert themselves more fully into a global market characterised and dominated by the interests of capital. This argument draws heavily on Phil Cerny's concept of the 'Competition State' (see later section of this chapter for a full discussion of this concept in theory) that, put briefly, forces states to conform to the imperatives of neoliberalism in order to secure much-needed investment that comes as a result of closer and more complete integration into the world's integrated capital markets. The oil-exporting states are largely independent of these imperatives of globalisation due to the room for manoeuvre given to them by international demand for oil and natural gas reserves that they control. Kirby stresses that there are important factors that muddy the waters of such a neat distinction: Brazil is a little different given the size of its internal market, Chile has long maintained a market-friendly economic stance in contrast with the more politicised discourse of other leftist governments, and Argentina stands somewhat apart given its relative lack of oil and natural gas, but with its demonstrated willingness to assert state authority over markets and its rejection of international capital (Kirby, 2010a).

This contribution by Kirby modifies an earlier distinction that he made (Kirby, 2003: 200). This earlier analysis distinguished between a 'conservative left', a 'reforming left', and a 'radical left'. The conservative left were represented by two groupings: communist parties and guerrilla groups inspired by the Cuban revolution, and national–populist governments such as those under Perón and Vargas. Both forms pursued a state-driven model of development through ISI, supported by organised working classes. The reforming left rejected conventional socialism and were more aligned to 'catch-all' groupings that were less demarcated along traditional class-based lines. The radical left challenged the prevailing political and socio-economic status quo. New parties and coalitions, such as the PT in Brazil or the Frente Amplio in Uruguay, pursued more overtly social democratic policies while maintaining their links with grass-roots social movements (Burton, 2009: 172). In identifying this radical left Kirby has offered invaluable analysis regarding their social base, yet falls into a similar trap when describing their goal within the social democratic paradigm. Indeed, a similar analysis is offered by Lievesley and Ludlam's *Reclaiming Latin America* (2009a). They argue that, 'some of Latin America's populist movements can be seen as particular vehicles of social democracy ... The same regimes later managed the turn to neoliberalism'. Additionally, Petras (2007) divides contemporary Latin American politics into four blocs. A 'radical left' that includes the Revolutionary Armed Forces of Colombia (FARC) guerrillas, a 'pragmatic left' that encompasses Chàvez, Morales, and Castro, 'pragmatic neoliberals' such as Lula, (the) Kirchner(s), and the Sandanistas, and 'doctrinaire neoliberal regimes' such as Calderón, Bachelet (and now Piñera?), and Uribe. Once again, such analysis reduced the different elements of the pink tide to traditional forms of political economy associated with social democracy or neoliberalism.

Leiva's (2008: 5) analysis places this left turn within the neo-structuralist paradigm. Such a paradigm suggests that 'international competitiveness, social integration, and political legitimacy can syn-ergistically be attained by swimming along with, not against, the swift currents unleashed by globalisation'. This is to be achieved through four core principles: first, a shift towards exports with higher value-added and an international competitiveness based on an increased produc-tivity and innovation; second, poverty, inequality, and low economic growth can be better addressed by ensuring a more dynamic entry into world markets; third, an explicit awareness that if market forces are to operate effectively they need to be complemented by non-market based forms of coordination; and fourth, active export-promotion policies such as technical innovation through partial subsidies and the promo-tion of strategic alliances between local and transnational firms (Leiva, 2008: 6–7).

Another attempt was again made by Kurt Weyland, Wendy Hunter, and Raúl Madrid (2010), in splitting this pink tide into dichotomous categories grounded in policy orientation. The so-called 'contestatory left', which is more antagonistic towards neoliberalism and the political system that implemented it, and the 'moderate' or 'pragmatic' left that has retained a strong pro-market orientation but has sought to condi-tion or qualify neoliberalism (Madrid, Hunter, and Weyland, 2010: 143; see also Kingstone, 2011: 103).

These analyses, once again, are not sufficiently sensitive to the nuance necessary to interpret these regimes accurately. For example, Madrid, Hunter, and Weyland (2010: 145) suggest that 'contesting' leftist presi-dents forged new electoral bases while in moderate cases presidents moved their parties to the centre to forge electoral coalitions built on pragmatic centrist votes (see also Kingstone, 2011: 106). However, much of this analysis is too general. The assertion that the 'contesting' left has a weaker commitment to macroeconomic restraint when compared to the moderate left does not stand up to scrutiny. In terms of government expenditure, productivity, and debt reduction, Néstor Kirchner's Argentina has done very well, yet is placed in the contesting group and labelled macroeconomically vulnerable (Kingstone, 2011: 116–17). In addition, this analysis deliberately avoids borderline cases – a fact that the book clearly acknowledges (Weyland, 2010: 5) – thus focusing solely on hand-picked unambiguous cases.

The use of these Western-centric analyses of political economy is not appropriate for analysis of contemporary Latin America and the pink tide. While elements of neoliberalism and/or social democracy (SMC) may well exist within the economic policies and political economy of the different regimes that constitute the pink tide in contemporary Latin America, they do not reveal their complete or true nature. As this chapter will go on to argue, such traditional meta-theoretical analyses are lacking, and other theories, not traditionally associated with Latin America, the US, or Europe must be considered.

One area of the literature that has begun to seriously engage with this research agenda is work that focuses on 'post-neoliberalism' in Latin America (see, for example, Arditi, 2008; Grugel and Riggirozzi, 2009; MacDonald and Ruckert, 2009). These contributions conclude that the contemporary left's agenda of redistribution of wealth and greater equity and 'dignity' is pursued without seeking to abolish capitalism, international trade, or liberal citizenship and is therefore 'more post-liberal than anti-liberal' (Arditi, 2008: 73). As Macdonald and Ruckert (2009: 6) suggest, 'post-neoliberalism should not be understood as an era after neoliberalism … [instead] the post-neoliberal era is characterised mainly by a search for progressive policy alternatives arising out of the many contradictions of neoliberalism'. Therefore, 'in the realm of economic policies there is a pragmatism that is neither excessively friendly nor totally ignorant of markets' (Heidrich and Tussie, 2009: 52). Grugel and Riggirozzi (2009: 2) express a desire to go into a 'fine-grained analysis which identifies the complexities of the new projects of economic and political governance alongside an engagement with developments at the level of regional political economy'. All these contributions provide invaluable research into the shape and nature of specific characteristics of the 'post-neoliberal' movement in contemporary Latin America and this book associates itself with the general tenor of their analysis. However, this research falls short of advocating an overall meta-theoretical approach that can invigorate and provide greater analytical leverage to the study of the pink tide, a task to which this book now turns.

The poverty of theory in the face of new Latin American political economy

The previous section of this chapter attempted to show how difficult it has been to characterise and theorise the contemporary political economy of Latin American pink tide governments. While a number of scholars have postulated a variety of different groupings and characterisations, with the most famous (and probably the least accurate) being that of Castañeda's 'good left' and 'bad left', none have been able to satisfactorily analyse these governments within dominant discourses and within political economy as a whole. It is the purpose of this section to outline the dominant theories of political economy present in Latin American history (and global history more widely), and then to challenge their usefulness as a hermeneutical device for providing analytical leverage and clarity in the pink tide debate. Therefore, this section will look at neoliberalism, SMC, and dependency theory and, in turn, reject each one in terms of its ability to characterise contemporary Latin American political economy. This allows the debate to move forward in the next chapter, and to begin a useful and original discussion of how alternative models of political economy could and should be drawn in order to appropriately locate these dynamics on the Latin American continent.

Neoliberalism

Neoliberalism is intellectually represented by Friedrich Hayek (1944) of the Austrian School, and later by Milton Friedman (1962) and the Chicago School. Hayek, in his book *The Road to Serfdom*, defends liberal democracy and capitalism against socialist and collectivist thought, especially emphasising the role and importance of liberty defined in terms of the rule of law as well as through property and contract rights (Gamble, 1996: 190). He argues that collectivism leads to tyranny by the faulty logic of central economic planning. Competition spontaneously and efficiently coordinates economic activity through price signals. This thinking received renewed intellectual focus after the 'failure' of Keynesian policies to manage inflation and unemployment in the 1970s through the work of Nobel Prize-winning economist Milton Friedman (1962; see also Lapavitsas, 2005). In his work he underlined the importance of the price system as a co-ordination mechanism, demonstrating a link with neoclassical economics – the approach in economics of analysing how individuals and firms should behave to maximise their own objective functions, assuming that activities are co-ordinated by the price mechanism, and that markets clear so that the economy is in equilibrium at all times (Black, 2002: 318).

This faith in neoclassical economics is complemented by a commitment to the 'Austrian-Libertarian' tradition as the source of political rhetoric (Chang, 2003: 77). This association suppresses the 'interventionist streak' inherently present in neoclassical economics due to its affiliation with welfare economics, which is a branch of neoclassical economics (Chang, 2003: 48). As a result, neoliberalism possesses three main strands of critique of the role of the state in the market. First, there is an affiliation with contractarian political philosophy in the sense that any extension of the role of the state beyond 'night watchman' is morally unacceptable. Therefore, economic efficiency should be sacrificed for the sake of individual freedom should the two clash (Friedman, 1962; Chang, 2003: 47). Second, state intervention in a complex modern economy is doomed to failure due to problems of informational costs and uncertainty. The suitable imperative to provide 'order' in an economy is that of the market, not state planning. 'If the fundamental uncertainties pervading the market process do not allow us to identify the ideal against which market failures are to be identified, namely, the neoclassical competitive equilibrium, the whole exercise in welfare economics becomes pointless' (Chang, 2003: 48). Third, neoliberals subscribe to the government failure approach, which rejects the welfare economics view of the state as a benign and omnipotent social guardian that maximises social welfare. The state is an agent that serves the interests of politically influential groups, which means that state intervention is likely to create allocative inefficiencies, 'organisational slacks', and rent-seeking, rather than the correction of 'market failures' (Munck, 2005: 60–1).

State–market dichotomy

For neoliberals government intervention in the economy and economic development is therefore a major source of price distortion that prevents markets from functioning properly and efficiently. Indeed, the very notion of *developmental* goals is made redundant by the neoliberals due to the theoretical primacy of 'static efficiency' over 'dynamic efficiency' (Chang, 1999: 184). Static efficiency is achieved when demand (or marginal private benefit) equals supply (or marginal private cost) as net benefit is maximised. In other words, when markets operate according to the laws of supply and demand and always tend towards equilibrium they will be statically efficient. Dynamic efficiency, on the other hand, considers the maximisation of net benefit over time, rather than simply as a series of static decisions, that is, measures to *improve* existing products, processes, and capabilities (Ghemawat and Ricart, 1993). Neoliberals contend that in their models of markets with perfect information, every short-run move is made after taking all its future consequences into account. Therefore, the distinction between the short run and the long run is meaningless, suggesting that the price mechanism is capable of achieving *both* short-run optimal allocative efficiency and long-run dynamic efficiency. Linked to this analysis is the neoliberal critique of the state as guardian of 'public interest' (Chang, 1999: 184). The concept of utility maximisation and self-seeking motives of individuals should also be applied to politics, which allows the state to be characterised as an organisation controlled by interest groups, politicians, or bureaucrats who utilise power for their own self-interests, producing socially undesirable outcomes. In other words, political determination of outcomes equals social waste through rent-seeking or dominance of minority interest over the majority interest (Krueger, 1974: 301–2; Rapley, 2008; Friedman, 1962).

Neoliberals therefore view the role of the state in the development process as facilitating the realisation of statically efficient markets. This is achieved through wholesale 'liberalisation', which in turn sets in train a process of 'getting the prices right' (Rapley, 2008). Domestically this means deregulation of the product and factor markets, while internationally this means opening up to trade and following the law of comparative advantage. Politically, this means the depoliticisation of the economic policymaking and implementation processes through the contraction or rolling back of the state through deregulation, and the destruction or restriction of the political influence of interest groups (Chang, 1999: 184). Therefore a competitive market populated by individually insignificant agents provides an objective solution that cannot be politically manipulated, whereas state intervention opens the door for sectoral interests to assert themselves through their influences on the state's decisions regarding the distribution of resources.

'Active' management of the economy should therefore be restricted to only a few areas. Firstly, the state should provide a legal and institutional environment in which markets can flourish. Secondly, the state should provide public goods where the contribution to social welfare is large, as these markets represent examples of where the price mechanism breaks down. Public goods in economics possess two characteristics that make them difficult, if not impossible, to operate in a traditional market mechanism. The first characteristic is 'non-rivalry', which means that consumption by one user does not reduce the supply available to others. The second is 'non-excludability', which is where users cannot be prevented from consuming the good. While there are very few true public goods (the air that we breathe perhaps), there are a number that are close enough that are key to economic development and must therefore be provided by the state (Thirlwall, 2008: 290); defence, law and order, roads, sewers, and clean water are all examples. Neoliberal economics is even cautious regarding these goods, however. Firstly, there is a belief that technology, or better-defined property rights (Chang, 1994: 8) may be the answer to the non-excludability issue; and secondly, while a problem may exist, it is not the state per se that should be the solution (Chang, 1994: 9). With regard to the non-rivalry issue often creating infrastructural and technological imperatives lead-ing to 'natural' monopolies – and thus transferring consumer surplus into monopoly profits and a societal dead-weight loss – neoliberal argu-ments (Palley, 2005: 29; Lapavitsas, 2005: 31) have suggested that the traditional anti-trust legislative role of the state could be brought into question. This is because they argue that even with state intervention there may not be efficiency gains, as well as the fact that cartels often occur in the first place through state intervention (Chang, 1994: 10).

A final area of intervention for neoliberal theory is in management of the macro-economy, which should be restricted to monetary policy (although the need for a 'stable' currency can also be formulated as a 'public good' issue). Neoliberalism assumes that the quantity theory of money is valid, and therefore that money is neutral in the long run, that is, it cannot influence the level and composition of output and employment (Mollo and Saad-Filho, 2006: 101). By tightening the money supply during periods of high inflation, and loosening it dur-ing times of recession, the state could help regulate and alleviate the economic cycle by regulating aggregate demand and therefore main-taining economic growth (Rapley, 2008: 64). Money supply could be manipulated through either exchange rate controls, or through the set-ting of interest rates, due to the relationship of the money supply to the liquidity preference curve. If interest rates are high then people tend to save more and spend less, and the high cost of loans discourages buying on credit. Less money chases the same supply of goods and therefore prices rise more slowly or perhaps even fall. During times of recession, low interest rates have the opposite effect, stimulating economic activ-ity that draws unemployed resources back into use. The manipulation of interest rates also fulfils three further objectives of a neoliberal state. First, for developing economies that adopt the neoliberal approach, it can help attract capital flows in order to help the balance of payments and achieve a target level of foreign currency reserves; second, and more generally, demand for government financing or public securities is regulated; and third, interest rates help set the desired level of domestic savings (Mollo and Saad-Filho, 2006: 102).

It follows that interest rates tend to be higher under a neoliberal government than under an alternative policy regime, where similar objectives may be pursued by a broader set of instruments. From the neoliberal viewpoint, this is not necessarily a disadvantage. High interest rates offer incentives to savers and increase the availability of investment funds, which should lead to higher growth rates in the long term. High interest rates in the poor countries also reflect their relative lack of capital, and the attraction of foreign savings should support higher levels of investment and global economic convergence (Palley, 2005: 20, 24; Lapavitsas, 2005: 35).

The neoliberal 'revolution' represented a partial return to the nineteenth-century laissez-faire tradition, supplemented by an Austrian emphasis on the limited transferability of knowledge and the role of entrepreneurship (Chang and Rowthorn, 2003: 36). The neoliberal approach therefore stresses the efficacy of the free market, and insists on the inefficiency and/or counter-productiveness of state intervention (Lapavitsas, 2005: 30). The failings of state intervention are ascribed either to an inherent shortage of information, the self-seeking behaviours of bureaucrats, or organised interests engaging in rent-seeking behaviour.

State–society dichotomy

The relationship between state and civil society and between politics and economics in neoliberal theory is that the two are analytically separate (Radice, 2008: 1164). Due to this separation in principle of economics and politics in neoliberal discourse exploitation – the idea that profit derives from the extraction of surplus value from wage labour – takes on a distinctly 'economic' semblance. Therefore:

> No explicitly political coercion need enter directly into the capitalist exploitation of labour, for it appears as a simple exchange of commodities in the market: labour-power is exchanged for a wage.
>
> Rupert (1993: 73)

In this analysis power is not political as capitalist class power is based directly on the given relations of production and state power, which 'defines the juridical conditions of private property, contract and exchange, thus entering implicitly into the constitution and reproduction of the economic sphere, as well as the class powers which reside in that sphere' (Rupert, 1993: 73). This allows a critique of the state, due to the relationship between the public and the private spheres. The historical creation of a private sphere is achieved through the creation of civil society, where individuals could be understood in abstraction from the society in which they were embedded, and thus be able to conceive and pursue their own private interests. The state is therefore defined in neoliberal theory as the social space that is distinct from civil society, and thus is naturally self-limiting. Therefore, the state is unable to challenge the separation of politics and economics as in doing so it would undermine the preconditions for its own existence:

> Insulated from explicitly communal and political concerns, the 'private' powers of capital are ensconced in the sanctuary of civil society, and from there implicitly permeate the public sphere, rendering it a partial, distorted and self-limiting form of community.
>
> Rupert (1993: 76)

This 'market based society', for Polanyi (1944: 60), means that '[i]nstead of economy being embedded in social relations, social relations are embedded in the economic system', or, in other words, 'a market economy can function only in a market society'. Therefore, the market continuously seeks to make a society in it own image (Munck, 2005: 61). Polanyi's *Great Transformation* was a story of industrial change in nineteenth-century Britain and showed that market society and market rules did not evolve naturally or through some process of self-generation (Munck, 2005: 61). Indeed, as Polanyi argues, 'the market has been the outcome of a conscious and often violent intervention on the part of the government which imposed the market organisation on society for non-economic ends' (Polanyi, 1944: 258). Polanyi and others such as Cox (1996) therefore demonstrate that government intervention was crucial to the making of markets in society, rather than the 'natural' processes as suggested by the likes of Hayek.

A historical materialist interpretation of this separation of politics from economics is that the state embodies political alienation due to the fact that its very existence as a specialised political entity 'testifies to the estrangement of community and communal powers from the daily lives and productive activities of people within capitalist social reality' (Rupert, 1993: 76). According to Rupert, the political economy of neoliberalism is therefore more than just an emphasis on markets and non-intervention, as it is embedded in a normative framework based on very specific epistemological and ontological foundations. Due to its grounding in positivism, neoliberalism claims to represent a product of objectivity reached through scientific methodology. Neoliberal economic theory and policy is therefore complemented by and dependent upon a number of contributions to philosophy, political theory, and politics.

Robert Cox's statement that 'theory is always for someone and for some purpose' (Cox, 1996: 87) points to the normative foundations of neoliberalism (indeed of all theory), and leads to a number of important insights into neoliberal theory. In asserting the primacy of the individual over society, and the private over the public, neoliberal policies have served to fundamentally redefine the respective roles of the public and private sectors and have resulted in the transfer of state functions to private enterprise (see also Clarke, 2005: 52–4). As analysed previously, neoliberalism asserts that the complexity of economic relations precludes 'deliberate planning' as no single, external body is seen to be capable to effect the mutual adjustment of individual agents and their actions in a way that maximises the use of scarce resources. It is only through engagement with the market mechanism that efficient outcomes can be realised. Therefore, in neoliberal discourse a close relation can be seen between the conceptualisation of the private individual and broader social changes. In this context, processes involving the continued marketisation of areas of social interaction and a shift in responsibility from the state to the individual seem appropriate. For example, markets and market competition have expanded dramatically, and into areas previously considered the realm of the public such as healthcare, education, pensions, utilities such as water and electricity, as well as law and order in the form of private prisons and 'security' firms (Williams, 2005).

The formal and informal linkages present in the social market capitalist model are missing and neoliberalism sees reliance on a welfare state as dangerous as it cripples freedom and erodes efficiency (MacGregor, 2005: 144). It is not the role of the state to intervene in a market mechanism that will operate perfectly well if left alone. Not being interested in de-commodification or in stratification effects facilitates this perception, as it is not the role of the state to engage in these activities of welfare redistribution, but markets.

In an era of globalisation state–society relations represent only half of the analysis necessary in order to fully understand the contemporary state with regard to development policy. This is also increasingly the case when considering welfare-regime analysis (MacGregor, 2005: 146). Therefore, the next section will analyse the role that international pressures play on the state in relation to the development process so that a complete understanding of the role of the state in the development process as understood by neoliberal theory can be developed.

National–international dichotomy

As Radice (2008: 1162) asks, what does it signify to add the qualifier 'global' to neoliberalism? Analysis suggests that within the very logic of neoliberalism is a drive towards globalism. The theory of comparative advantage is the justification for increasingly free global trade, and therefore integration of countries into the global logic of neoliberal capitalism. Indeed, this forms the basis of many criticisms of neoliberal capitalism as its role as a globalising project is in order to '[outflank] the bastions of collectivism in the welfare state and organised labour' (Radice, 2008: 1162). However, within the logic of neoliberalism, the globalising nature of its project is the spread of wealth through trade and specialisation. Therefore, much of the literature associated with this issue (see, for example, Held, 2000) analyses the process of evolution from the national to the global as it associates the development of local forms of social organisation equivalent to the principles of neoliberalism with their gradual spread through wider linkages in cultural and political affairs as well as in the economy and technology. Therefore, globalisation is treated as *within* capitalism (Radice, 2008: 1162), a fundamental logic of capitalism and the forces that its development unleashes on society. In other words, '[g]lobalisation is the ultimate expression of the will of the marketplace' (Karagiannis and Madjd-Sadjadi, 2007: 57), and neoliberalism is the theory that champions the primacy of the market in ordering social relations.

What therefore are the implications for our understanding of the neoliberal state? Globalisation is about the emancipation of the individual from the collective, and these processes have transformed the traditional role of the nation state. On the one hand, the decentralising effects on consumer sovereignty, that is, the fact that citizens everywhere acquire rights to access consumer goods and services regardless of country of origin make possible this emancipation; while on the other the homogenising effects of an increasingly complex supra-national institutional structure (the WTO, IMF, World Bank, and UN system) reinforce this emancipatory trend (Karagiannis and Madjd-Sadjadi, 2007: 58). Such homogenisation comes in the form of trade practices, or macroeconomic frameworks for example. Many traditional tasks of the nation state are thus surrendered to the international level, in order to help create a world in which capital can seamlessly and flawlessly transcend national boundaries. This process is deemed appropriate for a number of reasons, not least in order to facilitate economic development as understood in the theories analysed earlier.

One attempt to theorise how states react to neoliberal globalisation is Cerny, Soederberg, and Menz's (2005) concepts of 'internalising globalisation' and the 'competition state'. 'Internalising globalisation is about how people are changing their domestic political worlds in the context of growing complex interactions – economic, social, and political – across national borders' (Cerny, Soederberg, and Menz, 2005: 1). This process of internalising globalisation accelerates the process itself and further embeds it into domestic institutions and practices (Cerny, Soederberg, and Menz, 2005: 16). This process in turn propels, magnifies, reshapes and reorganises how technology, trading patterns, production systems, financial markets etc. impact on both politics and society. Such a transformation, therefore, has three main interlocking dimensions (Cerny, 2000: 22). The first involves a change in the character of the state's domestic tasks, roles, and activities. 'In particular, the aim of social justice through redistribution has been challenged and profoundly undermined by the marketisation or commodification of the state's economic activities and by a new "embedded financial orthodoxy"' (Cerny, 2000: 22), or 'embedded neoliberalism' (Cerny, Soederberg, and Menz, 2005: 16). The second dimension involves a fundamental reorientation of how states interact economically as well as politically with each other. 'Rather than perceiving the traditional "inside/outside" distinctions, state actors [politicians and bureaucrats] ... are increasingly concerned with promoting the competitive advantages of particular production and service sectors in a more open and integrated world economy' (Cerny, 2000: 22). This 'competition state's' main characteristic is 'that traditional policies aimed at achieving social justice through economic redistribution have been challenged and profoundly undermined by the marketisation of the state's economic activities and its focus on attracting and retaining capital flows' (Soederberg, 2005: 167). The third, and final, dimension involves the relationship between structure and agency. Cerny (2000: 23) suggests that such structural change is driven by agents who operate within previously structured but continually evolving sets of constraints and opportunities '... which can either severely restrict what actors can in fact achieve, or else enable them to exploit opportunities and even to construct the new spaces necessary to bring about wider changes'.

The core dimensions of the competition state therefore revolve around four principles (Cerny, Soederberg, and Menz, 2005: 15–17).

First is a logic that moves towards a more open world economy: this is facilitated by reducing barriers to trade and capital flows, and is also linked to the internationalisation of production. Second, there is a presence of an embedded financial orthodoxy and a neoliberal state: the embedded financial orthodoxy revolves around the control of inflation, balanced budgets, and supply side policy with an imperative of reducing marginal tax rates in order to stimulate productive investment. Third is the nature of regulation: often characterised as deregulation, a more accurate characterisation is pro-market regulation (due to the need to provide regulations and legal infrastructure that facilitates orderly conduct of exchange in the market), which comes in the form of 'arms-length' or 'light-touch' regulation based on providing the basic minimum legal and institutional framework for markets to operate and flourish. The final dimension concerns 'reinventing governance', which involves privatisation strategies as well as the development of schemes such as Public–Private Partnerships or Private Finance Initiatives (PFIs) as seen in the UK.

Neoliberalism in practice: The 'US Model' and the 'Washington Consensus'

The elections of Mrs Thatcher in the UK in 1979 and Ronald Reagan in the USA in 1980 can be viewed as inaugurating the formal period of neoliberal economic policy dominance. Such principles were then adopted by large parts of the developing world through Structural Adjustment Programmes (SAPs). The 30 years since have seen an application of neoliberal policy ideas within the economies of both industrialised and developing countries (Palley, 2005: 24). In the industrialised world this took the form of the 'US model', which, while far from implemented uniformly, broadly involved the deregulation of financial markets, privatisation, weakening the institutions of social protection, shrinking government, cutting top rates of tax, opening international goods and capital markets, and abandoning the goal of full employment in favour of the 'natural rate' (Palley, 2005: 25). Such prescriptions were based theoretically and methodologically on neoliberal theory.

The demise of the Keynesian era in the form of the Post-War Consensus, and the declining faith in ISI policies (refer to later sections for a full discussion of ISI) as a result of the debt crisis in the 1980s (Grugel, Riggirozzi, and Thirkell-White, 2008: 500; Colás, 2005: 75; Lapavitsas, 2005: 37), as well as the role of externally imposed SAPs, all paved the way for the resurgence of this neoclassical orthodoxy in the developing world, which would later converge in what was called the 'Washington Consensus' (Chudnovsky, 2007: 5). The term 'Washington

Consensus' was first coined by John Williamson (1990: 1) to describe a set of technocratic prescriptions that emerged from Washington, a phrase that for Williamson includes the international financial institutions (IFIs) – World Bank, IMF – the US Treasury, the Federal Reserve Board, senior members of the US administration and Congress, and think-tanks (such as the Institute for International Economics).

While responses to the crises in the 1980s were far from uniform, enough sites of convergence were identified to justify the use of the term Washington Consensus; although Williamson himself suggests that the use of the word 'consensus' may be too strong and perhaps a more 'accurate, if less memorable' phrase would be 'universal convergence' (Williamson, 1990: 2). Therefore, while individual developing nations often engaged in neoliberal reform, they did so with key idiosyncrasies due to the specific and individual nature of the economies and societies in which the reforms were taking place. However, despite this qualification by Williamson, he suggests that there are ten specific policy areas that collectively shape the nature of the Washington Consensus. These policies can be summarised as 'macroeconomic prudence, outward orientation, and domestic liberalisation' (Williamson, 1990: 1), but more specifically the ten areas are: fiscal deficits, public expenditure priorities, tax reform, interest rates, exchange rate policy, trade policy, FDI, privatisation, deregulation, and property rights (Williamson, 1990: 8–17). Therefore, the Washington Consensus was a set of neoliberal ideas, demanding of developing countries that they should achieve macroeconomic stability (typically by cutting government spending including subsidies to the poor), deregulating domestic markets, privatisation of state enterprises, and the opening of the economy to foreign trade and finance (Lapavitsas, 2005: 37–8).

In many instances such policy prescriptions were achieved through 'conditionality'. This was where the IMF or World Bank would withhold loans (in a context of a debt crisis in the developing world) unless the country receiving IFI money agreed on a series of structural reforms, collectively known as SAPs (Cornia, Jolly, and Stewart, 1987). Therefore, Munck (2005: 77) concludes that, 'for the weaker states and economies in the international system, neoliberalism arrived as an external force, principally in the shape of IFIs and through the mechanisms of SAPs in the 1980s (or PRSPs today)'. However, 'developing countries [were] not simply hapless victims or passive objects of global neoliberalism: they [were], like other states, populated by classes and social forces with their own interests and strategies, many of which [were] consonant with the ruling ideology of neoliberalism' (Munck, 2005: 78). Therefore, as Grugel, Riggirozzi, and Thirkell-White (2008: 502) conclude: 'while popular images of the Washington Consensus as a set of imperial policies forced on passive developing countries by the self-interested western powers are plainly a gross over-simplification, neoliberalism came to set the agenda for political economy globally in ways that narrowed the sphere of the possible and concentrated debate around questions about free markets to the apparent exclusion of other possibilities.'

As well as the nature of the implementation of the Washington Consensus principles, the prescriptions themselves also came under criticism. Such criticism can be grouped into two main areas: critique of the theory and methodology behind the prescriptions, and critique of the method and nature of the implementation of these policies (see, for example, Saad-Filho, 2005: 115). Detailed investigation of neoliberal theory has been conducted in previous sections of this book, but Saad-Filho (2005: 116) suggests four broad critiques. First, removing market 'imperfections' does not necessarily lead to increases in economic efficiency; second, the state was unable to address issues of poverty, unemployment, and rising inequality; third, there was a general lack of consideration of negative aspects of neoliberal policy; and fourth, the fact that rich countries did not become rich by following these neoliberal policies.

In terms of implementation problems, five main areas of critique can be identified in the literature (Saad-Filho, 2005: 116). First, the policies tended to favour large domestic and foreign capital at the expense of smaller capital and workers, which facilitated higher unemployment, wage stagnation, and concentration of income. Second, the rolling back of the state reduced the degree of co-ordination of economic policy activity. Therefore, market freedom increased the economic uncertainty and volatility, facilitating the onset of crisis. Third, jobs and traditional industries were often destroyed under the aegis of efficiency, which facilitated long run structural unemployment, greater poverty and marginalisation, disarticulation of existing production chains, and a more fragile balance of payments as the development of new industry was unable to compensate the loss of traditional industry. Fourth, macroeconomic strategy was orientated towards business confidence, which is subject to arbitrary change and therefore makes it difficult to invest due to the inability to plan effectively for the future. Finally, neoliberal policies are not self-correcting, that is, policy failure often led to the extension of IFI influence and intervention, often beyond economic policy, and into governance and the political process. Such mission creep undermines democracy and the basis of the social contract between the state and society (for an excellent overview of the critique of IMF implementation of SAPs, see Stiglitz, 2002).

As a result of these criticisms, and through the work of Joseph Stiglitz, the IFIs changed the prescriptions of the Washington Consensus – repackaging the policies as the 'post-Washington Consensus', and using the vehicle of Poverty Reduction Strategy Papers (PRSPs) rather than SAPs. The New Institutional Economics (NIE) critique by Stiglitz (2002) drew attention to the implications of market failure, as well as the institutional setting of economic activity, which can affect economic outcomes due to changes in these institutions (see later sections of this chapter for a discussion of the NIE school's contribution to the theoretical debate). Therefore, the post-Washington Consensus was supposed to reconcile open market policies with a commitment to democratic politics and poverty reduction (Grugel, Riggirozzi, and Thirkell-White, 2008: 503). However, such an approach shared the same methodological foundations as the Washington Consensus. The market is seen as natural and not a socially created institution, and the policy prescriptions that emerged from such considerations were broadly the same as those of the original Washington Consensus (Munck, 2005; Saad-Filho, 2005: 117).

The impact of the (post-)Washington Consensus on the developing world cannot be overestimated. While Williamson aimed to emphasise the technical, externally orientated, macroeconomic aspects of the 'counter-revolution' in development economics, the Washington Consensus went beyond deflationary adjustment, the need to counter balance-of-payments deficits, or controlling inflation and balanced budgets. Indeed, privatisation, liberalisation, and an attack on corporatism, labour organisation, and welfare regimes constituted a radical change in the basis of domestic legitimacy and state–society relationships (Grugel, Riggirozzi, and Thirkell-White, 2008: 501).

Neoliberalism and the pink tide

Neoliberalism, the driving force across much of the Latin American continent in the 1980s and 1990s, does not sufficiently capture a number of characteristics present in the contemporary political economy of the region. First, in terms of the state–market relationship, the economic reality of state interventions into the market through active industrial policies, as well as other macroeconomic interventions such as in foreign exchange markets (e.g. Argentina) are outside the logic of neoliberalism. Neoliberal emphasis on government intervention representing a major source of price distortion that prevents markets from functioning properly and efficiently (Chang, 1999: 184), as well as its critique of the state as guardian of 'public interest' (Krueger, 1974: 301–2; Chang, 1999: 184; Rapley, 2008; Friedman, 1962), provide ideological justification for *non*-intervention, rather than the pink tide states' attempts at manipulating the market for national developmentalist ends.

Second, the complex inter-relations between state and society are anathema to a political economy grounded in the analytical separation of state from society. As Panizza argues, and elaborated in much detail in previous sections, the Latin American pink tide has been characterised by renegotiations of traditional social contracts within states, incorporating non-traditional constituencies such as business interests or middle classes (Panizza, 2005: 725). The subsequent imbrication of the state with society through reinvigorated trade union movements, business associations, and civil society movements renders the neoliberal analysis of a state separate from society inappropriate for interpreting these contemporary processes.

Third, in terms of the state–international relationship, again the pink tide is not concurrent with neoliberal principles. Kirby's analysis (2010b) is useful here when he employs Cerny's concept of the competition state (Cerny, Soederberg, and Menz, 2005). While certain states within the pink tide are able to resist neoliberal imperatives due to their natural endowments of hydrocarbons (Venezuela or Bolivia, for example), others are not (Brazil or Uruguay, for example). Nevertheless, even those that do not have the independence gained as a result of a petro-economy are learning to use the phenomenon of globalisation more for national developmental goals, rather than being subject to a 'race to the bottom' (Argentina, for example).

Social market capitalism

Keynesianism formed the theoretical core of the reaction to the Great Depression and laissez-faire political economy, and became enshrined in the so-called Post-War Consensus. Massive state intervention by Roosevelt in the USA, coupled after 1945 with similar interventionist strategies in Europe pioneered the economic recovery of the Western world. Keynes himself was instrumental in the Bretton Woods process from which emerged the series of international institutions that operate to this day. His thought formed the intellectual underpinnings of the economic aspects of the Post-War Consensus, a consensus that was not broken until the 1970s when inflation and unemployment fuelled a desire for change, which came in the form of the neoliberal revolution. John Maynard Keynes believed fundamentally in the role of the market, and directly rejected central economic planning due to its incompat-ibility with his politically liberal views (Radice, 2008: 1166). However, this belief was tempered by the fact that he advocated an intervention-ist government approach to the economy to manage macroeconomic phenomena such as unemployment, recession, and inflation (Keynes, 1936). Keynesianism also supported a mixed economy, where both the state and private sectors had important, complementary roles to play in economic activity. Belief in the risk of market failure, and the need for the state to correct those failures, was coupled on an aggregate level with a Keynesian theory of the business cycle where volatile expecta-tions due to imperfect information and markets are the main source of macroeconomic fluctuations. This leads to an ideological justifica-tion for a further role of the state, which is one of smoothing these fluctuations in the business cycle through a variety of means (Chang and Rowthorn, 2003; Chang, 2003; Clarke, 2005: 58; Rapley, 2008; Thirlwall, 2008).

State–market dichotomy

Social market capitalists therefore see further roles for the state in addi-tion to those accepted by neoliberalism involving the provision of a legal and institutional environment and the provision of public goods. These additional roles include redistribution of income to create greater equality in society, state intervention to correct market failure, and state intervention in the macro economy in order to alleviate recession and smooth the business cycle for social benefit, especially in macro-economic ways through Keynesian-inspired policies such as 'fiscal pump priming'. Each of these will now be taken in turn.

For SMCs there is a role for the state in order to promote social equity, and therefore in protecting the vulnerable and ensuring an equitable distribution of income between people, between groups in society, between regions, and across generations. While neoliberalism believes this function is achieved through the 'trickle-down theory' of growth, SMC believes trickle-down can be augmented and complemented by the state (Thirlwall, 2008: 291). This is derived from a belief in a more 'positive' conception of liberty. This term is derived from Berlin's (2002 [1969]) distinction between 'positive' and 'negative' liberty. Negative liberty implies a 'freedom from' some kind of coercion, rooted in a Hobbesian notion of 'lack of external impediments to motion' (1966 [1651]), and translates into freedom to assembly, economic trade, and enterprise etc. Positive liberty is more far-reaching than this limited concept and embraces the idea of the freedom we experience when we possess the capacity to pursue some end or action (Fitzpatrick, 2001: 53). This is grounded in the development of modern political liberalism in the early twentieth century, and translates into rights to employment, housing, health, and education. There are a number of ways in which state intervention can proceed to achieve this: for example, redistributive taxation, welfare provision, investment decisions to alter future consumption levels, or intervention to encourage or discourage merit and de-merit goods respectively (Chang, 1994: 12). Neoliberal theory, due to its methodological individualism, views this 'state as social guardian' attitude as paternalistic, and argues that the belief that the state should decide on what individuals should produce and consume and in what ways is a first step towards 'the road to serfdom' (Hayek, 1944). However, McPherson (1984) responds by suggesting that denouncing any moral judgement other than those based on narrowly defined individualism is as meaningless as citing moral reasons for state intervention without discussing the role of morality in our social and economic life. Methodological individualism can also be critiqued through the revelation that it is based on two fundamentally unrealistic assumptions: that we all know our own interests all the time, and that we are all rational all of the time (Chang, 1994: 15). The neoliberal argument has also been criticised through an examination of economic history. Karl Polanyi (1944: 150) suggests that 'the road to the free market was opened and kept open by an enormous increase in continuous, centrally organised and controlled interventionism. To make Adam Smith's simple and natural liberty compatible with the needs of a human society was a most complicated affair'.

State intervention to correct market failures is justified by the fact that the conditions required for markets to perform their allocative and creative functions in an optimal manner are very stringent, and are unlikely to be satisfied in any economy. The true benefit of output may not be reflected in price because of externalities, price may not reflect marginal cost because of market imperfections, and many developmental goods (e.g. infrastructure) may not be produced at all because markets are incomplete or missing entirely (Thirlwall, 2008: 289). While neoliberals (Friedman, 1962; Palley, 2005: 27, 29; Lapavitsas, 2005: 34) agree that public goods represent examples of market failure and therefore there is a role for the government to play, individually rational decisions made in a decentralised manner in response to price signals can lead to collectively inefficient outcomes. This is because innovation often requires complex institutional arrangements that cannot be provided by market relationships and maximum price competition

(Schumpeter, 1942). Furthermore, market prices do not reflect the opportunity costs to society of using factors of production, or the value to society of the production of such commodities.

Externalities are another example of market failure. Externalities exist when there are some spillover effects from an individual's activities to those of others, leading to a discrepancy between the private cost/benefit structure and the social cost/benefit structure (Chang, 1994: 10). Most infrastructure projects, such as transport, power and water, and social capital, such as education or health, have greater social returns than private return and therefore the market under-provides these goods from a social point of view. Conversely, other activities confer negative externalities by imposing costs on society that are not paid for by the provider, and are therefore oversupplied by the market from the social point of view (e.g. pollution) (Thirlwall, 2008: 291). Therefore, the SMC approach would be for the state to subsidise the positive externalities and tax the negative externalities (Thirlwall, 2008). Friedman (1962) has provided a counter-argument which he calls the 'neighbourhood-effects argument', which suggests that correcting one set of externalities often leads to another set as, (1) it will introduce an additional set of neighbourhood effects by failing to charge or compensate individuals properly, and (2) it creates further externalities by 'threatening freedom'. The problem with Friedman's argument is that the calculation as to whether gains from eliminating externalities are smaller than the losses from newly created externalities cannot be determined a priori, as well as the fact that freedom can be limited just as much by not solving externalities in the first place (Chang, 1994: 11).

Both the left in the form of Marxist literature (Clarke, 2005: 58), and the right in the form of the Chicago School (Friedman, 1962; Palley, 2005: 29; Lapavitsas, 2005: 35), have critiqued the SMC approach for assuming that the state will always act in a role similar to Plato's philosopher-king. Chalmers and Hadiz (1997) have characterised the SMC state as a 'predatory state', or characterised its political economy as 'predatory capitalism', which suggests that the state is more a dynamic–independent force with its own objective function. This view can be critiqued, at least in terms of developed economies, due to the fact that the rich institutional context of most modern states makes this more difficult, as well as the fact that this kind of autonomy is very difficult across time, space, and issues (Chang, 1994: 19). Furthermore, an 'interest-group approach' could characterise the state as 'an arena within which economic interest groups or normative social movements contended or allied with one another to shape the making of public policy decisions about the allocations of benefits among demanding groups' (Skocpol, 1985: 4). This has been articulated from the left by Marx (1967 [1848]) characterising the state as 'the economic committee of the bourgeoisie', and from the right by 'regulatory-capture' literature (Stigler, 1971).

Keynes took particular issue with the conventional, classical economic assumption that during a downturn, labour prices (or wages) drop, causing demand for employment to rise and therefore for employers to hire more workers (Rapley, 2008: 16). The events of the Great Depression led Keynes to believe that high levels of unemployment could potentially exist perpetually, and therefore advocated the use of fiscal policy (Clarke, 2005: 58). The government could create jobs in a variety of ways, which would stimulate demand for goods and services, and therefore lead to the private sector expanding output creating both economic growth and employment. Once this virtuous spiral was in operation the government could keep the economy from overheating through natural leakage by saving. In short, Keynes' prescription for alleviating recession and improving the capitalist economy was for the state to spend while times were bad, and save while they were good (Clarke, 2005: 17).

State–society dichotomy

For proponents of SMC 'the state both represents and integrates society: it is not superordinate to or merely contiguous with society, but imbricated with it and a necessary part of societal self-regulation' (Radice, 2008: 1165). The question that therefore arises is that which was posed by Durkheim (Gough and Olofsson, 1999: 2): How is social integration and a well-functioning society possible in a differentiated and individualised social order? In other words, given its roots in classical liberalism, how does SMC integrate the concepts of negative and positive freedom, or of the individualism inherent in the market place and the socialisation necessary for social integration? One solution, often postulated by neoliberals, is society's 'invisible forces', free from political interference. Durkheim offered an alternative, a new 'organic solidarity' grounded in the moral experiences derived from the complementary nature of work roles (i.e. cooperation across the division of labour) and supported by a development of law and state institutions (Gough and Olofsson, 1999: 2).

Historically, the means that states have used to encourage integration and restrict differentiation (especially economically) were based on a kind of welfare economics as well as the political–sociological concepts of pluralism and corporatism. In politics pluralism is where power lies with neither the electorate nor elites. Rather, it is distributed between a large number of groups such as trade unions, business organisations, interest groups, and other social coalitions. Corporatism is the theory and practice of organising society into corporations subordinate to the state. According to corporatist theory, workers and employers would be organised into industrial and professional corporations serving as organs of political representation and controlling to a large extent the persons and activities within their jurisdiction. Throughout the analysis of the SMC state in previous sections the role of the state in development, facilitated theoretically by Keynes, can be understood in the context of SMC's understanding of state–society relations, that is, that an expanded interventionist role to alleviate the worst excesses of capitalist development is the responsibility of the state given its role in social self-regulation. Such an understanding can also be seen in the concepts of pluralism and corporatism. Both adopt the principle of creating links with society, for pluralism society as a whole, and for corporatism more with the economic world, which is both broad-based and inclusive of all economic interests. Such arrangements facilitate the integrated nature of the state and society through fostering backwards and forwards linkages that precipitate into the state providing for society's needs and wants accurately and efficiently.

Through its pluralist links with society the state adopts the aim of universal welfare, with the corporatist structures ensuring this is done within the capitalist framework and therefore with two central understandings. First, that workers require social resources, health, and education to participate effectively as citizens; and second, that social policies are a precondition for economic efficiency as they help promote the onward march of the productive forces in capitalism (Esping-Andersen, 1990: 12).

National–international dichotomy

Social market capitalism is necessarily national in character as the state is rooted in national social contracts among organised interests (Radice, 2008: 9). In other words, the development of citizenship rights was coterminous with that of the nation state (Fitzpatrick, 2001: 74). However, given the increasingly important role of globalisation and therefore the introduction of the national–international dichotomy into the analysis, what happens to citizenship rights? Ohmae (1995) has argued that citizenship rights are incompatible with globalisation and that it is only as market actors that we can exert influence on the global economy (Fitzpatrick, 2001: 75). Others such as David Held (see, for example, Held, 2000, or Ougaard and Higgott, 2002) have championed the concept of a global polity or cosmopolitan democracy, which suggests that global institutions that guarantee global rights, which are difficult for the nation state to enforce individually, can be constructed.

Greater problems exist in the social arena, and with social rights. Can there be a globalised form of citizenship that defines all humans as having rights to at least minimum levels or welfare and security? Or, what is the relationship between globalisation and welfare regime change (Ellison, 2006)? The answer(s) to this question are important, inter alia, in order to understand what role the character of contemporary globalisation plays in influencing state behaviour in relation to the development process.

One argument is that the economic nature of globalisation introduced a 'race to the bottom' for welfare states of countries trying to make their national economies the most attractive for foreign investment in a highly competitive market place. Indeed, a neoliberal drift has been identified by Ellison (2006: 49), which complements Giddens' (1990) argument that the increasing power of global capital constitutes by far the most serious difficulty for national governments struggling to manage welfare systems in increasingly open economies. The corollary to this is that in fact it is more *national* economics that has influenced welfare-regime change in the context of deindustrialisation and the shift towards a service economy. In addition, further analysis highlights the role of institutional structures in the state that can mitigate the pressures of globalisation. Ellison (2006) highlights the interplay between these two dichotomies of national and domestic, and economics and institutions. In essence, 'national welfare systems are changing as new economic pressures interact with existing institutional arrangements – political, social, and cultural – in ways that render the latter less stable' (Ellison, 2006: 2). Therefore, this argument contends that economic change at the global level is increasing, but the degree of pressure that it exerts on national welfare arrangements can be, to varying extents, accommodated by adjustment of institutional foundations in ways that do not fundamentally alter their character (Ellison, 2006: 48).

The introduction of the international, or the role of globalisation, into social market capitalist theory therefore offers some challenges to a concept of state–society relations grounded in national social contracts among organised interests. Attempts have been made, most notably by David Held (2000), to promote the use of global methods of governance to tackle global issues and promote global rights. However, such attempts seem to be difficult in practice as they remained based on nation state funding and willingness to enforce these rights nationally. More integrated approaches (see, for example, Colás, 2005; MacGregor, 2005), which stress the interplay between national and international pressures, as well as between economic and institutional perspectives, appear to offer the most sophisticated analysis. Such an approach suggests that nation states remain important in welfare regime articulation, and have a variety of institutional responses to alleviate/mitigate global pressures.

Social market capitalism and the pink tide

Social Market Capitalism theory is not appropriate either as a meta-theoretical interpretation of the pink tide. Keynesianism formed the theoretical core of SMC, and became enshrined in the so-called Post-War Consensus. John Maynard Keynes believed fundamentally in the role of the market. However, this was a belief tempered by a need for government intervention in order to manage macroeconomic phenomena such as unemployment, recession, and inflation (Keynes, 1936). Keynesianism therefore supported a mixed economy, where both the state and private sectors had important, complementary roles to play in economic activity.

Interventions in the economy in pink-tide states across Latin America have revolved around economic growth and development, rather than redistribution. It is true that a strong poverty reduction element has existed in some countries (most notably Brazil), but this is different from redistribution. The lack of policies to reduce inequality, combined with little to no interest in developing a comprehensive welfare state through the de-commodification of key welfare goods (Esping-Andersen, 1990) demonstrate the inappropriateness of interpreting the pink tide through such an SMC model relationship. Indeed, this conclusion is confirmed when analysing the state–society relationship. The absence of SMC-type social relations in the form of a social contract based on principles of redistribution or comprehensive poverty reduction (rather than a neoliberal style-social safety net approach), themselves the result of a different approach to the state–market relationship, results in contemporary Latin American pink tide states diverging from a SMC interpretation of their political economy.

Academics such as Weyland (2010: 9) have argued that pursuit of a social democratic agenda in Latin America is impossible as the region is incapable of replicating Europe's achievements in this area. 'An underdeveloped productive apparatus, deep social segmentation due to the exclusion of many workers from the formal economy, and the organisational weaknesses and shallow societal roots of many political parties and trade unions preclude a determined reform strategy that could profoundly alter the distribution of socioeconomic benefits in society' (Weyland, 2010: 9). Therefore, the northwest European experience cannot be replicated in present-day Latin America.

Dependency

The dependency school of thought arose in Latin America as a result of the failure of the ECLA (Economic Commission for Latin America) programme of the 1960s. The ECLA development strategy of protectionism and industrialisation through import substitution in the 1950s was widespread among populist regimes throughout Latin America. Under this 'ECLA Manifesto' Prebisch (1950), the head of ECLA, contended that reliance on exports of food and raw materials would inevitably lead to a deterioration of Latin America's terms of trade, which in turn would adversely affect its domestic capital accumulation. Therefore, industrialisation should be speeded up through substitution of current imports with domestic production; income from exported raw materials would be used to import capital goods and thus increase the rate of growth; and governments would actively participate as coordinators of the industrialisation programme (So, 1990: 94).

The purpose of this section is first to outline the dependency position through a synopsis of its critique of the nature of the international economic system that prevailed at the time, and its subsequent alternative economic policies that arose from this critique. Analysis will then move forward to the 'new' dependency school as represented by academics such as Cardoso and Faletto (Cardoso, 1973; Cardoso and Faletto, 1979). Once complete, a discussion of how these works influenced the political economy of Latin American countries through an analysis of populism will be conducted. In essence, the dependency school (and its political manifestation in Latin America through populist regimes) advocated state intervention in the market that went beyond the forms of state intervention advocated by Keynesianism and SMC, combined with a specific set of social relations in the state–society relationship present in these countries. While populism has been defined in both political and economic terms that complement the existence of such policies, this is insufficient due to the fact that populist regimes have also emerged from the right, as well as from both rural and economically developed nations. Therefore, these two concepts of dependency and populism, and the relationship between them, will be further explored further.

The original dependency theorists

By the 1960s many of those regimes that had engaged in the ECLA programme were plagued by inflation, currency devaluation, declining terms of trade, and other economic problems so that the ECLA Manifesto was discredited. The failure of the moderate ECLA programme prompted the dependency school first to propose a critique in an attempt to explain the failure of the ECLA program, and second to propose a more radical alternative programme structured around the implications of their critique.

Dos Santos provides the classic definition of dependency, arguing that the character of the relationship between two or more countries 'assumes the form of dependence when some countries (the dominant ones) can expand and can be self-starting, while other countries (the dependent ones) can do this only as a reflection of that expansion' (1971: 226). Therefore, the main observation of the dependency school is that dependency is an external condition, and therefore the main obstacle to development lay outside of the national economy (Gwynne and Kay, 1999: 112). This observation represented a fundamental critique of the modernisation school, which assumed that there were only internal problems to blame, associated with traditional culture, overpopulation, low investment, or lack of entrepreneurial ability (Frank, 1966). As Sunkel (1973) observed, modernisation theory saw the world as uniformly progressing towards an end point of development. In reality, underdevelopment is part of the structure of the economy and the result of structural elements. Therefore, the structure of the system changes as a consequence of exogenous factors, which are a product of the evolution of the hegemon in the international system.

These structural elements are the result of the legacy of colonialism. This historical legacy has resulted in less developed countries (LDCs) being totally restructured, and therefore altering their paths to development. There has been a 'development of underdevelopment' through a 'metropolis–satellite' relationship (Frank, 1966). Colonialism meant the structuring of LDC economies with the aim of facilitating the transfer of economic surplus to the West, which has produced the underdevelopment of LDCs, and development in the core. In other words, 'the historical process that generates development in the Western metropoles also simultaneously generates underdevelopment in Third World satellites' (So, 1990: 97). Dependency theory therefore suggests that these structural elements place fundamental structural limitations on the industrial development of LDCs (Dos Santos, 1971; Frank, 1966; Sunkel, 1973). Firstly, industrial development is dependent upon the existence of a primary product export sector because it brings in foreign currency to buy advanced machinery and capital from the West. Furthermore, this facilitates the maintenance of traditional oligarchic power structures in dependent states due to the fact that their power base lies in these primary product export bases that are maintained and perpetuated as a result of the dependency relationship. At the same time, there is a perpetuation of 'political dependence' (Frank, 1966) as these industries are often controlled by foreign capital. Political dependence is therefore the result of the 'close interconnection of the economy and the socio–political structure of the satellite with those of the metropolis. The closer the satellites link with and dependence on the metropolis, the closer is the satellite bourgeoisie, including the so-called "national bourgeoisie", linked and dependent upon the metropolis' (Frank, 1966).

Second, development is strongly influenced by fluctuations in the balance of payments, which are often in deficit because of three interrelated reasons. First, the high prevalence of monopoly in international markets for many traditional exports of LDCs results in depressed prices for raw materials and, at the same time, increasing prices for manufactured goods. Second, increased levels of foreign capital in dependent economies means that profits often go back to Western economies. Third, due to perpetuating balance-of-payments deficits LDCs increasingly rely on foreign loans and aid, therefore enhancing and perpetuating the dependency relationship (Kay, 1989: 41). While there was not much aid to Latin America in the 1960s this factor became increasingly significant in the 1970s and the 1980s with the debt crisis and subsequent restructuring of debt profiles on the continent.

Third, industrial development in dependent economies is contingent and conditional upon the technological monopoly of the West. Much of the technology and capital that is required for such a process is not simply sold to developing nations, rather it is rented through a system of royalties (maintained through patents) or the investment is carried out by Western corporations and therefore ownership remains with that company. The result is that the profits gained from such technology and investment is repatriated back to the core countries, therefore perpetuating the dependency condition of the host country (Pearson, 1985: Chapter 2).

In addition to the external conditions of international polarisation that create dependency, Sunkel (1973: 141) also points to sources of internal polarisation. These exist in a context of external dependency, and therefore ISI has not facilitated parity of Latin American countries with the global North, but merely changed the structure rather than the nature of the external economic relationship. Nevertheless they represent further means by which the dependency condition is perpetuated. Therefore, internal racial, political, social, and cultural discrimination in Latin America are important as they constitute substantial obstacles to the upward social mobility of important groups, and may even accentuate the marginal condition of certain groups over a longer period of time. As a result, 'marginality' – the shift towards a broader quest for an answer to the problems of mass, rather than individual, poverty (Bromley and Gerry, cited in Kay, 1989: 88) – arises out of a lack of access to stable income because of conditions limiting access to means of production, as well as their limited availability, and also because of discrimination. Therefore, among others, scholars such as Jose Nun (1969) and Anibal Quijano (1973) argued that there was a growing separation between a 'blue-collar elite' and the marginal masses. These marginal masses threatened social and political stability and exacerbated the 'great fear' (Gerassi, 1963), further fuelling perceived threats of a revolutionary overthrow forged by a marginalised lumpenproletariat (Fanon, 1963). For Sunkel (1973) the penetration of transnational capital into the Latin American economies was largely responsible for this, as it led to national disintegration by dividing society into two sectors: one which is integrated into the transnational system and one which is excluded from this system and which constitutes the marginal sector composed of the majority of the population. However, rising marginality in the Latin American context was also linked to ISI's inability to absorb the growing contingent of the labour force and its tendency to expel labour. This capital-intensive industrialisation process led to further income concentration and marginalisation of sectors of the population from the fruits of technological progress (Kay, 1989: 90).

In summary, traditional dependency as a body of literature possesses a number of fundamental characteristics. The main one, as discussed earlier, is that dependency is an external condition, although Sunkel also highlights important sources of internal polarisation that complements and reinforces this. Secondly, the nature of this dependency is fundamentally economic, although this does also lead to more political aspects such as the perpetuation of traditional oligopolistic power structures based around the power bases of traditional primary export sectors. Third, dependency can be seen as a component of regional polarisation. Therefore, underdevelopment in the periphery and development in the core are two aspects of a single process of capital accumulation, leading to regional polarisation in the global economy (So, 1990: 104). Fourth, dependency is seen as incompatible with development. While minor development can occur during periods of isolation, such as during a world depression or a world war (Frank, 1966), genuine development in the periphery is highly unlikely with the continual flow of surplus to the core. Finally, dependency is seen as a general process. The aim of dependency analysis is to outline the general pattern of relations in the Third World throughout the history of capitalism. Thus, some critics argue that national variations and historical complexity are downplayed in order to present the ideal type construct of dependency (So, 1990: 104).

The 'new' dependency studies

Many of these core assumptions of traditional dependency were challenged by the 'new' dependency studies, epitomised by the work of Cardoso (Cardoso, 1973; Cardoso and Faletto, 1979). Therefore, unlike the general analysis of the classical dependency school, Cardoso proposed a 'historical–structural' methodology. Therefore dependency is not a term to characterise the universal pattern of underdevelopment in LDCs, rather it is a methodology for the analysis of concrete situations in Third World development. As a result, this research agenda focuses more on the historic specificity of a dependency situation, and therefore how the specific constellations of dependency structures generate the possibilities for transformation. Thus, unlike classic dependency, which emphasises the structural determination of dependency, Cardoso views it as a much more open-ended process. If dependency structures delimit the range of oscillation, then political struggles of classes, groups, and the state can revive and transfigure these structures and may even replace them with others that are not predetermined (So, 1990: 136). Therefore, Cardoso (1973) argues that it is possible to have 'dependent-associated development'. Or, in other words, '[that] there can be development and dependency and that there exists more dynamic forms of dependence than those characterising enclave or quasi-colonial situations (Cardoso, 1977: 20).

Cardoso also highlights and emphasises the internal structures of dependency, as well as the external ones, and therefore supporting the idea of Sunkel outlined in the previous section. Instead of stressing the economic foundation of dependency, Cardoso is more interested in analysing the socio–political aspect of dependency, especially class struggles, group conflict, and political movements (So, 1990: 136). Therefore, analysis should not be restricted to the efficacy of different economic policies such as ISI; rather, the central issue for Cardoso is people's movements and consciousness of their own interests. Consequently, for Cardoso (1977: 14) 'what was significant was the movement, the class struggles, the redefinitions of interest, the political alliances that maintained the structures while at the same time opening the possibility of their transformation.' As stated, this complements Sunkel's analysis of the role of the internal situation in the dependent country as external domination appears as an internal force through the social practices of local groups and classes that try to enforce foreign interests because they may coincide with values and interests that these groups pretend are their own (So, 1990: 136), or what Cardoso and Faletto term the 'internalisation of external interests' (Cardoso and Faletto, 1979).

With the rise of neoliberal agendas in many Latin American states in the 1980s and 1990s the dependency school offered an alternative interpretation of that agenda. Commentators (Green, 2003; Rock, 2002; Gwynne and Kay, 1999) suggested that the essence of core–periphery relations has remained the same despite shifts in the economic sectors. Therefore, Latin America's endemic problems (of which the crisis in Argentina for example was a manifestation) of vulnerability to external forces, social exclusion and poverty have not been addressed by the neoliberal agenda. Indeed, the free market agenda has even exacerbated these issues (Gwynne and Kay, 1999: 4). Neoliberal policies in Argentina have increased inequality and therefore exacerbated tensions. Creation of part-time, insecure, and temporary jobs, combined with the fact that many of the new service sector jobs created are inferior to previous skilled manufacturing jobs, has led to the conclusion that 'labour deregulation' is not the key to poverty reduction (Green, 2003). Furthermore, Rock has analysed how core countries are able to regulate their foreign reserves through interest rates, while periphery nations have no such controls; and therefore their economies are controlled to a degree by policy in the nations of the core (Rock, 2002).

Theory to practice: Populism in Latin America

This evolution from ECLA structuralism to classical dependency and then to 'new' dependency informed more than just an intellectual debate, as many countries (especially in Latin America) adopted the economic prescriptions of this body of theory. Due to a redefinition of development away from the modernisation school's narrow concept of more industry, more output, and rising productivity towards one that put rising living standards for all people in the periphery at the top of the agenda, 'developmental programs should not cater to elites and urban dwellers, but should attempt to satisfy the human needs of rural peasants, the unemployed, and the needy' (So, 1990: 105). Consequently, some in the dependency school suggests that peripheral countries should disassociate with the core countries (Senghaas, 1979; Altmann, 1981). Instead of relying upon foreign aid and foreign technology, peripheral countries should adopt a self-reliance model – relying upon their own resources and planning their own paths of development so as to achieve independence and autonomous national development. Dependency theory therefore accepted the ECLA structuralist emphasis on ISI, but rejected its attempts to base development on a partnership between government and a foreign private capitalist sector. This was due to their negative interpretation of trans-national corporations (TNCs). Dependency theory suggested that TNCs use monopoly power to extract large profits and royalty payments from the host economies. Furthermore, this situation was exacerbated by the fact that many TNCs imported the capital goods necessary for the highly capital-intensive industrial techniques from the western economies. This led to the double impact of increasing pressure on the country's balance of payments, and increasing unemployment due to the increasing capital component of production (Jenkins, 1984: 222). As a result, TNCs displaced or incorporated nationally owned firms, prevented profit accumulation for domestic re-investment, and therefore prevented the growth of a dynamic Latin American middle class.

Many of these policies were adopted by what has been termed 'leftist–populist' governments in Latin America in the 1950s, 1960s, and 1970s. But what is the specific definition of populism? The dividing line between the left and populism is often blurred in Latin America (Heidrich and Tussie, 2009). Peron and the Peronist party are often portrayed as the quintessential populist movement, with leftist policies based on ISI and redistribution of wealth to workers. As a result, it is through these specific economic policies that a number of commentators have attempted to define populism. As Dornbusch and Edwards (1991: 7) have suggested, 'again and again, and in country after country, policymakers have embraced economic programs that rely heavily on the use of expansive fiscal and credit policies and an overvalued currency to accelerate growth and redistributive income'. In trade policy, populist policies would include 'increasing real rates of protection via non-tariff barriers, outright raising of tariffs to consolidated levels, grandstanding and nay saying posturing in trade negotiations to derail multilateral and regional trade talks, arbitrary controls on sources of hard currency, affecting trade volume and flows, plus conflating trade negotiations with declarations of standing up or caving in to US interests, or other sources of foreign capital present in the domestic economy' (Heidrich and Tussie, 2009). However, 'after a short period of economic growth ... bottlenecks develop provoking unsustainable macroeconomic pressures that, at the end, result in the plummeting of real wages and severe balance of payment difficulties. The final outcome of these experiments has generally been inflation, crisis, and the collapse of the economic system' (Heidrich and Tussie, 2009). Therefore, economic populism is an approach to economics that emphasises growth and income redistribution, and de-emphasises the risks of inflation and deficit finance, external constraints, and the reaction of economic agents to aggressive non-market policies.

However, over a 50-year time span populism in Argentina has been able to go from the historical leftist–populist nationalism of Peron to the neoliberal right wing policies of Carlos Menem. Indeed, Weyland (1999) and others have advanced the argument that Menem's administration, as well as Salinas' in Mexico and Fujimori's in Peru, were in fact populist governments with neoliberal agendas (Heidrich and Tussie, 2009). Therefore, it becomes apparent that populism must really be defined in terms of politics. While economic leaning has been significant, political roots also matter. The reintroduction of politics, or the emphasis on the socio-political nature of dependency, informed leftist–populist movements in Latin America, and therefore populism. Indeed, Kaufman and Stallings (1991: 16) have defined populism as a phenomenon that 'involves a set of economic policies designed to achieve specific political goals'. These political goals are: first, mobilising support within organised labour and lower middle-class groups; second, obtaining complementary backing for domestically orientated business; and third, politically isolating the rural oligarchy, foreign enterprises, and large-scale domestic industrial elites (Kaufman and Stallings, 1991: 16). Therefore, behind the economic policies is a political logic that propels the emergence of populist programs.

For some influential authors, populism is 'the very essence of the political' (Laclau, 1977: 222), 'the mirror of democracy' (Panizza, 2005: 99); the construction of a people is 'the political operation *par excellence*' (Laclau, 1977: 153). However, even with this positive view of populism there is no a priori guarantee that the will of the people will be lead to an appropriate form that could facilitate equitable development; yet the fact is that populism can represent the people as an oppressed part of a divided society makes for the recurrently blurred dividing lines in a continent marked by extreme income inequalities, poverty and political polarisation (Heidrich and Tussie, 2009). Yet, once again, this definition seems unable to include right wing as well as rural populist movements.

Other attempts have been made to forward a more functionalist definition: 'populism is an aberrant phenomenon produced by the asynchronism of the process of transition from a traditional to an industrial society' (Laclau, 1977: 147). However, as Laclau (1977: 158) points out, 'can populism therefore be assigned to a transitional stage of development? No because it has been present in developed societies', such as in Italy, France, or Germany. Laclau therefore concludes that the meaning of ideological elements identified with populism must be sought in the structure of which they are a moment, and not in ideal paradigms. These structures refer to the class nature of populist movements, to their roots in modes of production and their articulation. As a result, in order for this definition to hold true and therefore for a theory of populism to be postulated, the analysis must differentiate between the general problem of *class determination* of political and ideological superstructures, and the *forms of existence* of classes at the level of these superstructures (Laclau, 1977: 158). By defining classes as the poles of antagonistic production relations which have no necessary form of existence at the ideological and political levels, a theory can be postulated that is able to take into account left and right forms of populism, industrial and rural.

To sum up, traditional populism in Latin America can be considered in specific economic and political terms as outlined before. A focus on redistributive policies through macroeconomic policies in order to generate support among the working class, as well as significant sectors of the middle class, means that populism has connoted a reformist set of policies tailored to promote development without explosive class conflict. Programmes therefore normally responded to the problems of underdevelopment by expanding state activism to incorporate the workers in a process of accelerated industrialisation through ameliorative redistributive measures. This was true of Perón, as well as other leftist populist governments in Latin America during the twentieth century. However, such a definition is unable to take into account the populism of the right, which in Argentina emerged in the form of *Menemismo*. In order to incorporate all forms of populist regime, concepts such as those advanced by Ernesto Laclau must be considered. Such a consideration facilitates an understanding of populism as the poles of antagonistic production relations which have no necessary form of existence at the ideological and political levels. Populism in Latin America often arose as a response to the pressures of a globalisation that was characterised by liberalism and modernisation theory of the first half of the twentieth century. Therefore many populist regimes, especially that of Juan Perón in Argentina, were associated with economic policies that were championed by some dependency theorists and could be characterised as ISI.

Dependency and the pink tide

Some contributions have suggested that several governments of the pink tide represent a return to these populist regimes, many of which define populism in a very selective way with a highly normative agenda through a desire to place overwhelmingly negative connotations on the use of the word (see, for example, Castañeda, 2006). These contributions see many policies of elements of the pink tide as cynical attempts to win over the support of the masses at the expense of long-term stability and sustainability of the economy. They see not only a return to some aspects of traditional *desarrollismo* through ISI-like policies, but also a reflection of traditional dependency inspired state–society relations through clientelistic practices that co-opt elements of the working classes into supporting the governing regimes.

Such analyses are not sufficiently sensitive to the overall political economy of the pink tide. They represent essentially reductionist contributions that do not take into account all aspects of contemporary policy in a holistic manner. Therefore, as was argued for Latin America and the pink tide movement as a whole at the start of this chapter, and will be argued in detail for the specific case studies of Argentina 2003–7 and Brazil 2003–10 in Part II, detailed analysis reveals that new forms of state–market and state–society relationships have developed across the continent in the first decade of the twenty-first century.

The changes wrought to national societies as a result of 20 years of neoliberal restructuring, as well as the series of economic crises that beset the region, has transformed the social base of these pink tide governments, and thus the nature of the social contract under their regimes. The almost exclusive and hegemonic position of the organised working classes as seen under traditional *desarrollismo* governments has been replaced by broader based, more inclusive coalitions of support that include sections of society such as the unorganised poor, middle-class elements, and business associations. The policies that are advocated by these regimes are not a return to crude ISI, rather an attempt to pursue autonomous nationalist development in an era of globalisation characterised by the hegemony of international capital (for detailed analyses of these claims refer to Part II).

Conclusions: Latin America as a model of alternative political economy for post-crisis development

This chapter has argued that the new left in Latin America, known as the pink tide, has nothing to do with the old left, exemplified by the national–populist experiences that emerged in the 1930s or the 'guerilla romanticism of the sixties and seventies' (Lynch, 2007: 382). The pink tide is not about an anti-capitalist alternative but 'about generating an inclusive market economy that promotes investment and protects private property but simultaneously creates jobs and guarantees individual and social rights' (Lynch, 2007: 382). Furthermore, Lynch goes on to argue '[i]nternationally, this path does not mean subjection to the United States, but it does not encourage ideological polarisation against America either. On the contrary, as the governments of Brazil and Argentina have shown in recent years, the goal is to form regional blocs capable of negotiating better terms for international trade vis-á-vis developed nations' (Lynch, 2007: 382).

The pink tide is therefore a different path to those present in the history of Latin America. It is different from the national–populist regimes of the pre- and post-war period and also different to the neoliberal regimes of the late twentieth century that produced a series of systemic crises. Therefore, theories of political economy that centre on dependency or neoliberalism are inadequate to explain and contextualise contemporary Argentine political economy. In addition, SMC is also inadequate. This Eurocentric interpretation of political economy is not present in the constellation of state–society and state–market relationships, which instead is a product of the Latin American continent's history rooted in populism and neoliberalism. The Keynesian post-war consensus that dominated European political economy did not take root in Latin America, and subsequent experimentation with neoliberal restructuring, both nationally driven by domestic governments (as with Argentina, for example) and internationally driven by the IMF (through SAPs), has created a legacy where the institutions present in government and society do not constitute a SMC model.

This book argues that alternative theories of political economy must therefore be examined if greater analytical clarity is to be gleaned from examination of contemporary Latin America. Draibe and Riesco (2007) argue that the notion of the 'developmental welfare state' can capture the emerging arrangement of economic and social policy in Latin America. As Riesco argues (2009: 32) '[u]nlike twentieth century developmentalism, now the state is assuming a strategic and regulatory role, relying on emergent private enterprise for most economic matters'. Such an argument bears closer examination, and the next chapter will examine in detail the potential contribution of the Developmental Regime literature in political economy with regard to its efficacy in analysing and interpreting the pink tide in Latin America. Therefore, a theory that arose out of study of East Asia will be placed in the context of Latin America. Once this has been articulated in the next chapter, Part II will offer detailed case studies that will support these theoretical propositions.

All of this must also be placed in the context of economic crisis. The neoliberal era of the 1980s and 1990s in Latin America facilitated a series of systemic crises, from Argentina (1989) to Mexico (1994) to Brazil (1998) back to Argentina (2001) and Brazil (2002) again to name just the major ones. This book will argue that a fundamental shift in political economy has occurred in Latin America after the latest cycle of these crises at the turn of the century, a shift that has not only facilitated more stable growth and development strategies but has also ended a constant cycle of instability followed by further crisis. With the additional context of the 'Great Recession' and the 2007 global financial crisis, and the relatively lacklustre performance of post-crisis OECD economies, further credence is given to the strength of this new political economy with regard to strong post-crisis performance and strengthening of economic growth and development. These matters will be considered in detail in Part III of this book.

3
From Developmental States to Developmental Regimes: Lessons from Asia for Contemporary Latin America

The previous chapter demonstrated that mainstream meta-theories of political economy are inadequate when attempting to characterise and analyse the pink tide in Latin America. While elements of some or all of them may exist in different regimes across the continent, no one by itself can consistently and coherently capture the nature of these regimes. The chapter concluded by suggesting that the continent could represent fertile ground for articulation of alternative models of development, as well as alternative models of *post-crisis* development given the recent historical context of many countries in Latin America. It is the purpose of this chapter to outline an alternative model of political economy which, it will be argued, offers the necessary analytical leverage to interpret the contemporary political economy of Latin America's pink tide. This alternative is the 'Developmental Regime' (Pempel, 1998, 1999), itself a reformulation of traditional Developmental State theory. The Developmental State 'became by about 1990 the major ideological rallying point for those who wish to contest the appropriateness of neoliberalism and the Washington Consensus as a framework for effective governance and economic development in the global South' (Radice, 2008: 1153). Therefore, this chapter will seek to trace the contours of this theory and how it has developed. In doing so, this chapter will shed greater light on the nature of the pink tide, which was detailed in the previous chapter. Once complete, Part II will continue with in-depth case studies of Argentina and Brazil in order to further demonstrate the efficacy of a Developmental Regime approach when looking at Latin American political economy.

Origins of the Developmental State

The intellectual roots of this concept lie in mercantilism and the writings of Friedrich List (1983 [1841]). List wrote his work as a critique of free trade and classical liberalism, and contended that nations can have very different strategies concerning the role of government in development, and that the premises of liberalism are not self-evident truths but rather a set of choices to be made (Vogel and Barma, 2008: 25). This view was derived from the fact that the principles of development should be based on nation and nationality, rather than the traditional liberal emphasis on the principles of cosmopolitanism and individualism. Therefore, the national interest cannot be achieved by individuals focusing on their own *self*-interest. National power and national prosperity are to be achieved through stimulation of the 'productive powers', which are more important than individual wealth for the wellbeing of national economies (Vogel and Barma, 2008: 25).

In his work *The National System of Political Economy* (1983 [1841]) List distinguishes between the power of producing wealth and wealth itself, concluding that the former is more important than the latter as 'it insures not only the possession and the increase of what has been gained, but also the replacement of what has been lost' (List, 1983 [1841]: XII). He concludes from this that 'had he [Adam Smith] followed up the idea *productive power* without allowing his mind to be dominated by the idea of value, exchangeable value, he would have been led to perceive that an independent *theory of the productive power*, must be considered by the side of a *theory of values* in order to explain economic phenomena' (List, 1983 [1841]: XII, italics in original). The *theory of values* is what List terms Adam Smith's analysis in the *Wealth of Nations* (1974 [1776]) that concentrates on 'the science of exchange', or markets and the division of labour. By concentrating on this, and only this, List suggests that Smith has separated out 'mental forces from material circumstances and conditions, and thereby laid the foundation for all the absurdities and contradictions from which his school suffers up to the present day' (List, 1983 [1841]: XII). When this principle of the theory of productive power is extended to nations and national economies List is able to sketch out a series of historical examples, which show that economic development and levels of wealth across nations has been enhanced where the interest of individuals has been subordinated to those of the nation (List, 1983 [1841]: XIV), and therefore that the promotion of individual interests does not lead to the promotion of the common good in society (List, 1983 [1841]: XIV).

As can be seen, List frequently criticised the 'Smithsonian school' (as he called liberalism). However, his work was not a complete rejection of Smith, rather a caution against directly importing his ideas into countries that were less politically and economically developed than those Smith had analysed (Harlen, 1999: 739). Indeed, like contemporary liberals such as Smith, List saw universal free trade as a useful goal, but it did not represent a realistic vision for many economically weak countries in a world where free trade was the exception (Harlen, 1999: 742). Therefore, while the writings of List represent some of the intellectual origins of the Developmental State, his influence should not be overstated (Harlen, 1999: 734).

The historian Alexander Gerschenkron (1962) analysed the period of 'late development' in his book *Economic Backwardness in Historical Perspective*, and concluded that in a number of historical instances the industrialising process in less developed countries showed considerable differences, as compared with the more advanced countries, not only with regard to the speed of development but also with regard to the productive and organisational structures of industry that emerged from those processes (Gerschenkron, 1962). This was due to the fact that these late industrialising economies faced fundamentally different challenges than did Britain (the first nation to industrialise). This is due to the technology gap that these late developing nations faced, with the consequence that they did not have the luxury of industrialising slowly (as did Britain). As a result, rapid investment in heavy industry was necessary, something that was achieved in Germany through their industrial banks, or through the state, as in Russia. Therefore, Gerschenkron provided a further justification of state intervention based on the interaction of technological and institutional factors. He suggested that as a country embarks on a developmental process later and later, it needs to raise proportionally larger and larger amounts of savings as the minimum efficient scale of production grows larger and larger, which therefore needs a more and more powerful institution for industrial financing, the state being the most powerful of such institutions (Chang and Rowthorn, 2003: 22).

The central thesis of these works was that the state should play a central role in economic development. The modern manifestation of these classical arguments was to be found in the context of East Asian development, and it is to these works that this book now turns.

The Developmental State in East Asia

Developmental State theory emerged as a counter-critique to the neoclassical development paradigm and the neoliberal revolution of the 1970s and 1980s through a reinterpretation of the East Asian (the 'Newly Industrialised Countries' or NICs) development experience (Öniş, 1991: 110; Shaikh, 2005: 48). Although its origins lay outside the traditional left, it became popular among that community due to the fact that not only did it offer a critique of the neoclassical model, but it also placed the state at the centre of the analysis (Rapley, 2008: 135). Therefore, a new critique of the neoclassical model and the SAPs of the 1980s emerged that was not rooted in the traditional leftist discourse of structuralism and dependency. The central thesis of this body of literature (see, for example, Johnson, 1982; Deyo, 1987; Amsden, 1989; Wade, 1990) is clearly linked to List and Gerschenkron and stipulates that 'late development' should be understood as a process in which states play a strategic role in harnessing domestic and international forces to work for the national interest. Key to rapid industrialisation is a strong and autonomous state, providing directional thrust to the operation of the market mechanism, and it is this synergy between the state and the market that provides the basis for outstanding development experience (Öniş, 1991: 110). Chalmers Johnson (1982) in his book *MITI and the Japanese Miracle* termed Japan a 'Developmental State', thus becoming the pioneer of this concept. In this book he emphasises that Japanese institutions constituted a system that was favourable for economic growth, with the crucial ingredient being the role of the state in planning and guiding economic activity, through what came to be known as industrial strategy (Vogel and Barma, 2008: 240).

Both Amsden (1989) and Wade (1990) built upon Johnson with respect to industrial strategy and its impact on industrial performance. In the case of Taiwan, Wade (1990) suggested a 'governed market theory' of East Asian industrialisation as an alternative to the neoclassical 'free market' explanation. The essential elements of Wade's argument are that superior economic performance was largely the consequence of high levels of investment in certain key industries, higher levels than would have occurred in the absence of government intervention. This was the product of policies that enabled the government to guide or govern the process of resource allocation so as to produce a specific production and investment profile. This set of policies can be grouped under the banner of industrial policy, and, for Wade, are in turn supported by specific political, institutional, and organisational arrangements pertaining to both the state apparatus and private business as well as their mutual interaction (Öniş, 1991: 112).

Amsden's (1989) book *Asia's Next Giant: South Korea and Late Industrialisation* is an account of South Korea's Developmental State in action that contains strong parallels with Johnson's account of MITI and Japanese industrial policy, and to a lesser extent with Wade's account of the Taiwanese experience. Amsden argued that during the period in question South Korea could be characterised as a prototype case of a guided market economy in which market rationality was constrained by the priorities of industrialisation. Therefore, the government performed a strategic role in shaping domestic and international forces so that they were harnessed to national economic interests. Rapid industrialisation *per se* was the goal, rather than profit maximisation based on comparative advantage (Amsden, 1989). Key industries were selected (on the basis of potential for rapid technological progress, potential for labour productivity growth, and industries with high income elasticity of demand in world markets), promoted, subsidised, and exposed to global competition. Thus, the market was guided by a conception of the longer-term rationality of investment formulated by the state's elites. Furthermore, state intervention involved the creation of price distortions as well as more direct controls so that economic activity was directed towards greater investment. This was in contrast to the logic of neoclassical development theory, as a high degree of government intervention distorted relative prices so that the desired levels of investment could be channelled towards the strategic sectors (Amsden, 1989).

The central insight of Green and Amsden's analysis is that the government not only subsidised industries to stimulate growth, but also set stringent performance criteria in exchange for these subsidies. Therefore, while there were relatively high degrees of protection at first, that protection was incrementally withdrawn as the firms became more competitive so that they could gain access to foreign markets. Thus, the way in which industrial policy was implemented contrasted sharply with the more negative forms of industrial policy in certain West European countries, which usually involve subsidising declining firms or industries experiencing financial difficulties.

The formulation and implementation of strategic industrial policy in the cases of South Korea and Japan outlined before were facilitated by specific political and institutional arrangements. Contributions by Koo and Johnson in Deyo (1987) highlight the key distinction between the political basis for strong, autonomous developmentalist states and the institutional basis for state intervention and effective policy implementation. Analysis suggests that not only did this political basis exist in certain East Asian countries in the form of a specific socio-political context that facilitated strategy formulation conducive to rapid industrialisation and economic development, but that this basis, although separate from the institutions and structures through which policies are implemented, represented a fundamental aspect of development capacity (Öniş, 1991: 114). Therefore, the strategic power of the East Asian Developmental State depended on the formation of political coalitions with domestic industry, while successful state intervention relied on organisational and institutional links between politically insulated state agencies and major private sector firms.

Underlying these Developmental State imperatives were the two central features of unusual degrees of both bureaucratic autonomy and public–private cooperation. This facilitated the formulation of independent national goals by the state and its bureaucracy, as well as translating these broad national goals into effective policy action. Therefore, the coexistence of these two features was essential. For example, in the absence of bureaucratic autonomy public–private cooperation could easily degenerate into situations in which state goals are directly reducible to private interests. Argentina and Brazil during their bureaucratic–authoritarian periods could be examples of such a political economy, where close government–business cooperation materialised in the context of a weak state, in the sense that it lacked autonomy from powerful groups in society. The logic of the Developmental State therefore rests precisely on the combination of bureaucratic autonomy with an unusual degree of public–private cooperation, the central insight of which is that the degree of government–business cooperation and consensus on national goals is not purely the product of a given cultural environment but has been largely engineered by the state elites themselves through the creation of a special set of institutions (Öniş, 1991: 115).

The concept of the Developmental State therefore emerged from an analysis of late development tactics of specific states in East Asia. When attempting to explain why these states adopted this specific political economy many of these analyses concentrate on specific geopolitical factors such as the US confrontation with Communist China, or to specific socio-political factors within the Developmental States themselves, such as the relative egalitarianism present at the beginning of the industrialising process in Japan due to the Second World War. Alternatively, analysis centres on specific institutional formats, such as Johnson and his analysis of MITI in Japan. Therefore, the adoption of these specific tactics by the state was due to a combination of extraordinary threats in the geopolitical context of the time combined with a relatively egalitarian distribution of income prior to rapid industrialisation (Cumings, 1987: 44–83; Koo, 1987).

The Developmental State and Latin America

A body of literature developed during the 1980s and 1990s that attempted to analyse the different development experiences of states in Latin America and East Asia (see, for example, Evans, 1987; Gereffi, 1992; Haggard, 1990). Broadly speaking, both regions engaged in forms of state-led development. Indeed, one could suggest that the structuralist state presupposes a Developmental State (Jenkins, 1991). Gereffi (1992: 90) suggests that the debate has been caricatured into the East Asian development experience being driven by Export Orientated Industrialisation (EOI), while that in Latin America by ISI. However, Gereffi (1992: 91) goes on to suggest that 'inward-orientated' versus 'outward orientated' development strategies are not necessarily mutually exclusive. Indeed, historical analysis suggests that both strategies have been pursued in both regions at different times (Gereffi, 1992: 91), and this makes economic sense in terms of not wanting to overly rely on either domestic or international markets.

Evans' (1987) analysis concurs with this view in his attempt to draw lessons for Latin Americanists from the study of East Asian NICs. He suggests that '[t]he East Asian experience clearly contradicts the caricature of dependency theory … but so does Latin American experience' (Evans, 1987: 220–1). He goes on to say that '[w]ork by Latin Americanists has clear heuristic value in suggesting ways of analysing outcomes; East Asian sequences suggest intriguing directions for dependencista thinking' (Evans, 1987: 221). Therefore, both cases mutually reinforce theories on the role of the state: Latin America produced a variety of evidence in favour of the proposition that a more entrepreneurial state was essential for successful capital accumulation at the local level. The major East Asian NICs increase the evidence in favour of this hypothesis by offering cases where both the relative autonomy of the state apparatus and effective state intervention are well beyond what can be observed in Latin America – and where the success of local capital accumulation is also pronounced (Evans, 1987: 221).

However, study of the East Asian Miracle has also raised questions regarding the impact of state policy on inequality. Therefore, analysis in the East Asian NICs suggests that some study of Latin American development experiences within the dependency tradition has over privileged industrial class relations at the expense of others (especially rural), the role of geopolitics, and the role of autonomy in the state machinery (Evans, 1987: 223).

Evans concludes that '[i]f scholars working in the dependency tradition can avoid false lessons from East Asia while using the East Asian experience to expand their theoretical imagination, the result will be a more robust general understanding of dependent capitalist development. Whether we call the resulting approach an historical–structural analysis of the political economy of the Third World capitalist development or dependency does not matter as long as the useful insights of dependencistas are effectively used to construct future theoretical models' (Evans, 1987: 223). However, emphasis in the literature on such concerns as individual national and institutional factors, as well as specific constellations of international fracture points and cleavages, makes it extremely difficult to transport the Developmental State concepts out of these specific national contexts (Sørensen, 1991).

A further body of literature addresses the issue of whether this concept can be generalised across time and space (see, for example, Weiss and Hobson, 1995; Weiss, 2003). In *States and Economic Development* (1995: 2) Linda Weiss and John Hobson argue that 'non-economic – especially political – institutions are vital to the constitution, maintenance, and transformation of the modern market economy'. Through an historical and comparative political economy approach, the authors attempt to address the question: What makes some states better at development than others? Their answer lies in the construction of a framework for understanding state power, defined in an 'infrastructural' or 'penetrative–extractive–coordinating' sense. Therefore, state ability to facilitate economic change is defined in terms of its political capacity, understood in terms of their conception of power (Weiss and Hobson, 1995: 10).

The following section will outline the common principles that appear in the Developmental State literature, that attempt to transcend regional and temporal variations. These common principles are based around understanding the state's political capacity, and attempting to use and build on both dependency theory in relation to Latin American development experience, and Developmental State theory in relation to East Asian development experience. This is in order to attempt to generalise away from the specific context of East Asia so that the Developmental State concept can be transposed across time and space, so that its efficacy as a potential analytical tool for understanding contemporary Latin American political economy can be assessed.

Common principles of the Developmental State

From the existing literature a number of common principles can be extrapolated – common principles that can be used as a blueprint for understanding how the East Asian development experience could be generalised, and therefore applied to Latin America. All of these principles share a common understanding of the Developmental State which 'occupies the middle ground between strong states that utilise the military as the basis for their power and weak states that have been captured by the private sector and interest groups' (Karagiannis and Madjd-Sadjadi, 2007: 235). The first of these broad categories concerns industrial policy, the second the national business–state relationship, the third the role of state bureaucracies and wider considerations of the state–society relationship, and the fourth the role of authoritarianism versus democracy. Each of these will now be taken in turn.

Ha-Joon Chang (see, for example, 1993, 1995, 1999) has contributed more than most to the role of industrial policy and economic policies more widely within the Developmental State concept. His work has facilitated the argument that 'a fundamental characteristic of the Developmental State is having a strategic industrial policy organised around government directives that are broad-based in scope and leave the operational detail to the individual firms' (Karagiannis and Madjd-Sadjadi, 2007: 244). In addition to the points made earlier in this section, Chang points out that both national and transnational bourgeoisie in developing countries tend not to invest in new industries because they do not know whether other, complementary investments will come along; hence there needs to be a centralised co-ordination of investment plans (Chang, 1999: 192). State intervention can therefore reduce transaction costs, for example through 'indicative planning' (Chang, 1993: 53). Furthermore, infant industry arguments (the cornerstone of CEPAL's justification that underpins ISI) can be deployed. First, to raise an industry from the ground requires sums of capital beyond the reach of the private financial sector. The state, therefore, has a role to play, since through its actions it can raise the capital through borrowing, taxation, and the direction of export earnings (Rapley, 2008: 141). There is also a role to play in the accumulation of human capital. State investment in education, for example, allows for its population to develop the skills necessary to compete in a global market place. Second, to acquire, adapt, and alter production technologies imported from the developed world, firms must be given a learning period during which the state protects them from foreign competition. To make it possible for firms to move into a market in which penetration and brand loyalty favour established producers, the state may need to reserve its domestic market for local producers for a set period of time (Gerschenkron, 1962; Rapley, 2008: 143).

While the infant industry argument was deployed by the structuralists during the 1970s and therefore associated with ISI, the Developmental

State concept used it with important differences. First, rather than building an industrial base to satisfy local demand (the very raison d'être of ISI), it focused on building export industries in order to foster new comparative advantages based upon dynamic rather than static efficiency. Second, rather than provide local industry with indiscriminate protection, governments chose winners, strategically selecting a few companies in key industries that they would help raise to maturity, leaving the others to die (Amsden, 1989; Rapley, 2008: 143). A final point concerned the nature of industrial and agricultural development. Neoclassical theory has criticised traditional ISI for its urban bias (Rapley, 2008), for transferring resources from the rural sector to urban industry when their best comparative advantages lay in that rural economy. However, the early Developmental States of East Asia did not necessarily follow these practices, as they nurtured both agriculture and industry, with protection for agricultural markets also offered (Jenkins, 1991). The principle adopted by South Korea, for example, was to stimulate the primary sector and use these surpluses to fund manufacturing industry.

The Developmental State literature discusses the need for a successful Developmental State to have strength or to be hard (Rapley, 2008: 155). However, this strength should arise less from crude power and more from a marriage between a technocratic state and a well-organised indigenous capitalist class. To effectively guide economic development a state must enjoy the power to direct society and lead it through traumatic changes. Bureaucrats must be able to draft policies that promote national development, not the advancement of private lobbyists. Government may have to enact unpopular or even harsh policies in the name of development. More recent work (see, for example, Rapley, 2008: 162; Weiss, 2003) views the state as an entity closely linked to and permeated by society, as well as itself penetrating society. What determines strength is less the degree but the character of penetration; therefore, a strong society is a prerequisite of a strong state, because the state needs to have an equally organised, predictable set of social actors with which to relate. The conclusion from this is that states need not be authoritarian or remote from society in order to enact or institute development. From this one can deduce that government must develop a consensus in favour of reform or economic growth (Haggard and Kaufman, 1992). Therefore, strength is to be derived from the nature of the three remaining principles of the Developmental State: high degrees of administrative capacity (institutional analysis), the presence of a domestic capitalist class and its relationship with the state (business–state relationships), and a strong executive (authoritarianism).

This literature discusses how the costs of state intervention may be reduced, or how government failures can be corrected. Institutional schemes can be devised to reduce the costs of intervention, without foregoing the benefits of such intervention – for example, by mitigating the information problem through improving the decision-making capability of the state (Chang, 1994: 35), or reducing rent-seeking costs through reducing the ability of agents to influence the state, or introducing competition into the rent-seeking process (Chang, 1994: 38). The 'informational problem' can be described as the fact that, 'the state may be able to collect and process all the information relevant for the correction of market failures only at costs that are greater than the benefit of such a correction' (Chang, 1994: 25); this is related to the 'principal–agent' problem (Stiglitz, 1988). Rent-seeking occurs when state intervention creates additional wastes, which can be defined not only as traditional dead-weight losses but also as opportunity costs when resources are diverted into unproductive activities by private agents in order to capture rents generated by state intervention (Chang, 1994: 26). Rent here is defined as 'that part of the payment to an owner of resources over and above that which those resources could command in any alternative use' (Buchanan, 1980: 3).

In addition to these insights, NIE provides an analysis of the nature of economic costs relevant to the debate on state intervention in the development process. The infamous definition of economics by Robinson (1932: 16) suggests that 'economics is the science which studies human behaviour as a relationship between ends and scarce means which have alternative uses' (or the business of resource allocation in a world of infinite wants and finite resources). NIE critiques this definition by suggesting that the achievement of Pareto efficiency may in itself carry costs – independent of the hypothetical costs arising from not achieving efficiency (Chang, 1994: 46). Firstly, the literature on technical change points out that technology is not a blueprint but that it contains a lot of tacit knowledge that cannot be realised without a 'costly process of learning' (Chang, 1994: 47). Second, production is not merely an engineering process but also a labour process, and therefore may involve costs in the organisation of production (Chang, 1994: 46). Furthermore, in relation to resource allocation, two kinds of argument have been put forward. First, market exchange is not costless as assumed in neoclassical economics, because bounded rationality requires us to spend resources in order to establish safeguards against the 'opportunistic behaviour of the trading partner' – that is, the costs associated with writing and enforcing contracts (Eggertsson, 1990: 7–10). Second, the process of resource allocation by the state is not a costless exercise (Chang, 1994: 47; 2003: 82–3).

Achieving efficiency therefore incurs costs that have become known as transaction costs. 'If transaction costs are the costs incurred for the purpose of defining and redefining the property rights of economic agents, on the one hand, and of writing, monitoring and enforcing contracts within the existing rights structure, on the other, the costs of state intervention may also be reinterpreted as transaction costs' (Chang, 1994: 48). In neoclassical economics,[1] however, the allocation of resources is a costless process whether it is achieved through the market or through state intervention. The government failure school compared the ideal market, which is costlessly run, with the state, whose activities incur costs. NIE suggests that both state intervention and market transaction incur costs (Chang, 1994: 48). Therefore, the question identified by this analysis is whether the state can achieve the same allocative efficiency at a lower cost than the market can, and not whether state intervention is costly *per se*. The role of the state in the economy, therefore, is (in part) to lower transaction costs in the economy. Indeed, it may even be appropriate to incur higher transaction costs through state intervention, if there were savings to be made on other costs that more than offset them. Concrete measures can be achieved through instituting a well-defined property-rights system and effectively enforcing it (North, 1981: VI; Lapavitsas, 2005: 36). Also, reducing macroeconomic instability of the economy through aggregate demand management is important (Simon, 1983: 19–20). Increased macroeconomic instability retards the ability of agents to make rational calculations, and therefore requires them to incur costs through actions such as financial hedging activities or inventory holding (Richardson, 1972; Chang, 1994: 49).

This NIE approach therefore possesses six important elements or contributions to the intellectual debate regarding the role of the state in the economy (Chang, 2003: 97–100). The first is the rejection of the assumption of market primacy that underlies neoclassical economics. Under this view, the market is seen as a natural institution that spontaneously emerges, with other institutions such as states or firms as emerging only when the market fails. Viewing the market as an institution with no ontological primacy (or predetermined characteristics) facilitates an ability to understand the relations between market, state, and other institutions in a balanced and historically more accurate way. Second, due to multiple views on what the ideal market can do, the assumptions underlying arguments regarding theories of the market must be made explicit in order to judge the merit of a specific position.

Third, it understands that capitalism as a socio-economic system is more than a collection of markets, and is made up of a complex myriad of different institutions. Therefore, market failure is no longer seen as a failure in the whole economic system. Fourth, the market is a fundamentally political construction. A market cannot be defined except with reference to the specific rights/obligations structure that underpins it; and because such rights/obligations are determined through a political process, all markets have a fundamentally political origin. Fifth, this implies the need to build a theory of politics that takes a broader and more balanced view, rather than one that is merely an extension of market logic as with neoliberalism. Lastly, it draws attention to the institutional diversity of capitalism and therefore understanding the role of the state is critical, not simply because the international differences in the mode of state intervention are a major source of this diversity, but also because the exact institutional form of corporate governance or labour representation, for example, will be legitimised in the eyes of the market participants through formal or informal processes of the state (Lapavistas, 2005: 37; Chang, 2003: 100).

Research on the nature of the business–state relationship in a Developmental State centres on the presence of a domestic capitalist class through the development of a common interest via interest groups and chambers of commerce, so as not to reduce itself to crony capitalism (Wu, 2008) and patrimonial politics (Rapley, 2008). Furthermore, as well as organisation, capitalists make up for their shortcomings, which in a developing country centre on the fact that they do not yet contribute large amounts to the national economy, by linking their organisations to entry points in the state. This produces a two-way information flow as not only can the capitalists express their concerns to policymakers, but policymakers can communicate more effectively with chief players in the economy (Rapley, 2008).

These considerations complement research that attempts to provide more holistic analysis by including considerations of the nature of state–society relations. Traditional Developmental State theory views the state to be necessarily separate from society in order to insulate it from competing interests, and those who may bear the costs of economic development incurred due to the lack of perfect mobility of factors of production. Further work was conducted, chiefly by Peter Evans (1995), which led to a characterisation of the state–society relationship as one of embedded autonomy. Evans takes as given the necessity of state intervention in the economy, and concludes from this that state involvement in economic transformation has two significant implications. First, the state becomes involved in the process of capitalist accumulation, and second, the role of the international system as a division of labour and the state's place in that division is highlighted. From this Evans derives two ideal types of state, characterised by the nature as well as the results of their intervention: the predatory state and the Developmental State (Evans, 1995: 12). While the predatory state extracts at the expense of society and therefore undercuts development, the Developmental State presides over transformation in which it arguably played a role.

In identifying the characteristics necessary for a successful Developmental State, Evans concludes that the most appropriate central feature is embedded autonomy. Yet Evans falls into the same circular reasoning as the early Developmental State theorists through emphasising the role and character of the state's bureaucracy at the expense of other explanatory factors. His argument suggests that a Weberian-style bureaucracy in the sense of selective, meritocratic entrance requirements and independent long-term career rewards gives them autonomy. However, here he departs from Weber and suggests that far from being insulated from society, 'they are embedded in a concrete set of social ties that binds the state to society and provides institutionalised channels for the continual negotiation and renegotiation of goals and policies' (Evans, 1995: 12). For Evans this embedded autonomy facilitates best the state's role in industrial transformation, yet he reduces the basis of legitimacy for this intervention to bureaucratic links with industrial capital. The possibility of legitimacy based on other forms of state–society relationship, or indeed multiples and combinations of different relationships, is not considered.

The final area of consideration is that concerning the nature of democratic governance in Developmental States. Johnson (1987) has argued that while there is no necessary connection between the Developmental State and authoritarianism there is an 'elective affinity' between the two, echoing the work of O'Donnell (1973) and his analysis of the connection between bureaucratic–authoritarian regimes in Latin America and their emphasis on heavy industrialisation. However, this link between authoritarianism and the Developmental State has been questioned by a number of scholars, with a whole literature on democracy and the Developmental State emerging (see, for example, Robinson and White, 2002). With regard to this link Bruce Cumings (1999: 69) argues that 'theoretically speaking ... there is no reason why this [the link between the developmental state and authoritarianism] has to be'. He outlines four reasons for this (1999: 69–70). First, authoritarian dictators and military regimes cannot supply the rationality required in industrialising states. Second, in the industrial epoch military power has always been less important than other forms of power. Third, weak states may be highly authoritarian. Immanuel Wallerstein (1983: 56–7) articulates this point when he says: '[s]tates have been located in a hierarchy of effective power which can be measured neither by the size and coherence of their bureaucracies and armies nor by their ideological formulations about themselves but by their effective capacities over time to further the concentration of accumulated capital within their frontiers as against those of rival states'. The fourth and final point is that strong military power has often been the product of industrialisation, and history has shown that it is a relatively ineffective method of industrialisation (e.g. Japan and Pearl Harbour).

In this early literature democracy was perceived to be a luxury that was feasible only in countries that had achieved developmental success. Democratic politics were considered to be a barrier to sustained development since unbridled political competition could generate pressures that led to deviation from the appropriate path necessary for sustained economic development (Robinson and White, 2002: 1). Recently, a compatibility argument has developed (e.g. UNDP, 2002) that is premised on the assumption that democracy and socio-economic development are complementary. However, aside from its questionable empirical foundations, the compatibility argument is premised on restricted notions of both democracy and development. Democracy is usually defined in a limited, procedural sense based on competitive elections decided through a universal franchise. Participatory notions of democracy, which are premised on the ability of citizens to take a full and active role in decision-making, play a secondary role to representative democracy (Luckham, 2002). Moreover, development is often considered simply as economic growth and material well-being through market-led growth. Therefore, the compatibility argument rests on the assumption that developmental democracy means capitalist procedural democracy.

While developmental democracy is not an assured outcome of a simultaneous process of economic and political liberalisation, it should not be totally discarded. The political and institutional basis for a number of states that have demonstrated broad-based sustainable development combined with a legitimate and inclusive democracy lies in the form of the 'democratic Developmental State' (White, 2002). There are two critical ingredients in constructing a successful democratic Developmental State (White, 1995). First, an effective Developmental State requires a particular mix of politics and institutions that can create, maintain, and deepen democratic structures and shape developmental outcomes in both productive and equitable ways. Second, there is the presence of the mutually reinforcing concepts of both participatory democracy processes and redistributive and inclusive development (Robinson and White, 2002: 5). In other words, the deeper the democracy and therefore the more widespread and representative the representation, the greater the likelihood that there will be societal pressures for policies to reduce poverty and enhance social welfare (Sklar, 1996).

The national–international relationship

Developmental State and neo-institutionalist literature, which theorises about the national–international dichotomy, attempts to integrate that theory into the existing corpus of literature. For example, Cumings (1999: 21) argues that 'the Developmental State is unthinkable apart from its relationship to the external world, in particular to the hegemonic power, which opened its market.' The characterisation of globalisation as 'for capital, of capital, and by capital' (Karagiannis and Madjd-Sadjadi, 2007: 55) means that globalisation is to be understood as the ultimate expression of the marketplace (Karagiannis and Madjd-Sadjadi, 2007: 57), and state action should be understood with this characterisation in mind.

As a result of this characterisation of the contemporary world order and the nature of the global political economy, three significant constraints on Developmental State activity present themselves. Firstly, there is the role of debt. High levels of debt in the third world has given the IMF and the World Bank (as well as the Paris Club of Creditors) enormous amounts of leverage over developing states. The traditional use of structural adjustment and later use of PRSPs, by the IFIs as vehicles for introducing (or deepening) neoliberal-style reforms along the lines of the Washington Consensus have represented, and continue to represent, powerful tools by which these institutions can effect real structural economic change on debtor nations.

Second, the third world has a deficit of market power. As Rapley (2008: 174) states: 'competing with numerous other countries in the sale of a small range of goods for which demand is relatively elastic, and for which the market is dominated by one [monopsony] or a few big purchasers'. Therefore, high degrees of competition, coupled with the prices for many of the commodities determined in global markets and denominated in US dollars, results in many LDCs being tied to the vagaries and whims of international markets, with limited options to ameliorate their situation.

The third point concerns the role of Foreign Direct Investment (FDI) and other activities by TNCs. Many neoliberal commentators actually see this activity as wholly and unreservedly beneficial, 'promoting the integration of developing countries into the emerging network of globalised production and thus enhancing their efficiency and growth' (Chang, 2003: 248). This is due to the increasingly large amount of global FDI flows and the example of countries (especially in East Asia) that embraced these activities and thus facilitated economic growth and development. However, Chang (2003: 250–4) points out that the bulk of FDI occurs among and between developed countries, and that the use of East Asian developing countries as examples of countries with pro-TNC policies involves a very selective use of evidence. Indeed, '[m]any countries in East Asia, while not against hosting TNCs in certain areas, have had rather restrictive policies overall to FDI' (Chang, 2003: 252). Therefore, 'there is a growing consensus that accepting a package of finance, technology, managerial skills, and other capabilities offered by TNCs may not be as good for long term industrial development as encouraging national firms to construct their own packages using their own managerial skills – with some necessary outsourcing' (Chang, 2003: 256).

These three factors result in the room for manoeuvre of states, and therefore their ability to engage in independent development strategies, being severely restricted and any attempt to understand national development strategies must be considered in this context (Chang, 2003: 265). However, while the apparent consequence of globalisation is to strip states of their power to intervene in the market (both in institutional terms and ideologically), the Developmental State still has scope for action. Therefore, as the ability of states to alter their competitive advantages is limited by globalisation's tenets, each state must become more creative in how they approach industry and social policy (Rapley, 2008: 76). For example, '[w]hile the WTO has brought about significant changes to global trading rules, there is still much room for national policy intervention. Industrial strategy is still very important with an array of policies with a view to increasing production and productivity of the national economy in the long run' (Karagiannis and Madjd-Sadjadi, 2007: 7). In other words, 'while the tools of industrial policy often undergo change as circumstances alter, states constantly adapt their instruments to the new tasks' (Weiss, 2003: 296). Furthermore, policies towards FDI and other TNC activity can complement this industrial policy. Therefore, long-term productive enhancement may be better achieved by an industrialisation strategy that puts emphasis on building local managerial and technological capabilities and uses TNCs in a selective, strategic manner to accelerate that process (Chang, 2003: 260).

Limitations of the Developmental State approach and the Developmental Regime[2]

It is the contention of this book that a more nuanced and holistic analysis can be derived through an examination of the concept of the Developmental Regime (Pempel, 1998, 1999). But why so much emphasis on a single word: regime? Critics of the Developmental State concept have argued that it is inadequate as a general theory of development, due to its reliance on spatially and temporally specific explanatory factors in the developmental success of its subjects, the NICs or East Asian Tiger economies. As shown in previous sections, there have been admirable efforts to transpose the Developmental State principles out of those specific contexts. The four principles of the Developmental State that render the concept transferable outside of the East Asian context have developed and changed over time on the basis of further research and scholarly debate. The economic tools of finance and industrial policy can be read and understood outside and independent from their manifestation in the NICs. Furthermore, the deployment of the concept of transaction costs as defined in NIE suggests that complex state institutional arrangements can be employed to lower these costs, and therefore Developmental State intervention can be economically rational once the net outcome of such intervention is considered. The capacity of the Developmental State can be measured through the character of its penetration into society, as well as the degree. Therefore, business–state relationships can form part of this institutional complex, allowing entry points between the state and key elements of society. Also, the democratic Developmental State literature shows that the pains associated with the developmental process can be managed by political forms of societal organisation other than authoritarianism.

There is therefore much good scholarly work that can be built upon. However, as a theory of development the Developmental State concept has an inadequate understanding of both state–society and state–international relationships. Pempel's (1999: 157) analysis captures this well through highlighting three interrelated shortcomings. The first shortcoming is that the Developmental State literature privileges the political and economic role played by state bureaucrats. This is because they are treated as totally de-politicised, socially disembodied, and in rational pursuit of a self-evident national interest (Pempel, 1999: 144). In the words of Chalmers Johnson (1982: 356) 'politicians merely reign, whereas the bureaucrats actually rule'. This led Bruce Cumings to suggest that the state then emerges as a 'web without a spider' (Cumings, 1999: 61). This can be critiqued through the observation that 'if not from the politicians from whom do bureaucrats get their sense of direction?' (Cumings, 1999: 145). Bureaucracies may well be rational, but in whose interests are they rational? One answer could be the national interest, derived from the possible interests of the politicians or at least of those in power. This opens the door to the possibility of multiple capitalisms and therefore many varied versions of economic development. Or, in other words, many different capitalisms or forms of development, each promoting the interests of different specific socio-economic groups (Pempel, 1999: 145). As a result, different Developmental Regimes are possible, based on different constellations of socio-economic interests rooted in state–society relationship(s).

The second shortcoming is derived from the first as it concerns Developmental State theory's preoccupation with the insulation of state bureaucrats as key to economic development. As Pempel (1999: 147) suggests, 'bureaucratic autonomy and mandarinate competence in the absence of numerous other conditions are thin reeds on which to rest a strategy of economic development'. Due to the assumption of the apolitical nature of the bureaucracy, the concept implies support for bureaucratic authoritarianism (O'Donnell, 1973), which provides few guarantees of positive economic development. By understanding the state as a social relation, and through subsequent integral state–society analysis, Pempel's 'Developmental Regime' concept overcomes this critique as it facilitates a more appropriate analysis of socio-economic relationships and coalitions present in the state–society relationship.

The third critique is the lack of a complete discussion and understanding of the international political environment within the Developmental State concept. Most Developmental State literature focuses on the domestic context, yet the modern state, like the mythological Janus, has two faces: one looks inward toward domestic society, the other turns outwards towards the international arena (Pempel, 1999: 147). When introducing the role of the international to this debate the analysis of the previous section provides a theoretical framework. First, because the fundamental goal of a Developmental Regime is the improvement of its economic conditions, any country aspiring to development must choose its strategy within the broader context of regional and international power balances (Pempel, 1999: 147). Therefore, economic conditions will be highly contingent on the broader external arena within which any developing nation must operate. Second, the nature of the contemporary global order must be considered. As analysed earlier, the contemporary nature of globalisation is shaped by changing patterns of hegemony. Therefore, by considering the nature of contemporary global order, the character and nature of contemporary globalisation can be revealed. This is important due to the ways in which globalisation shapes state behaviour and action in the development process.

The Developmental Regime approach attempts to overcome these theoretical inadequacies, while at the same time recognising the fact that it is through the work on the Developmental State that such an approach is possible. The use of the term regime is crucial both in the sense of representing a break with traditional Developmental State theory, and due to the implications of the word itself. 'Regime' involves a sustained fusion among the institutions of the state, particular segments of the socio-economic order, and a particular bias in public policy orientation (Pempel, 1999: 157). This term therefore refers to a 'middle level of cohesion in the political economy of a nation-state' (Pempel, 1998: 20). In other words, to talk of a regime is to denote the fact that in the relation between state and economy a complex of legal and organisational features are symbolically interwoven (Esping-Andersen, 1990: 2). The term therefore implies less than a political system or constitutional order, but more than an administration. This is crucial in facilitating a more complex understanding of state–society and state–international relationships, and therefore overcoming traditional deficiencies in the Developmental State approach.

It is worth noting here that this use of the term regime is not concerned with its use in regime theory in international relations. Beginning in 1982 in a special issue of the journal *International Organisation*, with key contributions by Krasner (1982a, 1982b), the international regime approach in IR has been 'the principle analytical device though which to study the traditional problem of rules, norms, and institutions in IR' (Crawford, 1996: 33). As well as the journal articles Krasner's book *International Regimes* (1983) outlines an approach to particular sets of formal agreements, norms, customs, institutions, and beliefs commonly accepted by a group of nation states when dealing with specific problem areas such as trade, monetary regimes, the environment, and security. Pempel uses the term in the context of a focus on domestic political economy, and therefore with comparative politics. His concern, and that of this book, is therefore with continuities and discontinuities in the political, economic, and social biases within single countries (Pempel, 1998: 225), and in the context of this book, Argentina and Brazil.

Another body of literature in political science and comparative politics has attempted to theorise about regimes (see, for example, Denison, 2006), stemming from earlier studies of totalitarianism and authoritarianism (Linz, 1973). Such works developed typologies of regimes, using labels such as party-based regime, military regime, and personalist regime (Brooker, 2000: 36–58), as well as others such as *caudillismo*, *caciqismo* (Linz, 2000: 156), or sultanistic regimes (Denison, 2006: 20). The term regime in this context therefore often carries negative connotations, as it is associated with forms of non-democratic (and often violent) rule. Its usage by Pempel and in this book carries no normative agenda and is value-neutral, simply referring to the 'shape, coherence, consistency, and predictability of a country's political economy over time' (Pempel, 1998: 30).

Derived from Pempel's analysis, and therefore for the purposes of this book, regimes are based on the interactions of specific social sectors and key state institutions (Pempel, 1999: 158). In turn, these 'fusions of state and society are reflected in specific public policy profiles', which result in the character of a regime being 'determined by the societal coalition of that state, and the institutionalisation and bias of the public policies that result' (Pempel, 1999: 158). The three essential elements of a regime are therefore: socio-economic alliances, political–economic institutions, and a public policy profile (Pempel, 1998: 30). 'Underpinning any regime is a specific set of relationships among important socio-economic sectors' (Pempel, 1998: 22). The sectors and groups that underpin any regime are those that empower, and are empowered by, the public policy profile (which will be elaborated later). Typically, the prevailing public policy mix sustains and reinforces the dominant socio-economic power base as well as a particular set of political and economic institutions (Pempel, 1998: 21). Therefore, there is a complex interrelationship between these three elements, which can be in flux and therefore suggesting that regimes may have little or no enduring stability. In order to further elaborate the regime concept and thus demonstrate further the ways in which it builds upon the Developmental State concept, each of these three elements will now be examined in more detail.

The idea that socio-economic alliances underpin, and are underpinned by, the state is not a new concept. At a theoretical level Marxist analysis of the state as (in its most basic form) the executive committee of the bourgeoisie reflects this opinion well; this is also equally true of

Weberian pluralist analysis which emphasises perhaps more social alliances as well as economic ones. At an historical level this has also been demonstrated. For example, Alexander Gerschenkron demonstrated that authoritarianism in Germany was derived from the alliance of 'iron and rye' (read: Saxony/Rhineland industrialists and Junker landlords) (Gerschenkron, cited in Pempel, 1998: 23), or Collier and Collier's work on showing how labour's inclusion or exclusion from such alliances shaped the political evolution of eight Latin American countries (Collier and Collier, cited in Pempel, 1998: 23). What a regime approach suggests therefore is that long-term historical alliances between the state and certain sections of society, which are the result of specific policies of the state as well as becoming policy in the first place due to such alliances, facilitate a potentially consistent set of relationships that forge one of the legs of the tripod of a regime.

The second leg of the tripod is institutions. For the purposes of Pempel's regime analysis these can be defined in terms that are congruent with political science, that is, the formal organisations of the state and society. Pempel outlines three types of institution that are important to a regime: government institutions, economic institutions, and those that connect government, economy, and society (Pempel, 1998: 23–6). Government institutions include areas such as the civil service, courts, parliaments, cabinets, the military, and the police. Economic institutions broadly express how the state interacts with the market, both domestically and internationally. Therefore a highly individualistic market-driven agenda will produce different economic institutions to those that express extensive concentration and coordination of market power by the state. Such constellations will be reflected in areas such as central banks, corporate structures, legal economic frameworks, and patent regulations. Institutions that connect the government, economy, and society include areas such as electoral systems, interest associations, party systems, and economic policy networks. Historically such institutions have been prominent mainly in theorising constellations described as corporatist, but other constellations are possible such as more fluid structures based on grass-roots movements in civil society. In summary, institutions here are sets of rules, both formal and informal, that emerge from society and in turn structure social and political interactions. They specify what can be done, by whom, and to whom, and they define the sanctions for breaches of the rules behaviour (Kingstone, 2011: 129).

Institutions regularise the organisations of decision-making through which the regime channels and manifests its power. They therefore are more than simple rules of the game and procedures that must be followed. Their efficacy depends on the possibility of governing over individual or collective behaviour and of incorporating values, preferences, and expectations of human beings in interaction (Boschi and Gaitán, 2009: 18). Such institutionalisation of a regime is essential to ensure longevity beyond any single administration. While a regime can, and indeed must, begin with one administration its longevity beyond a single administration relies heavily on the continuity facilitated by the presence of institutions. Institutions ensure 'organisational mechanisms that remain relatively invariant in the face of turnover of individuals and relatively resilient to the idiosyncratic preferences and expectations of individuals' (Pempel, 1998: 23). Such continuity and relative invariance of organisational mechanisms at the government, economic, and societal levels reflect the presence of a regime. In terms of a *Developmental Regime*, institutions are important insofar as they incorporate a pro-development orientation in their daily operation, with the aim of inaugurating a virtuous cycle of growth.

The third, and final, leg of any regime is the presence of a public policy profile. In the short run, a regime's public policies (both in the political and economic spheres) are 'tangible manifestations of the regime's power configuration' (Pempel, 1998: 27). Therefore, public policy necessarily, and by definition, delivers benefits to the regime's supporters. These supporters in turn form the basis of the regime's power; they are manifested in socio-economic alliances of their own, and support the regime not only through electoral politics, but also through the other conduits by which state power is exercised. This support is derived from the objective economic consequences of policy profiles (Baker, 2009: 15). In the longer run 'they reinforce and solidify institutional arrangements and coalitional alliances, guaranteeing systemic and semi-permanent rewards' (Pempel, 1998: 27). Thus, public policies play a critical role in the constitution of any regime as they represent the glue for socio-economic coalitions and institutions (Pempel, 1998: 27). Through such an interaction public policies can become more than just policies, as they become interwoven within and characteristic of the state–society, state–market, and state–international relationships. They become what Durkheim calls 'social facts' (Durkheim, cited in Pempel, 1998), or Gramscian 'hegemonic projects' (Gramsci, cited in Pempel, 1998).

The character of the regime that constitutes this hegemonic project is reflected in the three essential elements of socio-economic alliances, institutions, and the public policy profile as outlined earlier. As these three elements are wide-ranging, theoretically they could generate a wide range of possibilities, as well as the fact that regimes can experience little or no enduring stability. However, as a theoretical tool the concept of regime remains useful due to the analytical clarity that it brings to characterising the complex nature of state–market, state–society, and state–international dichotomies. One such example is the concept of a Developmental Regime.

The Developmental Regime approach offers an alternative under-standing of state–society and state–international relationships as expressed in the Developmental State literature through the term hardness. The developmental part of the label therefore reflects an understanding of the state–market relationship as analysed by tradi-tional Developmental State literature. The regime concept represents an attempt to generate more complex understandings of the state–society and state–international relationships where the principles of the Developmental State reside only in the state–market realm. Such work can trace its origins to the Developmental State literature on capacity, a term that the Developmental Regime approach builds upon. Rather than talk about capacity, Pempel (1999: 140) highlights a characteris-tic that he calls the primacy of politics. This characterisation allows analysis to concentrate on how economic development results from a politically constructed project aimed at improving national economic competitiveness. This is the result of three key observations.

First, political power can contribute positively and effectively to a nation's economic well-being. This echoes the NIE approach to under-standing the net result of state intervention in the economy through institutional analysis, rather than the neoliberal assumption that state intervention equals inefficiencies, or the SMC assumption that the state is neutral and largely benign. Second, political representatives can be key shapers of economic transactions, and third, they can think in a longer-term (developmental) perspective. This point allows analysis to move away from explanatory factors such as national culture, as was the prob-lem with early Developmental State theory in its discussion of the NICs. Pempel points to the role of the international in shaping a state's options, therefore defining dependency as 'less a determinant international struc-ture and more a set of shifting constraints within which individual nation-states have room to maneuver' (Pempel, 1999: 143). He thereby moves away from traditional Developmental State literature and analysis by inte-grating an understanding of the dynamics of the international sphere.

In order for this concept of a Developmental Regime to be appropriate, a state must reflect a number of key characteristics (Pempel, 1999: 157).

The first is that it must forge a socio-economic support coalition that commands more in the way of politically relevant resources than the coalition(s) supporting its opponents. Second, a regime must be able to define the central issue in politics and therefore set the content of the nation's agenda. Third, it must put forward a legitimate ideology that plausibly presents the interests of its supporters as general or common interests. Fourth, it must be able to deliver benefits to its supporters that reward them for their support. A regime is sustained to the extent that these supporters are given long-term benefits, not simply short-term profits (Pempel, 1999: 178).

Such a framework differs from that of the Developmental State literature, which traditionally views the state–society relationship as 'mutually embedded' (Evans, 1995: 13). Embedded autonomy, the term coined by Evans, is where the state possesses a strong bureaucracy with a 'corporate coherence' (defined as meritocracy and long-term career options within the organisation) that is not insulated from society, rather 'they are embedded in a concrete set of social ties that binds the state to society and provides institutionalised channels for the continual negotiation and renegotiation of goals and policies' (Evans, 1995: 12). For Evans, these links are predominantly with industrial capital rather than society in general (Evans, 1995: 17).

The concept of Developmental Regime as previously outlined begins to sketch out an understanding of this relationship that moves beyond Evans' conceptualisation of the Developmental State. At the same time, the analysis provided by the Developmental State literature on state–market relationships remains appropriate. However, the more subtle and complete analysis of Pempel (1998, 1999) suggests that the Developmental State's concept of capacity can be reformulated, with much more complex state–society and state–international relationships present, which are expressed in the concept of a Developmental Regime.

With the appropriate general and theoretical foundations laid, the book can move on to discuss the specific case studies of the post-crisis administration of Néstor Kirchner (2003–7) in Argentina and Lula (2003–10) in Brazil. After laying out the evidence, both qualitative and quantitative, these case studies will attempt to place Kirchner's and Lula's regimes within the same theoretical framework articulated and developed in this chapter.

Part II
Surveying the Landscape: The Cases of Argentina and Brazil

4
The Economic Policies of Néstor Kirchner's Argentina 2003–7

In order to understand the impact of the multifaceted crisis of 2001–2 on the contemporary Argentine political economy, that crisis itself must first be outlined, analysed, and interpretations offered. However, the anger expressed during *El Argentinazo* had deep roots, and the specific events leading up to it had echoes in the past. Therefore, this chapter will begin with a brief characterisation of the crisis of 2001–2 (dubbed the 'Tango Crisis' by international commentators, or '*El Argentinazo*' by the left inside Argentina) before analysing the political economy of the post-crisis regime of Néstor Kirchner. Such analysis will be concerned with the policies of the Kirchner administration and their impact(s) on the recovery, structure, and make-up of the Argentine economy. Attention is focused on the most active areas of Kirchner's policies, which have been in the macroeconomic and industrial policy arenas. Further analysis is also offered on important spheres that include MERCOSUR and international trade more widely. Thus, this chapter will display a panorama of the evolution of the Argentine economy post-crisis, presented thematically. Once this is complete, and a full picture of Kirchner's policies has been understood and analysed, the next chapter will move on to explore the implications of these policies for Argentine development in terms of a changing political economy. Part III then considering the regional and global implications of such analysis, in the context of the theoretical framework outlined in Part I.

After an opening section on the crisis this chapter will enter into a discussion of the broad macroeconomic environment during the 2003–7 period, exploring the nature and the dynamics of the recovery through an investigation of the sources of growth in the context of Kirchner's specific polices. This will be complemented by a discussion of the sustainability of this model through an investigation of the Argentine investment profile during this period. Analysis will also include a consideration of Kirchner's policies that sought to restructure the basis of the Argentine economy through an emphasis on what Kirchner called 'production and work', and therefore a shift towards the export of goods and a corresponding shift of emphasis away from the financial sector. The extent to which this has been the result of specific government policy or the result of changing international conditions will be considered. Further analysis of exchange rate policy, fiscal accounts, debt, and inflation will expand upon these considerations.

Analysis then moves away from macroeconomic considerations and investigates anti-poverty strategies. The role of *Plan Jefes y Jefas de Hogar* will be investigated, as well as other government policies such as *Planes Trabajar*. This will be further developed by consideration of wage and employment policy, followed by trade policy in the context of MERCOSUR. The chapter will then conclude by considering the question of continuity and change, suggesting that elements of both can be identified in his record. Such an analysis provides the necessary starting point for an attempt in Chapter 5 to understand both these policies as a cohesive programme, or a *Kirchnerismo,* and to place such a programme in the theoretical context as developed in Part I of this book. Once complete, and the efficacy of a Developmental Regime approach to post-crisis Argentina has been established, a similar exercise will be conducted with Lula's Brazil (2003–10). Part III will be then be able to consider the wider regional and global implications of these conclusions in the context of post-crisis political economy and development strategy.

The financial crisis of 2001–2

During December 2001, Argentina bore witness to a series of remarkable events. In the space of a mere 15 days, the country saw five presidents, the largest debt default the world has ever seen, the abandonment of the ten-year-old currency exchange regime which had formed the contractual basis of the whole Argentine economy since its inception in 1991, and the devaluation of the peso. And all of this happened in the midst of a profound socio-economic crisis.

In the context of this economic turmoil, spontaneous protests broke out all over Argentina. The state unleashed a strong wave of repression against these, including the declaration of a national 'State of Emergency' by President Fernando De la Rúa (of the Radical Party). Approximately 30 people were killed and 4500 detained (Filippini, 2002: 2). During the conflict, many businesses were sacked and looted, generally by groups of the unemployed. The state was impotent to control this climate of destruction and De la Rúa, who had held office for approximately two years, was forced to resign from the presidency in the worst moment of the crisis, fleeing the *Casa Rosada* in the presidential helicopter. After a brief interregnum in which the President of the Senate, Ramon Puerta (Peronist), took office provisionally, the Governor of the province of San Luis, Adolfo Rodriguez Saa, (Peronist) assumed control of the National Executive Power as President. However, after only one week of taking office, he too was forced to resign due to severe social dislocation and unrest, an abortive economic recovery plan based on a new currency, and the appointment of unpopular figures.

After another brief interregnum in which Eduardo Camaño (Peronist), President of the National Chamber of Deputies, took charge, the legislative assembly designated Eduardo Duhalde (Peronist) as President. Duhalde oversaw the management of the crisis until popular elections were held in 2003, elections in which Duhalde did not stand. By the time of these elections the worst effects of the crisis had run their course. However, any incoming president would have had to deal with an Argentina that had been driven to its knees economically, financially, politically, and socially, with many expecting the road to recovery to be both long and hard.

Interpretations of the economics of the crisis by mainstream commentators and academics have gravitated towards a consensus that places emphasis on the exchange rate regime in explaining the crisis. This is because the exchange rate regime and associated factors such as external shocks were essentially large barriers to economic growth in the Argentine economy (see, for example, Perry and Serven, 2003; Feldstein, 2002; Chudnovsky, 2007).

The first of these 'barriers' was *Convertibilidad's* role as an adjustment mechanism. Carrera suggests that there was a trade-off in adopting this system as while there was a 'successful reduction in nominal volatility … it made the behaviour of the automatic adjustment mechanism more difficult to reduce output volatility' (Carrera, 2002: 7). In other words, an initial overvaluation of the Real Exchange Rate (RER) led to successful stabilisation of the hyperinflationary situation, but at the expense of international competitiveness. The RER is the rate at which one country's real goods and services can be changed into those of another (Black, 2002: 391), and is useful as it is able to take into account changes in the relative prices of goods and services. Even more accurate is the calculation of a country's Real Effective Exchange Rate (REER). This is calculated by an average of the country's bilateral RERs with each of its trading partners, weighted by the respective trade shares of each partner (Catao, 2007). Therefore, an overvalued RER (or REER) implies that the costs of Argentine goods on the international market (i.e. exports) are expensive relative to others on the market, and the opposite effect with imports being relatively cheap. Therefore, levels of imports increased, exports decreased (or increased at a slower rate), the current account suffered, and eventually the crisis was precipitated as the economy failed to grow. For Carrera (Interview with Carrera, 2007), this is the central issue in the crisis: 'I consider the most important reason for the crisis is the loss of competitiveness that the economy had in the last part of Convertibility.' Heidrich also argues that 'basically, the convertibility scheme was an anti-inflationary mechanism. Peg the currency to the dollar at a fixed rate and you allow for inflation to run out [down] in the initial period 1991–2. However, eventually that implies an overvalued RER' (Interview with Heidrich, 2007).

To go beyond the strictly economic reasons for the financial crisis, one must look at the magnitude of the socio-political crisis, and the profound social impacts and political turmoil that engulfed Argentina during this time. The institutional fragility of both the Argentine state apparatus (Wolff, 2005; Schweinheim, 2003), as a result of neoliberal reforms in the 1990s, and the *Alianza*, due to its coalitionist nature and neglect of institutions, meant that events became uncontrollable and institutional safeguards and social safety nets were not there to catch people when they started to fall into poverty. All of these factors combined to produce the unique events of *El Argentinazo* during December 2001 and January 2002, and its dramatic consequences for the people of Argentina.

One must also look to the unique nature of Argentine *Convertibilidad*, and understand that the scheme was so much more than a fixed exchange rate system (Chudnovsky, 2007: 158). Indeed, *Convertibilidad* represented the fundamental lynchpin of confidence and stability in the Argentine economy through its role as an inflationary anchor. Many contracts were denominated in US dollars, including many loans and therefore much of the private debt held by Argentines. Therefore, when the system collapsed the central pillar of the economy collapsed too and, combined with the political factors outlined before, facilitated one of the most spectacular financial crises and economic collapses in Argentina's history.

The economic characteristics of Argentina, 2003–7

When the GDP figures are examined for the Kirchner administration it is clear that Argentina experienced a dramatic recovery in terms of economic growth (see Figure 4.1). The reasons for this dramatic recovery change according to which period one examines but Damill, Frenkel, and Maurizio (2007: 18) identify three stages to the recovery. The first stage is the immediate recovery period of the second and third quarters of 2002. The actual GDP recovery during this period was relatively weak, and GDP levels remained significantly below pre-crisis levels until 2004, due to suppressed aggregate demand as a result of falling employment, falling wages, liquidity constraints as a result of the *corralito*,[1] and economic uncertainty (Riggirozzi, 2009: 103; Bezchinsky et al., 2007: 19). The second period of recovery from the last quarter of 2002 to the second quarter of 2004 was very much to do with increases in aggregate demand (Heymann, 2006: 58). Employment ceased falling, wages began to increase again, liquidity returned to the economy as the *corralito* was finally totally lifted, and some sense of normality and certainty began to return (Damill, Frenkel, and Maurizio, 2007; Bezchinsky et al., 2007: 21).

The third and final period of recovery, from the third quarter of 2004 onwards, was due to the fact that exports started a period of faster expansion. This can be attributed in no small part to the government's

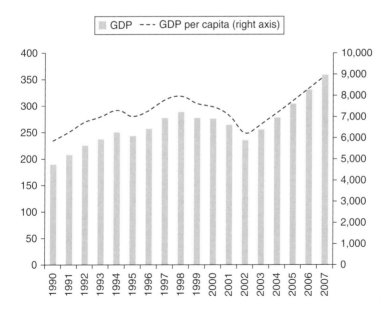

Figure 4.1   GDP and GDP per capita in US$ (billion) at 1993 prices
Source: Ministry of Economy and Production, 2009.

interventions in the foreign exchange market and the stated policy of maintaining a competitive exchange rate (Damill, Frenkel, and Maurizio, 2007: 20; CEPAL, 2006: 69), although other factors were certainly involved; these include the rise in global primary commodity prices and the reversal in the terms of trade both for Argentina and Latin American countries as a whole (Petras and Veltmeyer, 2009: 11–13; Panizza, 2009: 225–49), as well as stronger external demand (CEPAL, 2006: 70).

The three main sectors that fuelled this growth were construction, agriculture, and industrial manufacture. The dynamism of the construction and industrial manufacture was reflected in both massive Gross Fixed Capital Formation (GFCF) and in the imports of capital goods (Bezchinsky et al., 2007: 21). As a weighted index where 1997=100 construction activity increased from a crisis low of 57.8 in 2002 to 134.3 by 2007, thus far exceeding pre-crisis highs in the 1990s (refer to Figure 4.1). Therefore, while the economic recovery had a consumption component, investment across sectors played a significant role in the return of growth (Gerchunoff and Aguirre, 2004: 4). Agribusiness grew by 11.9 per cent and industrial manufacturing grew by 7.7 per cent (CEPAL, 2007b) in the 2004–5 period, with a weighted index of the physical volume of industrial manufactures growing from a crisis low of 70.2 in 2002 to 121.9 by 2007 (INDEC, 2007).

Figure 4.2 shows that in the context of a fast-growing economy GFCF as a percentage of GDP increased to 19.6 per cent by 2006, exceeding pre-crisis highs of 19.1 per cent in 1998 (CEPAL, 2006: 71). GFCF has not been the only driver of investment in Argentina, with overall investment levels in the economy increasing from a crisis low of 11.96 per cent of GDP in 2002 to 23.35 per cent in 2007 (Ministry of Economy and Production, 2009), with high volumes of capital goods imports improving productivity (CEPAL, 2007a). These latest levels of investments equalled the investment peak in the 1990s (Kosacoff, 2008: 38).

There also appears to have been a shift in emphasis in the management of the Argentine economy since 2003. This shift in emphasis has been to encourage production, more specifically the industrial sectors of the economy, at the expense of the financial sector, especially the banking and capital markets (Ferrer, 2005: 370–1). Heidrich (2005) terms this a 'competitive change', and states that the motivation behind this is that Kirchner saw Menem as focusing overly on the financial sector, the legacy of which was social exclusion and poverty present in contemporary Argentina. There have been dozens of mechanisms and promotion programmes that have offered tax breaks, subsidies, sponsored credit, and technical assistance that have formed the core of Kirchner's

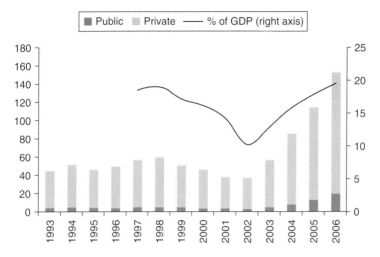

Figure 4.2 Gross fixed capital formation pesos (billion) and percentage of GDP, 1993–2006
Source: Author's elaboration of data from Ministry of Economy and Production, 2009 and CEPAL, 2007a.

industrial policy, and thus facilitated this change in the structure of the Argentine economy (Baruj and Porta, 2005; see also Ortiz and Schorr, 2009: 5). In addition, there have been a number of public works programmes such as road building, bridge construction, etc. (Interview with Heidrich, 2007) in order to promote private levels of economic activity (EIU, 2007; Heidrich and Tussie, 2009). The structural shifts that this policy has facilitated are reflected in Figure 4.3, with industry and the goods-producing sectors contributing an increasingly large amount to GDP. This represents a key source of change in the structure of the post-crisis Argentine economy in comparison to the Menem period. Banking and capital markets that took centre stage during the 1990s, while not actively discouraged, were relegated in importance in comparison to industry and the real economy broadly defined. This 'active' industrial policy will be analysed in detail in the next section.

The third phase of recovery also involved a substantial expansion of Argentine exports. This expansion represents a centrally important feature of the nature of the economic recovery in Argentina, and has also had a major impact on the structure of the Argentine economy. This is due to the fact that throughout the post-War period there has been a structural imbalance in the economy of Argentina: the

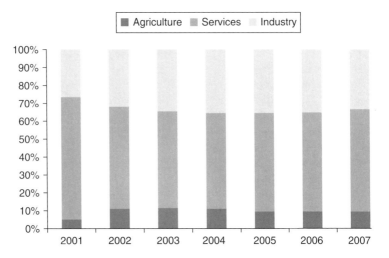

Figure 4.3   The structure of the Argentine economy as a percentage of GDP
Source: World Bank, 2009.

asymmetry between the export contribution (to GDP) of the smaller agricultural sector and that of industry (Di Tella and Dornbusch, 1989: 6–7; Chudnovsky, 2007). Under Kirchner, as Figure 4.4 shows, the value of exports rose steadily from the start of 2003 onwards, and, unlike the period preceding the crisis in 2001, the total value of exports exceeded the total value of imports, which is reflected in the Argentine current account surplus post-2001 crisis.

Not only did the value of exports rise but, as Figure 4.5 demonstrates, as a share of GDP Argentine exports increased from a maximum of 10 per cent of GDP throughout most of the 1990s to between 22 and 25 per cent of GDP from 2003 onwards. While part of this is certainly down to the massive contraction of GDP experienced by the crisis, as well as the statistical effect of the devaluation of the peso, the coefficient has remained above 20 per cent through into 2006 after GDP recovered to pre-crisis levels. Therefore, manufacturing exports form a large and growing part of the Argentine economy for the first time (Heymann, 2006: 55).

Exports of primary products represented 71.3 per cent of total exports, and manufacturing represented 28.7 per cent in 2004 (CEPAL, 2005: 105–6). Figure 4.6 demonstrates the increasing level of exports, as well as the increasing share of manufacturing as a percentage of total exports. The most recent figures available from the United Nations Development

Figure 4.4 Imports and exports of goods and services (US$m)
Source: Interview with Heymann, 2007.

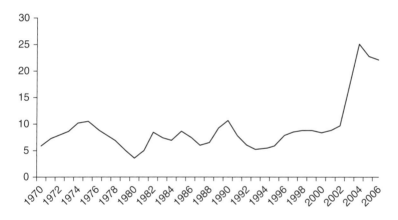

Figure 4.5 Coefficient of exports to GDP in constant US$
Source: Interview with Heymann, 2007.

Programme (UNDP) also mirror these trends, with Table 4.1 showing a drastic increase of exports as a percentage of GDP from 10 per cent in 1990 to 25 per cent from 2003 onwards. Furthermore, a growing proportion can be attributed to exports from a manufactured origin, growing from 27 per cent in 1990 and 2003 to 31 per cent by 2005.

The contribution of increasing global commodity prices should not be underplayed, and certainly represents one of the reasons for such

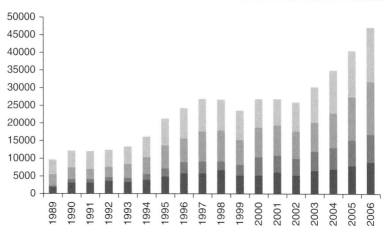

Figure 4.6   Exports by type of good in Argentina, 1989–2006 (US$bn)
Source: Bezchinsky et al., 2007.

Table 4.1   Structure of Argentine trade

Year	Exports of goods and services (% GDP)	Primary exports (% of merchandise exports)	Manufactured exports (% of merchandise exports)	High-technology exports (% of merchandise exports)
1990	10	71	27	7.1
2003	25	72	27	9
2004	25	70	29	8
2005	25	68	31	6.6

Source: UNDP, 2005, 2006, 2007–8.

significant increases in agricultural exports in particular. Indeed, it was
not only Argentina that experienced a strong growth record grounded
in exports but also much of Latin America as a whole during this
period, with the continent growing at an average of 5.6 per cent in
2006 (CEPAL, 2007a: 1). This growth was fuelled by a highly favourable external environment (Petras and Veltmeyer, 2009: 84; CEPAL,
2007a: 18), which included the steady expansion of the world economy

Table 4.2   Public accounts of Argentina under the Kirchner Administration, 2003–7

Year	Income (millions of pesos)	Surplus (millions of pesos)	Primary surplus (millions of pesos)	Surplus (% of GDP)	Primary surplus (% of GDP)
2003	77,214.5	1805.3	8688.1	0.5	2.3
2004	105,106.0	11,657.8	17,360.8	2.6	3.9
2005	126,426.3	9418.1	19,661.2	1.8	3.7
2006	158,521.1	11,623.0	23,164.8	1.8	3.5
2007	164,073.5	90,23.2	25,718.6	1.2	3.1

Source: Columns 1–3: Ministry of Economy and Production, 2009; Columns 4–5: EIU, 2007.

(prior to the onset of the global financial crisis in 2007–8), China and India's increasing importance in world demand, and the role of increasing commodity prices creating increasingly favourable terms of trade for Argentina and Latin America as a whole. CEPAL calculations suggest that these factors were the equivalent to 3.4 per cent of GDP growth for the Southern Cone region in 2006 (CEPAL, 2007a: 11).

In fiscal terms the administration of Kirchner saw a significant and sustained improvement, leading to both a primary surplus and a surplus in the public accounts throughout the administration. Table 4.2 clearly shows this, with not only significant improvements in the surplus and primary surplus but also as a percentage of GDP in a growing economy.

On the other side of the balance sheet is expenditure. Both primary and non-primary spending increased at approximately the same rates, demonstrating that interest payments on debt have not been chiefly responsible for the increases seen in spending as they were in the 1990s. Furthermore, while spending has increased fairly dramatically in absolute terms, as a percentage of GDP government spending has changed very little. Sound public finances were therefore the chief characteristic of the Argentine fiscal situation in the period 2003–7.

During Kirchner's administration there was a reduction of the external debt from US$164.6 billion in 2004 to US$107.8 billion in 2006 (see Table 4.3). Furthermore, the relationship between total debt and GDP improved, falling from a high of 153.6 per cent in 2003 to 62 per cent in 2006 (CEPAL, 2007a: 104). The relation between exports and debt also improved, both as a result of falling debt obligations and rising exports. Interest rate payments as a percentage of exports fell from 29 per cent

Table 4.3   Argentine debt after the crisis

Year	Total Gross External Debt (US$ billions) (1)	Total External Debt as a % of GDP (2)	Total Accrued Interest as % of Exports[a] (3)	Total gross External Debt as a % of Export (4)
2001	166.3	–	39.4	533
2002	156.7	–	35.6	538
2003	164.6	153.6	29.0	479
2004	171.2	127.3	24.6	431
2005	113.8	111.8	14.2	245
2006	107.8	62.0	9.8	197

Source: Columns 1 and 2: CEPAL, 2007b; 3 and 4: CEPAL, 2007a.
Note: [a] Includes interest due but not paid.

in 2003, or a high of 39.4 per cent in 2001, to 9.8 per cent in 2006, reflecting both rising exports and the increased sustainability achieved by Kirchner's negotiations in the debt swap of 2005. This renegotiation of the external debt was an especially important contributor to this improvement and will be discussed in detail in the next section.

Immediately after the crisis there was a large spike in inflation, as prices adjusted to post-*Convertibilidad* conditions. At the time there were widespread fears that the economy would enter a hyper-inflationary period similar to that experienced in the late 1980; this did not occur mainly due to suppressed demand through reduced wages and high unemployment. Since this period inflation has been rising steadily, with increased prices for both goods and services in a context of high and sustained economic growth. From a base of 100 in 1999 the CPI (Consumer Price Index) had reached 194.89 by 2007 (Ministry of Economy and Production, 2009). In percentage terms, from 2003 onwards Argentina experienced official annual year on year rates of approximately 10 per cent.

Under Kirchner, Argentina saw large falls in the unemployment level, which was largely the result of sustained economic growth after 2003. This also resulted in a significant decline in unemployment and underemployment in Argentina from over 20 per cent and 12 per cent respectively, to around 7 per cent and 6 per cent by Q4 2007, leading Beccaria, Esquivel, and Maurizio (2007) to conclude that the intensity of the net generation of jobs associated with the recovery constitutes the most remarkable characteristic of the period. Furthermore, much of the new employment generated has been in the private sector, with public employment expanding less than 5 per cent since 2003 (Heidrich and Tussie, 2009).

Real wages were hit particularly badly after devaluation in January 2002 and the subsequent change in relative prices. Due to the inflationary pressures on the economy present at the time, the government was very conscious of not wanting to add to them through wage increases (Interview with Carrera, 2007), as well as the fact that Kirchner wanted to contain public expenditure (Heymann, 2006: 52). Public sector salaries were almost static throughout 2003 and 2004, and real salaries were still 40 per cent below their 2001 levels in 2006 (Heidrich and Tussie, 2009; see also Riggirozzi, 2009: 89–113). Therefore, one of the main effects of exit from *Convertibilidad* was the change that resulted in relative prices and the subsequent enormous cost that this entailed for the working class due to the fall of real wages to an historic low in the last thirty years. The end result was that the average remuneration for work by the second quarter of 2005 was 17 per cent below 2001 (i.e. pre-crisis) levels and 9 per cent below in the more dynamic manufacturing and construction sectors (Beccaria, Esquivel, and Maurizio, 2007).

The economic policies of the post-crisis administration of Néstor Kirchner

Growth and investment policy

One of the main themes in the literature is that the dramatic recovery and growth experienced by Argentina in the 2003–7 period was more due to the convergence of international conditions, rather than the result of proactive and successful government policy. However, while international conditions have clearly been favourable their role should not be overstated. While exports in Argentina grew impressively from 2003 onwards, gross domestic investment grew at much higher levels (Ministry of Economy and Production, 2009; Tussie, 2009: 72). This was mostly due to the construction boom and the subsequent increases in GFCF, as well as strong growth in manufacturing. This strong growth in manufacturing also demonstrates that not all export growth in Argentina during the period 2003–7 was in the primary sector, with exports of manufacturing origin representing a significant proportion of the growing export base (Bezchinsky et al., 2007). Therefore, manufacturing growth has served to help a limited decoupling of the Argentine economic recovery from international commodity prices. However, agriculture remains Argentina's chief source of export revenue and therefore the limited nature of this decoupling should be stressed.

Some commentators (Petras and Veltmeyer, 2009: 55–95; Ferrer, 2005: 369; Heidrich, 2005; Levy, 2004: 134) have argued that the high levels of growth experienced up to the mid-2000s are unsustainable in the medium- to long-term because of a lack of appropriate investment in the economy. Increased exports and national savings, as well as flat international capital prices, facilitated increased and sustainable investment (CEPAL, 2006: 72). Sustained medium- to long-term investment without facing foreign exchange shortages has long been a challenge of Argentine investment (Gerchunoff and Aguirre, 2004: 15). However, much of the investment came from either national savings (at greater purchasing power due to flat international capital prices) or the foreign exchange proceeds from increased exports. The government policies that underpinned this export boom, both those that have fostered it such as the Stable and Competitive Real Exchange Rate (SCRER) and those that seek to create long-term gains from it such as the rise in foreign exchange reserves, suggest that there is a degree of sustainability and stability in the longer term growth environment in Argentina.

The picture is not uniformly secure, however, due to the existence of key bottlenecks in the economy. Such bottlenecks were arguably a direct result of Kirchner's policies of price controls (Ferrer, 2005: 368; Haselip and Potter, 2010: 1173; Lowenthal, 2007: 50; *The Economist*, 21 August 2008), as well as his failure to create a suitable climate for investment. This suitable climate is in terms of an appropriate legal framework coupled with a government that will not engage in over-regulation or even expropriation. Therefore, while investment was sustained by SMEs, particular problems remained with large private infrastructure investment (outside of construction), especially in the power sector (Heymann, 2006: 63).

Kirchner's administration has therefore not only engaged in successful management of the economy, in order to take advantage of these benign international conditions but has also implemented several deliberate macroeconomic policies that have served to stimulate growth relatively independently of those conditions. The rest of this section will now explore those policies in subsections further, which this chapter argues have facilitated this story of recovery.

Exchange rate policy

One of the most striking changes in the Argentine economy has been the role of exports. Kirchner has facilitated this structural shift that occurred after abandoning the currency peg through a proactive policy in the form of intervention in the foreign exchange markets.

Immediately after default and devaluation in 2002, and until the middle of the year there were rises in the nominal exchange rate. From mid-2002, and up until mid-2003, there was a period of appreciation that only came to a halt as the result of a deliberate policy decision by the Kirchner administration: the maintenance of an SCRER (Frenkel and Rapetti, 2008; Damill, Frenkel, and Maurizio, 2007: 3; CEPAL, 2007a: 104–5). In practice this has resulted in an exchange rate with the US dollar of between 2.8 and 3.1pesos, and a steady depreciation of the RER.

This maintenance of an SCRER can therefore be argued to represent the administration's single most important contribution to Argentine GDP growth over the last five years (Frenkel and Rapetti, 2008: 215). Indeed, this policy was intended not only to aid the import substitution process that had begun after devaluation, but also to promote exports (especially those of a manufacturing origin) and therefore accelerate the growth of the economy and thus the recovery (Riggirozzi, 2009: 103; Interview with Heidrich, 2007; Interview with Heymann, 2007). This strategy can also be read as a desire to restructure the economy in order to reduce dependence on international commodity prices through the promotion of exports of a non-traditional origin for Argentina, namely those of manufacturing origin. Furthermore, this policy also reduced Argentine dependence on the global economy by facilitating the accumulation of foreign exchange for debt servicing (Interview with Finkmann, 2007; Interview with Carrera, 2007), giving Argentina a financial cushion from potential future external shocks.

In summary, Kirchner's exchange rate policy not only served to clearly distinguish him from Menem's *Convertibilidad*, but also has arguably been the foundation upon which his political economy has been formed. The maintenance of an SCRER was a cornerstone policy under which Kirchner's administration has been able to begin the process of restructuring the Argentine economy, specifically in favour of exports of non-traditional, manufactured products. Therefore, while some of this growth in export earnings can be put down to a buoyant global market in commodities there is a dynamic proportion of those exports that are manufactured goods and therefore independent of the reversal in the terms of trade during this period. This has stimulated economic growth that, in turn, facilitated large increases in fiscal revenue that allowed Kirchner's administration to engage in a judicious drawing down of debt and fiscal conservatism (see next sections). While incomplete sterilisation has led to some leakage into the economy, and therefore exacerbated upward inflationary pressures, this has not been to an extent so as to cause associated problems in the economy (see later section on inflation).

Industrial policy

The extent to which the change in the economic structure of the Argentine economy has been the result of deliberate policy planning on behalf of the Kirchner administration, or the result of shifts in the economy that were the product of the crisis 2001–2 is not clear. Indeed, Ortiz and Schorr (2009: 3) suggest that industrial policy was based largely on the movements of the exchange rate post-*Convertibilidad* rather than any active industrial policy on the part of the Kirchner administration, which only involved very specific measures 'bounded in its effects and poorly coordinated'. Nevertheless, programmes did exist and represent aggregate demand stimulation policies based on Keynesian principles of fiscal pump priming, where the government could create jobs in a variety of ways, which would stimulate demand for goods and services and therefore lead to the private sector expanding output creating both economic growth and employment (Clarke, 2005: 58).

The efficacy of such an approach in the Argentine context has been brought into question. Fernando Porta (2005) has suggested that much of the industry in Argentina suffers from the twin problems of low value-added production and low levels of complementarities. Ortiz and Schorr (2009: 5) complement this analysis as their suggestion of a lack of co-ordinated industrial policy led to an absence of active policies aimed at strategic reconstitution of production chains. Therefore, while on a quantitative level the structure of the Argentine economy has shifted post-*convertibilidad* in a qualitative sense it has stayed the same. The change in the exchange rate and the associated decreased cost of labour, while having encouraged the development of activities historically neglected has not substantially changed the relationship between different production linkages within the industrial network (Santarcángelo, Fal, and Pinazo, 2011: 103). In summary, the trend of declining industrial output relative to total output that occurred in the 1990s was partly reversed but the configuration of the industrial sector did not change in a meaningful way (Bugna and Porta, 2008: 41). Therefore, taking advantage of the shift in currency and some limited industrial policies have aided the macro level in terms of industry's share of GDP but there has been limited progress in support of a reindustrialisation that would redefine Argentine specialisation in terms of its profile of production, nor has there been therefore a drastically different insertion of Argentina into the international division of labour (Azpiazu and Schorr, 2010: 136).

Fiscal policy

There are several reasons for the turnaround in the public accounts during the 2003–7 period, which had been plagued by deficits in the years running up to the crisis and in the recession period after the crisis in 2001–2. By far the largest impact on the surplus was the improvement due to debt restructuring. Interest payments on debt as a percentage of GDP fell from a high of 3.8 per cent in 2001 to 2 per cent in 2007, a level comparable with the median average of developing countries (World Bank, 2004). This is due to Kirchner's policies with regard to debt restructuring, which will be addressed in the next section.

The improvements in the primary surplus were derived from increasing tax receipts. There was a steady increase in tax receipts since 2003, partly the result of a growing economy and partly the result of increased efficiency of tax collection and consequent reductions in tax evasion. In 2006 alone, tax receipts rose by 25.85 per cent (CEPAL, 2007a: 104), and as a percentage of GDP, tariffs on exported goods rose from an insignificant 0.02 per cent in 1998, to 2.5 per cent in 2007 (Ministry of Economy and Production, 2009). These increases in tax receipts have been the result of Argentina's export boom and have been especially beneficial to the fiscal surplus created by the agricultural sector due to the boom in international primary commodity prices during that period (Petras and Veltmeyer, 2009: 61; CEPAL, 2007a: 11).

Favourable international circumstances for major Argentine primary commodity exports have certainly contributed to these increases. However, favourable international circumstances are not the only reason for this expansion of revenue from export tariffs. Kirchner's SCRER can be interpreted as deliberate government policy to stimulate exports of a manufacturing origin (Interview with Heymann, 2007; Gerchunoff and Aguirre, 2004: 6), combined with increasing the competitiveness of agricultural exports, partially due to the same policy. Therefore, this increase in the competitiveness of Argentina's exports can be traced directly to deliberate government policy.

Debt policy

The fundamental reason for the sound public finances was the result of Kirchner's renegotiation of Argentina's debt burden. Debt was used as a way of funding the current account deficit throughout the 1990s and combined with the recent experience of the largest debt default in history on 23 December 2001 it was clear that Argentina not only required a major reappraisal and restructuring of its international debt portfolio but also a change in attitude towards debt in order to facilitate the conditions for a sustainable future in the form of a long-term, sustained reduction of the debt. Both of these issues were addressed by Kirchner, managing to negotiate both a significant haircut (i.e. a partial cancellation) of its outstanding debt and a favourable restructuring of interest and maturity (Tussie, 2009: 73; Damill, Frenkel, and Maurizio, 2007; Kosacoff, 2008: 39) as well as removing the stress on sustainability (Interview with Heymann, 2007; see also Riggirozzi, 2009: 102–4).

This policy of hard negotiation and the eventual removal of Argentina from IMF-inspired economic policy represented a departure from the history of Argentine policy since the *Desarrollismo* govern-ments of Frondizi (1958–62) and Illia (1963–6). For example, IMF advice was taken by Frondizi and Illia when attempting to tackle inflation in the economy, and *Convertibilidad* in the 1990s was maintained under continued IMF advice. Reaching a peak during the Menem years, many Argentine commentators, including Kirchner himself, blamed the IMF and its policies in Argentina for the crisis of 2001 and its aftermath (Tussie, 2009: 73; Tresca, 2005). Therefore, in both related policy areas of debt reduction and IMF influence, the Kirchner administration repre-sented a substantial departure from the 1990s under the administration of Menem, as well as from earlier administrations as this accumulation of debt in the economy and associated IMF influence in its economic affairs has been a trend from much earlier in history.

Employment, anti-poverty, and wage strategies

Kirchner's strategy of job creation through economic growth resulted in a relative lack of specific anti-poverty measures. While poverty reduced significantly from its crisis highs (see Table 4.4), this was largely due to the employment trends, with the effectiveness of Kirchner's anti-poverty strategies fairly limited. During his administration he main-tained and partially extended minimal social safety nets, the universal policy of *Plan Jefes*, which originated in the Duhalde administration in response to the extreme poverty impact of the 2001–2 crisis, was actu-ally run down throughout his administration. This programme was replaced with other, much smaller schemes such as *Planes Trabajar* and *Plan Familias*. Therefore, despite his traditional Peronist power base, and his extensive use of associated rhetoric, this was not backed up with sys-tematic attempts to deal with poverty. Instead, Kirchner preferred to use expansions in employment and private wages in order to help reduce the very high levels of poverty in Argentina.

Despite demonstrating this relative lack of systemic intervention, the Kirchner administration was proactive in its minimum wage policy. The minimum wage in Argentina had been at the same level since 1993, until Duhalde increased it in 2002. This policy was continued by Kirchner with incremental increases throughout his presidency (see Table 4.5). These steady rises in the minimum wage had an important

Table 4.4 Social indicators under the Kirchner administration

Year	Urban poverty rate (households %)	Urban poverty rate (persons %)	Urban unemployment rate (%)	Urban under-employment rate (%)	Registered private sector wages (2001=100)	Unregistered private sector wages (2001=100)	Public sector wages (2001=100)
2003	36.5	47.8	14.5	11.4	135.32	104.23	106.23
2004	29.8	40.2	12.1	9.7	150.21	116.25	110.78
2005	24.7	33.8	10.1	8.4	189.20	130.88	125.06
2006	23.1	31.4	10.4	8.1	215.68	146.97	132.55

Source: Ministry of Economy and Production, 2009.
Note: Wages are in money terms (i.e. non-inflation adjusted).

impact on extreme poverty, especially, as in March 2003 the minimum wage of 200 pesos represented 29.9 per cent of the money needed to purchase what was considered a basic basket of goods; whereas, by September 2007 the minimum wage of 900 pesos was 100.4 per cent of that same basket in real terms.

Other areas of active policymaking have been in the areas of pension reform. In 2005 state pensions were increased, and in 2007 Kirchner allowed holders of individual accounts in the private sector to switch back to the state system at no charge. Account holders numbering 1.2 million proceeded to do so (*The Economist*, 23 October 2008). In addition, the *Ley de financiamiento educativo* (Ley 26075) of 2006 provided an infrastructure for increased government funding of education, including teacher's salaries, which had been hit hard by government austerity measures in the run-up to the crisis of 2001–2 (Carollo, Bregia, and Brizuela, 2006). All of these measures together can be read as government designed catch-up policies in order to facilitate increasing purchasing power of key socio-economic groups in Argentine society.

Inflation

The issue of inflation represents the single greatest challenge for contemporary Argentine macroeconomic policy given the task of maintaining high growth rates through a depreciated RER in the context of an open capital account. This problem represents the classic 'trilemma' or 'impossible trinity' where in the absence of capital controls and a

Table 4.5 Minimum wage compared to the basic basket of goods for a typical family (constant pesos)

Year	Basic basket of goods (1)	Minimum wage	Minimum wage as a % of the basic basket
Mar 2003	668.87	200	29.9
Sept 2003	656.61	270	41.1
Mar 2004	672.02	350	52.1
Sept 2004	684.82	450	65.7
Mar 2005	720.36	450	62.5
Sept 2005	754.37	630	83.5
Mar 2006	799.25	630	78.8
Sept 2006	810.57	780	96.2
Mar 2007	854.18	800	93.7
Sept 2007	896.57	900	100.4

Source: Ministry of Economy and Production, 2009.
Note: (1) Estimation for the total country based on INDEC data and the 2001 Census.

policy of a fixed exchange rate regime, governments give up sovereignty of monetary policy. The solution therefore for a number of analysts is for the central bank to concentrate more on price stability by raising interest rates and letting the peso appreciate (Frenkel and Rapetti, 2006: 21). In the short run, Argentina has been able to deal with this dilemma from the currency side of the equation (i.e. preventing real appreciation of the peso) through using its fiscal surplus to buy foreign exchange generated by the trade surplus and using it to pay foreign debt or accumulate foreign exchange reserves (Mercado, 2007: 11). The inflation issue, however, is more difficult in the context of high GDP and decreasing spare capacity. From the supply side the relatively low investment levels, especially in the energy sector, has reduced the elasticity of supply over time (Mercado, 2007: 12; Interview with Heymann, 2007) This has been exacerbated by the demand side, as the increases in consumption and investment associated with accelerated growth, as well as the continuing trade surplus, have all put short-run pressures on the rate of inflation (D'Amato, Garegnani, Paladino, 2007: 7; Mercado, 2007: 12; Interview with Heymann, 2007).

The traditional levers of inflation dampening, increasing interest rates or an appreciation of the exchange rate, are unavailable to Argentina given its stated policies of a low RER – the result of the unholy trinity issue. Instead, monetary policy involved sterilisation efforts to limit the growth of monetary aggregates (Frenkel and Rapetti, 2006: 22) and limited capital controls introduced in June 2005, inspired by Chile's policies in the mid-1990s to discourage short-term capital inflows. Fiscal policy has also played a role in the inflation conundrum of contemporary Argentina. As analysed elsewhere in this chapter, fiscal discipline and conservatism, as well as a reluctance to see large wage increases and the management of inflation expectations through price controls, have all served to help dampen inflation. Indeed, according to Martin Redrado (2008), former governor of the Argentine central bank, the evolution of fiscal and wage policy is critical along with monetary aspects when making judgements about the Argentine macroeconomy.

Many have commented that the levels of inflation under Kirchner, and in contemporary Argentina, are not problematical, given the expansion of GDP (Mercado, 2007; Frenkel and Rapetti, 2006; Interview with Heymann, 2007; Interview with Carrera, 2007). Notwithstanding alleged attempts to manipulate the official rate through presidential bribes to the government statistical body INDEC (due to large amounts of newly denominated debt being linked to domestic inflation) (Petras and Veltmeyer, 2009: 85), and the subsequent perception on the street that prices are rising much higher than the official rate and creating wage demands in the workplace, this is true. However, the historical mechanisms for previous hyper-inflationary situations were government deficits and upward pressures on the exchange rate, two factors that are not present in the contemporary macroeconomic framework of Argentina with a government fiscal surplus, and an exchange rate that was not appreciating. Combined with a trade surplus and a high level of foreign reserves the situation in Argentina did not show the typical triggers for an explosion of inflation. Nevertheless, these indicators are likely to change over time, and many of the measures adopted by the government were short-term solutions at best. This has been reflected by the increasing problem of inflation in the Cristina Fernández de Kirchner presidency, and longer-term solutions are becoming increasingly urgent.

Conclusions: Continuity and change

One of the main sources of change in post-crisis Argentine economic policy is that strong growth has been accompanied by twin surpluses in the fiscal and current accounts. This chapter has suggested that these dynamics point to a conclusion that the current surge in GDP growth is not (yet) another bubble but rather a sustainable trajectory. Furthermore, in contrast to the Menem years of *Convertibilidad*, this trajectory has been in the context of a significant reduction in national debt, both foreign and domestic. Whereas the currency peg of the 1990s strangled exports and stimulated imports due to an overvaluation of the peso, with the resulting current account deficit being funded through debt, the post-crisis policy of an SCRER has stimulated the economy and facilitated a judicious drawing down of debt. A further effect of the SCRER policy, again in contrast to the 1990s, has been the stimulation of exports. This complements the previous conclusions due to the resultant effects on the trade surplus, the fiscal situation, and the changing debt profile. The exit from *Convertiblidad* generated a change in relative prices and incentives in the Argentine economy that stimulated the industrial sector at the expense of the financial sector, especially in the export industries as suggested earlier, which fostered change at a macro level. This chapter has demonstrated that while a significant proportion of this expansion was due to favourable international circumstances in the form of increasing commodity prices and international demand (and the associated improvement in the terms of trade), specific policy on the part of the Kirchner administration was also responsible. The

SCRER stimulated both agricultural and manufacturing exports, and the twin surpluses fostered a stable macroeconomic environment that also stimulated domestic consumption and investment.

While change has therefore been present, there is also continuity. The expansion of industry, facilitated to a large degree by the new exchange rate regime and to a lesser degree by industrial policy, simultaneously led to the consolidation of two major legacies of the pre-crisis model of capital accumulation present in Argentina. Firstly, disjointed and truncated industrial sectors skewed towards relatively low value-added production and a lack of complementarities in intra and inter industries, and secondly, the continuing redistribution of income away from the workers towards capital. This second point was exacerbated by the post-crisis administration's wage policy that discouraged increases in public sector salaries in particular, partly in order to manage inflation expectations. Furthermore, the relative lack of systematic poverty-reduction strategies meant that improvement in the poverty figures were largely the result of an expanding economy and associated expansions in employment rather than pro-active government intervention. Therefore, the administration of Néstor Kirchner is not so much a question of continuity *or* change but continuity *and* change, with Kirchner having run an economy based on pragmatic, gradualist, and developmentalist principles while maintaining a neoliberal, Menemist social safety-net model. It is to the impacts of these changes on Argentine political economy and its subsequent development trajectory that this book now turns.

5
Argentina, *Kirchnerismo*, and *Neodesarrollismo*: Argentine Development under Néstor Kirchner, 2003–7

The previous chapter identified sources of continuity and change in the economic policy record, or the state–market relationship, of Néstor Kirchner. This was so as to form the analytical basis for this chapter, which will examine the implications of these sources of continuity and change with regard to Argentine political economy. It is the contention of this chapter that in the years 2003–7 there was a *Kirchnerismo* present in Argentina, and this *Kirchnerismo* possesses a number of characteristics that represent departures from previous forms of political economy in Argentina. This chapter will also seek to place *Kirchnerismo* within a suitable analytical and theoretical framework in order to generate an understanding of this development experience that could be transposed across space and time. Therefore, this chapter will also seek to locate *Kirchnerismo* within the Developmental Regimes literature as articulated in Chapter 3.

The labelling of Néstor Kirchner's Argentina as 'developmental', or as a Developmental State, requires more than examination of economics and economic policy. Indeed, as Fine's (1997: 3) critique suggests, the Developmental State concept is in danger of being reduced to the statement that '[w]herever there is or has been development, there must have been a Developmental State'. Therefore, this chapter will complement the state–market analysis of the previous chapter by also looking at the changing nature of state–society relations in Argentina, rooted in an examination of political economy. Such an analysis will facilitate an understanding of Néstor Kirchner's Argentina that centres on his fundamentally Peronist politics. This will be achieved through consideration of factors such as the nature of Kirchner's political power and how his policies have cemented their support, as well as analysis of his distinctive rhetoric. In addition to examination of the state–market and state–society relationships, analysis will cover the state (national)–international relationship, as this expanded role for the state in Argentina 'is being carved out in the context of a globalised and market-led economy' (Grugel and Riggirozzi, 2007: 88). Therefore, factors such as the role of the IMF, debt, dependence on global commodity prices, and foreign investment will all be discussed. Consideration of the role of the three mutually influencing dichotomies of state–market, state–society, and state (national)–international overcomes weaknesses present in some of the Developmental State literature, and will facilitate an understanding of Néstor Kirchner's *neodesarrollismo* state within the context of Pempel's (1999) concept of a Developmental Regime. The central proposition is therefore that the administration of Néstor Kirchner 2003–7 is a Developmental Regime adapted to a continuing Peronist politics, which, somewhat paradoxically, represents both leftist and neoliberal components.

State–society relations under Néstor Kirchner: *Kirchnerismo*?[1]

Points of departure between *Peronismo* and *Kirchnerismo*

Peronismo was an ideology that contained many manifestations, but during the first two administrations (1946–55) of Perón at least some important key principles can be located. *Peronismo* included both authoritarian and populist components, which were a blend of the ideologies of the 1930s and a traditional Argentinean style of leadership (a charismatic strongman leading from the front). Perón and Peronism therefore represented a form of leftist–populist nationalism that is rooted in what Laclau (1977: 158) called 'the structure of which they are a moment', which in the context of Argentina during this period meant an urban working class movement that was allied to elements of the domestic bourgeoisie as well as the military. Therefore, for Portantiero (1989: 18) '[t]he first Peronist administration based its legitimacy on a pact between the trade unions and the armed forces, but its most important axis was the arbitrating figure of Perón as a symbol of the new state'. Perón's economic model of the late 1940s and 1950s was based on a *desarrollismo* model, and therefore favoured national over foreign capital, and urban wage labour over agro-exporting elites (Vellacott, 2006; see also Gambini, 2007). Indeed, Torre and Riz (1991: 78) outline Perón's economic policy as having three core objectives: 'the expansion of public spending, giving the state a stronger role in production and distribution; the alteration of relative prices to encourage a more egalitarian distribution of national income; and the progressive accumulation of a system of incentives and rewarded activities orientated towards the internal market and discouraged production destined for international markets'.

These economic policies of ISI initially produced an impressive growth record, and combined with his generous legislation in favour of worker rights and redistribution of the proceeds of growth to the workers, generated huge popularity. Peronism's fundamental political appeal therefore lay in its ability to redefine the notion of citizenship within a broader, and ultimately social, context (Blanksten, 1969: 249; Di Tella, 1983: 15; Portantiero, 1989: 17; Gambini, 2007). Citizenship was not defined in terms of individual rights and relations within political society, but was redefined in terms of the economic and social realms of civil society (Di Tella, 1983: 17). Citizenship, therefore, was more about social equity, rather than the individual pursuit of wealth (Segura-Ubiergo, 2007: 60–1; Gambini, 2007). This social equity, however, was limited to the urban working classes due to the institutional links of the PJ (*Partido Justicialista*) with the trade unions. As Grugel (2009: 50) puts it, 'since social policies and labour law during the ISI period had reinforced the links between governments and trade unions and social protection had been mainly directed to the workforce (rather than the poor), the social policy regime had tended to neglect the rural population and the poorest groups in society'.

The first major difference between *Kirchnerismo* and Perón's policies is in the nature of the link between citizenship and social welfare. As summarised by Grugel and Riggirozzi (2007: 88), 'Peronism changed the terms of citizenship in Argentina by establishing the *pueblo*, made up of unionised workers the urban poor, and the lower-middle classes, as a political actor with rights to economic and social inclusion'. Despite using rhetoric that echoes this link between citizenship and social welfare, Kirchner has not engaged in widespread social programmes, instead preferring to target specific social groups (Petras, 2006: 283; Grugel and Riggirozzi, 2007: 98; Beccaria, Esquivel, and Maurizio, 2007). Therefore the welfare programmes present in Argentina in the 2003–7 period such as *Plan Familias* and *Planes Trabajar*, combined with the running down of *Plan Jefes y Jefas* were not designed as proactive policies to systematically tackle poverty in traditional Peronist constituencies, as the state–society relationship under *Kirchnerismo* is not based on such principles; rather, they have much more in common with neoliberal style safety-net models of social welfare, designed to catch individuals and prevent them from falling into complete poverty and destitution

(Beccaria, Esquivel, and Maurizio, 2007). This stands in contrast to Perón's policies of providing social protection and political patronage through clientelism for the urban working classes as a whole.

A second change concerns the role of corporatist practices. Svampa's analysis (2008: 83) that *Kirchnerismo* represents a return to old Peronist style-corporatism does not tell the whole story, as *Kirchnerismo's* relationships with business and the trade unions possesses qualitatively different characteristics from old Peronist relationships, such as the top-down associations and institutional links between Perón himself, the PJ, and trade union movements. This has led Etchemendy and Collier (2007) to term Kirchner's distinct approach as 'neocorporatism', or, more specifically, 'segmented neocorporatism'. This is defined (Etchemendy and Collier, 2007: 366) as 'a pattern of peak level negotiation in which monopolistic unions, business associations, and the government coordinate on inflation-targeted, sector-wide wage agreements and minimum wage floors, which apply to a substantial minority of the labour force'. It is corporatist due to the tripartite nature of the relationship (government, organised labour, and business), it is 'neo' due to the redefinition of this relationship (see further), and it is segmented due to the fact that the agreements reached only applied to a minority of the workforce (formally employed, organised labour).

A new pattern of tripartite negotiations is therefore present under the administration of Kirchner that is different from the *Peronismo* of Perón. Whereas the relationship between the *Confederación General de Trabajo* (CGT) and the government under *Peronismo* was very much top down, *Kirchnerismo* is characterised by more autonomy from both the state and the increasingly fragmented party system (Etchemendy and Collier, 2007: 365, 381). The formal links between the Peronist party and the CGT and the political appointments of CGT members to government posts under Juan Perón that facilitated this top-down relationship are not present in *Kirchnerismo* (Interview with Andrés Mendez, 2007). While there are links and conduits between the Kirchner administration and organised labour movements they are much more diffused, informal, and decentralised (Interview with Andrés Mendez, 2007; Etchemendy and Collier, 2007: 381. This is demonstrated by the fact that individual unions have engaged in industrial action (strikes) in order to manipulate the outcome of negotiations, often against the wishes of government officials (Etchemendy and Collier, 2007: 381; see also Figures 5.1 and 5.2). These figures demonstrate that strikes in Argentina have consistently exceeded the levels of the presidency of Menem (see later sections), and certainly represent more than during Perón's first two administrations

(1946–55). Figure 5.2 also reflects Kirchner's ability to re-institutionalise protest politics in the aftermath of the 2001–2 crisis, with non-union led protest dropping dramatically during his administration and in the aftermath of the 2001 crisis. In sum, 'Peronist unionism has displayed in the last three years a degree of autonomy from an allied government and from the Peronist party arguably unknown in Argentine history' (Etchemendy and Collier, 2007: 381).

There is also difference in another aspect of the tripartite relationship, that between the government and the business community. The 'genuine participation of business' (Etchemendy and Collier, 2007: 382) in these tripartite negotiations stands in contrast to the governments of Perón, where the genuine involvement of business participation in tripartite negotiations was rare. Even during periods of Argentina's history where directly populist governments were not in power the involvement of business associations has been fragmented. For example, the most important business associations did not support the outcome of the negotiations in the wage bargaining rounds of 1973–6 and 1987–9 (Etchemendy and Collier, 2007: 382). Under the administration of Kirchner such negotiations were more systematic, with both the sector-wide wage agreements and the minimum wage agreements of 2005, 2006, and 2007 enjoying the support of the most important sectoral and national business associations.

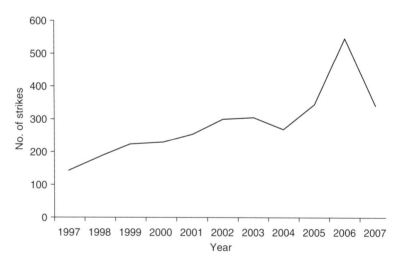

Figure 5.1   Number of strikes in Argentina (1997–2007)
Source: Etchemendy and Collier, 2007.

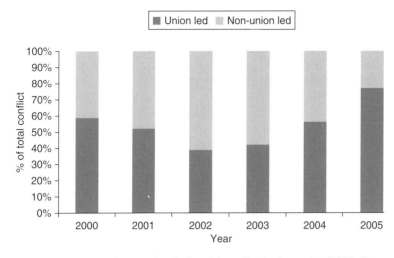

Figure 5.2   Union- and non-union-led social conflict in Argentina (2000–5)
Source: Etchemendy and Collier, 2007.

Systematic negotiation and agreements with both organised labour and domestic business have been part of Kirchner's greater goal of economic development, due to the need to contain inflation, or more specifically one of the main traditional drivers of Argentine inflation: excessive wage increases. The traditional Peronist and *desarrollismo* policies in Argentina led to sustained wage increases for skilled workers that were ultimately eroded due to periods of systemic inflation. This led to the classic debate between the monetarists and the structuralists, a debate that was won by the monetarists and the IMF, who therefore gained control over the direction of Argentine economic policy. Therefore, there is an important difference here between the dynamics of *Kirchnerismo* compared to those of traditional *Peronismo.* The prioritisation of controlling inflation over wage increases for the (organised) working-class is not only demonstrated by this relationship with the unions. Indeed, it is also present in Kirchner's relationship with the business world. His extensive use of ad hoc price controls can be interpreted as helping in negotiations with the unions over wages as such price controls reduce inflationary expectations (Etchemendy and Collier, 2007: 379, 381).

This prioritisation of inflation control over wage increases for the working classes also reveals a third difference between *Kirchnerismo* and *Peronismo.* Traditional Peronism 'was unable to construct a social consensus around the principles of nationalist/statist development' (Panizza, 2005; Grugel and Riggirozzi, 2007: 89; Roberts, 2007; Riggirozzi, 2009: 102). As Riggirozzi (2009: 90) puts it: 'the nationalistic rhetoric and the political economy of Peronism redefined citizenship in terms not of individual rights but as economic rights and social inclusion'. State intervention was about control over the key sectors of the economy and to engage in social programmes in line with the state–society relationship present. *Kirchnerismo*, on the other hand, was a strategy for growth based on selective protectionism and targeted state intervention in order to facilitate macroeconomic stability and economic growth through stimulation of an export industry (see previous chapter) and limited diversification away from traditional reliance on agro-exports. The state took on the responsibility for economic growth, and specifically facilitated this through the SCRER policy and stimulation of exports (Frenkel and Rapetti, 2008), as well as an accumulation of reserves to create confidence in the domestic economy (Grugel and Riggirozzi, 2007: 97–8).

A fourth and final difference concerns the issue of poverty. The rise in poverty in Argentina first under Menem (see next section), and then as a result of *El Argentinazo*, was spectacular. While these levels have receded from crisis highs under Kirchner's administration, this has been largely due to decreasing unemployment in the context of high and sustained economic growth (Grugel and Riggirozzi, 2007: 104). Therefore, the middle-class elements that were driven into poverty as a result of the events of 2001–2, and who joined the ranks of the 'new poor', were relatively quick to recover. However, high degrees of poverty that were created in the 1990s as a result of structural reforms – as well as the result of the process of neoliberal globalisation and greater international competition – have remained, with individual poverty and indigence at 20.6 per cent and 5.9 per cent respectively in 2007 (Ministry of Economy and Production, 2009). This poverty was not systematically addressed by Kirchner's administration (Beccaria, Esquivel, and Maurizio, 2007). Such policies would perhaps require a more fundamental shift in political economy, and *Kirchnerismo* is characterised by a strategy of 'bending and moulding' the existing political institutions and economic model rather than changing it altogether (Panizza, 2005: 15).

Points of departure between *Kirchnerismo* and *Menemismo*

Menemismo in the 1990s was very different to traditional *Peronismo*. Despite being elected on a Peronist platform, as soon as he was in power he initiated a programme of 'neoliberalism by surprise' (Stokes, 2001). Consistent with this project, Menem himself expressed the intention to 'pulverize the crisis'. He warned his fellow citizens to brace themselves for 'a tough, costly, and severe adjustment', requiring 'major surgery without anaesthesia' (Smith, 1991: 46). Indeed, 'from a deceptively simple assumption that the state – understood as a complex social and political process as well as an economic one – was to produce development in the 1950s and 1960s, it came itself to be seen as the principal obstacle to development, responsible for both crisis and stagnation' (Grugel and Riggirozzi, 2009: 5).

The neoliberal regime installed in Argentina, and Latin America more widely, had a distinct four-point agenda (Munck, 2003: 53). First, trade liberalisation was pursued, which culminated in the creation of MERCOSUR in 1991 (Argentina, Brazil, Paraguay, and Uruguay). During this time (1991–7) Argentina dismantled or removed many of its remaining tariff and non-tariff barriers, thus opening its economy to international markets and competition. Trade liberalisation had actually begun under Alfonsín in 1988, and served to reduce the weighted average tariff rate to 48 per cent (from a high of 141 per cent in 1959) (Chudnovsky, 2007: 34). Menem therefore carried out a 'second phase' of trade liberalisation, which served to reduce the weighted average tariff rate to 19 per cent by 1991.

Second was the promotion of privatisation and a consequent reduction in the role of government. Due to the legacy of ISI and *Peronismo* Argentina at the start of the 1990s was dominated by state-owned enterprises (SOEs) – for example, YPF, *Gas del Estado*, *Ferrocarriles Argentinos*, *Empresa Nacional de Telecomunicaciones* – and nationalised industrial sectors. Therefore, privatisation saw the transfer of ownership of huge swathes of the Argentine economy, including the telecommunications sector, water and sewerage, natural gas distribution, electricity generation and distribution, state firms in the manufacturing sector including steel and petrochemicals, ports, airports, railways, the postal service (*Correo Argentino*), the national airline (*Aerolíneas Argentinas*), and a number of provincial banks. These mass privatisations, generated substantial cash reserves and were used to help fund consistent balance-of-payments deficits due to the suppression of exports as a result of the currency peg (*Convertibilidad*). However, there were also more political reasons for such actions. 'Privatisation was considered a powerful instrument that could be used to gain a good reputation, quickly, among the local and international establishment' (Chudnovsky, 2007: 66). This need to gain a good reputation was crucial in the context of a traditionally populist party in government and the fact that it had come to power in the middle of hyper-inflationary conditions.

Third, labour reforms to introduce flexibility so as to lower the cost of labour were implemented. New controls over the labour movement were therefore introduced (Grugel and Riggirozzi, 2007: 91). In 1991 fixed-term and special training contracts were introduced for the young (Law No. 24,013), as well as creating an unemployment benefit system. Employer wage taxes were reduced in 1994, and in 1995 Law No. 24,013 was expanded and introduced a six-month trial period into new employment contracts (Chudnovsky, 2007: 90). These reforms helped to deregulate the labour market, and increase the flexibility of the labour force. At the same time, it also served to increase the precariousness of employment (Cortés, 2009: 57).

Fourth, and finally, policies of financial liberalisation involving liberalisation of cross-border capital movements, and domestic bank deregulation to promote greater integration into the international capital market were introduced. Therefore, the Argentine economy was further linked to the global economy and was prone, as scholars such as Ffrench-Davis and Reisen (1998), Rock (2002), Dinerstein (2002: 21), and Stiglitz (2002) argue, to speculative flows of financial capital. For O'Donnell (1973: 122) and Ferrer (2005: 107) this has been a long-term structural characteristic of Argentine economic history. Initially the result of Argentine prosperity resting on the export of agricultural products under Menem was the result of increasing incorporation into the global economy through tariff reduction, both in industrial sectors and, importantly for understanding the impacts of *El Argentinazo* in 2001, in the financial sector.

To achieve these goals Menem constructed and maintained a coalition between the economic right and the working class, forged through an emphasis on a discourse around the idea of economic emergency. The context of hyperinflation and chronic instability that ensued allowed Menem to persuade these groups that desperate times called for desperate measures (Tedesco, 2002: 474–5; Chudnovsky, 2007: 65; Grugel, 2009: 39). Indeed, Menem sought to put 'politics directly at the service of economic priorities' by presenting economic stabilisation as the most important means to steady democratic society (Tedesco, 2002: 478). He therefore manipulated politics in order to achieve economic ends. Combined with the generally worsening situation in terms of unemployment, poverty, and widening income inequality, this contributed to the erosion of the traditional bonds between the poor/working class and Peronism. However, these bonds were, while reduced, still very much present, and help explain the populist redistribution policies and use of patronage to mitigate some of the costs of labour restructuring and unemployment (Grugel and Riggirozzi, 2007: 91).

While *Menemismo* contained important populist elements, it also contained distinctive elements that could be characterised as neoliberal. Indeed, state–society relations in the 1990s under Menem were often considered to be distant and this was manifested in removal of social safety nets and the deregulation of the labour market. Kirchner did not engage in policies involving redistributive taxation, inequalities increased or simply stayed the same depending upon the sector, and the structures of socio-economic power stayed in place. Therefore, 'Kirchner has not distributed property income or power – except among different segments of the capitalist class' (Petras, 2006: 284). *Kirchnerismo's* approach to poverty also reflects a continuation of the Menem era (Petras, 2006: 283), as 'welfare essentially remains in the safety-net model of neoliberalism which can at best only ameliorate some of the worst manifestations of poverty' (World Bank, 2001: 10-11; Grugel and Riggirozzi, 2007: 105).

Despite these similarities, there are a number of points of departure within the state–society dichotomy that allows for a characterisation of the Kirchner administration 2003–7 which is different to *Menemismo*. The first concerns the emphasis under Menem on stability, through controlling inflation via the *Convertibilidad* regime, and increasing efficiency through policies of liberalisation of the economy and privatisation. This was achieved through moving towards a separation of the state from society in the political economy of *Menemismo*, and thus the erosion of the bonds between the poor/working classes and the Peronist party as represented by *Menemismo*. Kirchner and *Kirchnerismo*, as analysed previously, 'has forged a relationship based more on nationalist/statist development' (Godio, 2006: 35, 58; Grugel and Riggirozzi, 2007: 89) combined with a nationalistic political project (Riggirozzi, 2009: 89).

These different understandings of the state–society relationship are also reflected in *Kirchnerismo's* relationship with the trade unions. The links and conduits between the Kirchner administration and organised labour movements are different to the Menem years, and have facilitated much more cooperation and agreements than under *Menemismo* (see Figure 5.3; Etchemendy and Collier, 2007: 381). This in turn feeds into differences in the tripartite relationship. Genuine cooperation and negotiation between the business community and organised labour under *Kirchnerismo* was not present in the Menem years, due to the nature of his relationship with the trade unions.

In summary, in terms of state–society relations, or the social contract, *Kirchnerismo* can be seen as a *form* of Peronism, one that reflects

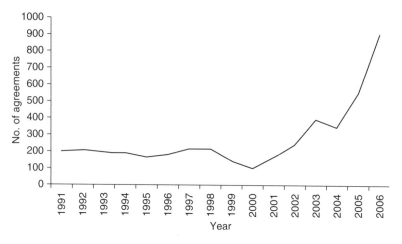

Figure 5.3   Number of Government–Union Agreements in Argentina (1991–2006)
Source: Etchemendy and Collier, 2007.

the influence of *Menemismo* and contemporary processes of neoliberal globalisation. These factors lead to the conclusion that a distinctive *Kirchnerismo* is present in the period 2003–7, a *Kirchnerismo* that possesses many similarities to *Peronismo* or *desarrollismo*, but also important differences, which possess some similarities with *Menemismo*, but once again is clearly different. This has led Grugel and Riggirozzi (2007) to suggest a characterisation of a form of *neodesarrollismo*, constituted fundamentally in principles of statist development; or Riggirozzi (2009) to term it as 'open economy nationalism', a blend of market-friendly economics and a nationalistic political project to help structure state–society relations. Such characterisations are indeed appropriate to the extent that they accurately reflect Kirchner's forging of new state–market and state–society relationships in Argentina in the period 2003–7. These characterisations however, fall short of promoting the idea of a *Kirchnerismo* as an institutionalised or coherent form of governance due to reservations regarding 'the extent of democratic revitalisation, the concentration of executive power in policymaking, and the enduring vulnerabilities of the economy' (Grugel, 2009: 21). Such limitations are therefore appropriate areas for further analysis and discussion, but it is the contention of this chapter that there *is* a *Kirchnerismo* as a coherent form of political economy.

The international dimension of *Kirchnerismo*

Analysis of the national–international relationships reveals important, indeed essential, elements of *Kirchnerismo* that facilitate an holistic understanding of his regime, and also show further points of departure from both traditional Peronist politics and *Menemismo.* Therefore, Argentine relations with the IMF, the role of debt, the issue of dependence on global commodity prices (especially in the context of government stimulus and emphasis on the export sector), and foreign investment will all be discussed in this section.

Argentina's relations with international capital have fundamentally changed under Kirchner. The sovereign debt default after the 2001 crisis altered the national (Argentine)–international capital relationship, and Kirchner's actions between 2003 and 2007 served to cement these changes. First, his tough negotiations with the IMF and other creditors (most of which are represented by the Paris Club of creditors) over the restructuring of the defaulted debt served to isolate Argentina from international capital markets. As a result, much new national debt was issued to the domestic market, or to Hugo Chavez's Venezuela. This judicious drawing down of Argentine debt to much more manageable levels represents an attempt to break the structural nature of debt in Argentine economic history, and is arguably unique to *Kirchnerismo* as both Peronism and *Menemismo* oversaw large increases in the Argentine debt burden. Furthermore, the early repayment of the entire outstanding US$9.8 billion debt facility that Argentina had with the IMF meant that IMF influence, a factor shaping national–international relations in Argentina since the end of Perón's first administration, has all but disappeared. Indeed, the IMF even closed its regional office in Buenos Aires as there was no more need for it after the repayment of the outstanding debt. While this decision 'owes much to the government's need to create an image inside Argentina of a sovereign state' (Grugel and Riggirozzi, 2007: 99), the desire to shrug off IMF influence over economic policy and engage in rhetorically nationalist economic policy was also a strong motivation (*The Economist,* 20 December 2005). However, Kirchner has been careful not to preside over a total rupture with the international community. While he engaged in hard negotiations with international creditors, a restructuring agreement covering the vast majority of owners of defaulted debt was achieved. In its totality Kirchner's policy managed to renegotiate Argentina's relationship with the forces of international capital, or, as Riggirozzi (2008: 140) put it, rewrite 'the financial rules of the game'. Given that this was in the context of the 2001 period, crisis management was fundamental in forging a new space for dissent from global rules; yet, at the same time, without falling into outdated, anti-capitalist economic autarky (Riggirozzi, 2008: 141).

This desire to strengthen the Argentine economy in relation to international institutions such as the IMF was matched by a desire to foster relations with other countries in Latin America (Grugel and Riggirozzi, 2007: 99). This is the result of push factors such as the desire to forge greater economic independence for South America, as well as perhaps more pull factors, such as the need for the Venezuelan government to purchase Argentine bonds due to international capital markets being closed off. Such an attitude has resulted in the pursuit of closer relationships with Venezuela, Brazil, Chile, and Bolivia through MERCOSUR (Interview with Diana Tussie, 2007), and a commitment to a regional energy market in April 2005 (Grugel and Riggirozzi, 2007: 99). However, events have presented this policy with some major challenges. The cutting off of gas exports to Chile during the energy shortage in the winter of 2007 (*Clarin*, 22 July 2007), as well as the role of *las papeleras*[2] (paper mills) (*Clarin*, 13 April 2006), have created points of tension that have damaged Kirchner's desire to improve regional relations.

The cornerstone of *Kirchnerismo* rests on the development of Argentina's export economy, largely facilitated through the maintenance of an SCRER. This represents a fundamental break with the Peronist model. *Peronismo* was based on ISI, and therefore largely closed to external economic forces through tariff and non-tariff barriers to trade (NTBs). *Kirchnerismo* stands in stark contrast to this model, with active promotion of an open economy though effective state management (Grugel and Riggirozzi, 2007: 106; Gerchunoff and Aguirre, 2004). This is also in contrast to the Menem years, where the maintenance of an overvalued RER through the *Convertibilidad* regime choked the competitiveness of Argentina's export industry. However, Grugel and Riggirozzi (2007: 106) identify the key challenge of 'how to manage fiscal and monetary policies in order to sustain Argentina's export successes, in the context of a globalised economy and historically vulnerable commodity prices'. Kirchner's policies have gone some way in addressing these needs. For example, an average of 11.1 per cent growth in the 2003 to 2006 period has been experienced in the manufacturing sector, and therefore has begun a process of decoupling from the declining terms of trade trap first identified by Raul Prebisch (1950). Furthermore, Kirchner's debt policies have served to reduce external vulnerability through the stabilisation and rationalisation of Argentina's debt burden. This has reduced Argentina's external vulnerability by reducing the potential pressure of a traditional currency/balance-of-payments crisis. Finally, the accumulation of large reserves as a result of the SCRER policy has also served to give Argentina a cushion against falling export prices or volumes.

The final consideration in the nature of the national–international relationship in *Kirchnerismo* is that of foreign investment, and relations with foreign business – namely TNCs. While Néstor Kirchner was happy to accommodate foreign companies that had existing interests in the domestic economy, he was more hostile towards TNCs looking to initiate interest in Argentina (Interview with Heidrich, 2007). This approach is different to more traditional policies associated with *Peronismo*, which viewed almost all TNC activity in the domestic economy as potentially damaging. Such an approach by Kirchner was also mirrored in the financial sector. While Kirchner maintained links with the sector in order to help his plans to expand personal credit to facilitate the consumer boom (Interview with Finkman, 2007), and there has been no hostility towards the banks in particular (Interview with Finkman, 2007), there has not been the active promotion of their interests as experienced during the Menem years through institutional links with the state such as personnel in the administration or the central bank. For example, one commentator[3] suggests that 'there are not the kind of people in the financial sector who move in government circles and can therefore be in a position to influence policy anymore'.

In sum, analysis of the international dimensions of *Kirchnerismo* reveals further points of departure from previous forms of political economy in Argentina, and thus complements the analysis of this chapter as it points to a distinct *Kirchnerismo*. Such a *Kirchnerismo* has a fundamentally different relationship with international capital. Due to the promotion of exports as a path to sustained economic growth being pursued as a development strategy, Argentina's external relationships are fundamentally different from both the ISI of *Peronismo* and *Desarrollismo*, and the era of *Convertibilidad* under *Menemismo*. This has also fed into Kirchner's policies regarding foreign debt, global institutions (most notably the IMF), and foreign investment through TNC activity.

Bringing in analysis of both the national–international and state–society relations facilitates a more holistic understanding of *Kirchnerismo*. Such an understanding overcomes some of the problems associated with traditional Developmental State literature as outlined in Part I. More traditional concepts of capacity that revolve around state bureaucracies, and the state being insulated from society through authoritarian regime or embedded autonomy, have been shown to be both spatially and temporally specific. Therefore, the next section of the chapter will explore the theoretical concept of the Developmental Regime (Pempel, 1999) (see Chapter 3), itself derived from the Developmental State literature, in order to determine its efficacy as a transferable framework for understanding *Kirchnerismo*.

Kirchnerismo as a Developmental Regime[4]

Kirchnerismo and the key characteristics of a Regime

As discussed in Part I of this book, the term regime in this analysis is derived from the work of Pempel (1998, 1999). Regimes are based on the interactions of specific social sectors and key state institutions (Pempel, 1999: 158). In turn, such fusions of state and society are manifested in public policy. Therefore, the character and nature of a regime is determined by the three inter-related concepts of socio-economic coalitions, the institutions of the state, and the bias of public policies that result and serve to act as the glue between the coalitions and institutions (see Chapter 3; see also, Pempel, 1998: 30). It is the purpose of this section to demonstrate how Pempel's use of the term regime is useful for understanding, contextualising, and theorising *Kirchnerismo*, as outlined in the previous sections of this chapter. This process will both provide analytical clarity to the characterisation of Néstor Kirchner's administration in Argentina 2003–7, and further develop and enrich the Developmental Regime approach. In order to achieve these tasks Pempel's approach, as analysed in Chapter 3, will be applied to Néstor Kirchner's administration of 2003–7; and in that process demonstrate how it is more appropriate to talk of Néstor Kirchner's regime rather than his administration.

The socio-economic alliances that help forge the state–society relationship under Néstor Kirchner have been detailed in previous sections of this chapter. Drawing support from and making alliances with different sectors of society from trade unions to the domestic bourgeoisie, middle class elements and elements of the poor and working classes, *Kirchnerismo* and its policies have served to provide access to the state for such groups and facilitated a public policy profile that in turn is beneficial to the economic and political interests of these groups. Such benefits have been derived from the unifying factor of neodevelopmentalism, or *neodesarrollismo* (Grugel and Riggirozzi, 2007; Grugel, 2009), and the benefits of economic growth being channelled to Néstor Kirchner's supporters through a consumer boom and expanding employment.

Such constellations of power are also reflected in the institutional structure of *Kirchnerismo*, with a number of its key elements demonstrating varying degrees of institutionalisation, for example his segmented neocorporatist approach to state–labour and state–business relations (Etchemendy and Collier, 2007). This approach has been partially institutionalised through the creation of conduits of communication between the state and key interests, and also through cementing his support with key labour unions by allowing them to maintain traditional patronage networks through using those unions as the mechanism by which to channel relief payments made under the *Plan Jefes y Jefas de Hogar.* Another example has been the passing of successive amendments to the minimum wage law, increasing its level to the point where it was commensurate with the minimum basket of goods deemed appropriate for a minimum standard of living. This has facilitated the continued support of both key labour elements as well as the trade unions. A more recent example, from the administration of Cristina Fernandez de Kirchner, has been the changing of the constitution of the Central Bank to include economic growth alongside inflation control in the Bank's remit, mirroring the responsibilities of the current US Federal Reserve as opposed to those of the UK Bank of England, which is only responsible for controlling inflation.

There are just as many examples of key policy areas that form the basis of *Kirchnerismo's* approach to development that have not shown levels of institutionalisation that would fully embed and secure the Developmental Regime in Argentina. Key pillars of Kirchner's Developmental Regime, such as his SCRER, are policies that were pursued due to the personality of Néstor Kirchner himself, but have not been reflected in the political and economic institutions of Argentina. Another is the example of maintenance of tight fiscal discipline, a key cornerstone of Kirchner's state–market relationship. The ability to maintain such discipline throughout his administration was due chiefly to the personal interventions of Kirchner himself and his desire to not oversee runaway public expenditure. Kirchner's style of leadership and government was very personal and highly centralised, with Kirchner himself taking many day-to-day decisions and ruling through Presidential Decree. Such a style of leadership and therefore lack of institutionalisation of such practices leaves Argentina's embryonic Developmental Regime vulnerable to fluctuations in the public policy profile. These fluctuations could lead to an alternative path being followed, or to a different regime being constructed. This relative lack of institutionalisation will be discussed further in the section on limitations in the conclusions of this book.

The final essential element of a regime as defined by Pempel (1998, 1999) is that of a public policy profile. As discussed in Chapter 3, the public policy profile of a regime is the glue that binds together the institutions and socio-economic alliances of that regime. In the articulation of Pempel's first two essential elements of a Developmental Regime with reference to Argentina earlier, examples of Kirchner's public policy profile were used to demonstrate how they served to act as this glue, delivering benefits to key supporters and thus facilitating their support of the regime, which in turn is reflected in the institutionalisation of such norms and behaviours. Such institutionalisation is an ongoing project, through which to ensure the relative stability of Kirchner's specific constellation of these essential elements, and therefore of his regime.

Kirchnerismo and the key characteristics of a Developmental Regime

If the specific constellation of socio-economic alliances, political–economic institutions, and public policy profiles present under Néstor Kirchner during the 2003 to 2007 period facilitates the use of the term regime for Argentina, then what is the significance of using the qualifier developmental? This book demonstrated in Chapter 4 that the state–market relationship under Néstor Kirchner can be best encapsulated by the term developmental, and interpreted through the Developmental State literature as outlined in Chapter 3. For example, the stimulation of an export industry through an SCRER policy, combined with an industrial policy centred on production and work, represents an interpretation of key Developmental State tenets.

Developmentalism is much more than simply an economic strategy based around growth, as it is an approach to development that is reflected in both state–society and state–international relationships in addition to state–market relationships. Analysis of the Developmental State's contributions to these areas earlier in the book revealed weaknesses based on the primacy of government bureaucracy and authoritarianism has been at the cost of supportive state–society relations and state–international relations. This has largely been due to the traditional characterisation of the Developmental State's relationship with society as 'embedded autonomy' (Evans, 1995). Furthermore, in terms of state–international relationships, traditional Developmental State literature overly focuses on the role of specific geopolitical factors, such as the role of US largesse towards South Korea in the 1950s and 1960s. Work subsequent to the first wave of literature on the Developmental State has moved the analysis forward in interesting ways. The work of Linda Weiss on the role of institutions in forming state power, defined in an 'infrastructural' or 'penetrative-extractive-coordinating' sense (Weiss and Hobson, 1995: 10) in order to generate specific developmental outcomes, or the work by Robinson and White (2002) on political systems and the Developmental State, can all be built upon to generate a more nuanced and complex understanding of state–society and state–international relationships.

Pempel's concept of the Developmental Regime generates this nuanced and complex understanding of these relationships present in Argentina in the period 2003–7. As outlined in the previous section, the regime concept is able to capture the specific nature of state–society and state–international relationships; and it is the task of the rest of this section to complement and build upon the analysis in both Chapter 3 and the previous section in order to demonstrate how Pempel's concept of the Developmental Regime can be applied to *Kirchnerismo* and why this is an appropriate exercise. Such a course of action will therefore both contribute to the understanding of Argentina under Kirchner, and enrich the concept and theory of the Developmental Regime (Pempel, 1998, 1999) through an investigation of its ability to accurately interpret and reflect the empirical evidence presented in previous chapters.

Pempel (1999) outlines three key characteristics of a Developmental Regime, which will be examined in relation to the administration of Néstor Kirchner in Argentina during the period 2003–7, concluding that in all three areas the evidence shows that the synergies facilitate the understanding of Kirchner's administration in terms of the Developmental Regime concept.

Pempel's framework will be examined in reverse order, and therefore the first key characteristic to be analysed is the benefits that the regime delivers to its supporters (1999: 178). As analysed in the previous section Kirchner forged an alliance between the old Peronist working-class base, the consuming middle-classes, and local bourgeoisie and big business (chiefly domestic manufacturing business). This realignment of the Argentine social contract after the 2001 crisis was achieved by Kirchner through policies that delivered benefits to each of these groups. The acquiescence of the unions, and therefore the working class base, was firstly gained through the dramatic economic recovery over which Kirchner presided. This facilitated large increases in employment and decreases in poverty, both phenomena that fundamentally helped the Argentine working classes. The specific character and nature of Kirchner's relationship with the unions can be characterised as segmented neocorporatism, as analysed earlier in this chapter. Furthermore, Kirchner's freezing of utility prices was enormously popular, and helped the poorer classes more due to the relative price inelasticity of energy demand. Third, his policies of infrastructural investment and a renewed emphasis on production and work both served to appeal to the traditional Peronist base of his support, and deliver benefits in the form of employment in the newly emerging export sector, complemented by Kirchner's SCRER policy. In addition, in synergy with these domestic policies, Kirchner's relations with international capital have earned him a lot of respect and political capital domestically due to his hard-line stance on the defaulted Argentine debt with the IMF and the Paris Club of creditors. His early repayment of the US$9.8 billion outstanding IMF arrears, and therefore the removal of the ability of the IMF to influence Argentine economic policy, was enormously popular domestically.

The middle classes also benefited from Kirchner's Developmental Regime. The creation of macroeconomic stability after the 2001–2 crisis and the resumption of investment restored consumer confidence, and therefore domestic consumption. In addition, the loosening of personal credit (facilitated through government policy) aided this consumption growth. The bourgeoisie more widely, as well as the domestic business community, has benefited as a result of the same macroeconomic stability and growth of investment under Kirchner, facilitating private investment in an economy that was 25 per cent larger by the end of 2007 than its pre-crisis peak in 1998 (CEPAL, 2008: 105). While this support has not been universal across sectors, with the example of the energy industry standing out due to its investment strike as a result of Kirchner's use of price controls for domestic energy consumers, Kirchner has nevertheless demonstrated a willingness to deal with domestic capital and those bourgeoisie who sought to invest in the economy.

The regime's creation of conduits between itself and elements of domestic industry and business has facilitated political access for these groups. This has therefore given them a stake in the regime, as well as delivering benefits through preferential access to government institutions. This relationship has been present also in the relationship with the trade unions, facilitating a characterisation of segmented neocorporatism, a characterisation that fits Pempel's framework well, as it looks to supply benefits to its supporters in both labour and business. Labour achieved gains through access, (modest) wage increases supported by policies to reduce inflation, minimum wage increases, and government policies to stimulate employment. Business gained due to its own conduits, especially in relation to domestically owned capital, as well as the sound macroeconomic environment facilitating an investment environment. Finally, his forging and cementing of relationships with TNCs that have historically invested in Argentina, and his relative hostility towards the involvement of new TNCs entering Argentina's market place, served to shape the conduits and relationships that he had with different sectors of international capital.

The next characteristic outlined by Pempel is that a Developmental Regime legitimates ideology. This means that the regime puts forward an ideology that plausibly represents the interests of its supporters as general or common interests. This legitimating ideology is *Kirchnerismo*. Based around the specific set of national and international relationships discussed previously, *Kirchnerismo* has articulated an alternative for the Argentine people that has represented their interests, and generated benefits for them. In his articulation of an alternative, Kirchner has sometimes served to produce some domestic tension with the opponents to his regime (see Conclusions for more details on limitations), often with opposing international interests. Indeed, the rhetoric of Kirchner can often be understood in this context. Producing enemies abroad can often galvanize support domestically, and also in this case allows for the articulation of *Kirchnerismo*, and its opposition to the forces of global neoliberalism in the form of both old neoliberal Menemist policies, and contemporary relations with the IMF.

The final characteristic of a Developmental Regime as understood by Pempel is that it defines the central issue in politics, and therefore sets the content of the nation's agenda, defining and pressing its own issues at the expense of its opponents (Pempel, 1999: 158). As demonstrated in the previous chapter, Néstor Kirchner has been able to forge a social contract based on development, or what Grugel terms *neodesarrollismo*. Stimulation of export industries through his SCRER policy, the expansion of domestic credit to facilitate a consumer boom, and measures to curb inflation that included low public sector wage increases and price caps have all served as policies to define this central issue and characteristic of *Kirchnerismo*. Furthermore, the nature of the Kirchner administration's decision-making structures, and his relationship with the media, are useful here. As discussed previously, Kirchner's strong grip on the government apparatus and highly centralised decision-making processes are not unique to this period of Argentine history. However, they have allowed Kirchner to set a strong and unified agenda. Combined with his relationship with the media, that is, almost exclusive use of supportive popular media to express his message, this has allowed Kirchner to dominate and set the national agenda. Political opponents were few and far between. This has been due to both Kirchner's ability to dominate the agenda, as well as the virtual destruction of the main traditional opposition, *Los Radicales*, by the events of 2001–2.

The Developmental Regime approach therefore helps to both interpret *Kirchnerismo*, providing both analytical clarity to its different characteristics, and enriching the Developmental Regime approach. Rather than viewing the policies of Néstor Kirchner as simply a series of decisions made in reaction to events, or as opportunistic pragmatism, the Developmental Regime approach provides the analytical leverage with which to interpret the approach of *Kirchnerismo*. Furthermore, such leverage facilitates an understanding not simply based on broad concepts of populism, nor on overly narrow interpretations such as traditional Developmental State theory, but on a holistic interpretation of the three interrelated and mutually reinforcing developmental dichotomies of state–market, state–society, and state–international.

Conclusions: Kirchnerismo and the Developmental Regime approach

Kirchner's Developmental Regime has facilitated sustained economic growth, with the level of GDP exceeding pre-crisis highs by the end of 2004. Furthermore, a significant amount of this new growth has been in the manufacturing sector, and therefore represents diversification away from Argentina's traditional export base of agricultural commodities. This serves to help remove the fortunes of the Argentine economy away from the cycles of commodity prices, although not from the international economy in general (indeed, on the contrary perhaps) due to the fact that much of this new industrial growth has been in export sales. The long-term benefits and prospects of this growth are healthy due to a sustained, stable macroeconomic environment, sustained growth and increased investment, although key investment bottlenecks in the energy sector in particular could well result in limiting economic growth in the future. Increased profitability and decreased dependency on international commodity prices has also been facilitated by a highly beneficial debt restructuring and repayment, leading to increased growth in the manufacturing sector. However, it must be stressed that this is a process that has not yet reached completion, and the Argentine economy is still dominated by the agricultural export industry. This fusion of national relationships and policies with a distinct international strategy based around reducing debt, a reformulation of the relationship with the IMF, and political preference for national industry could be labelled as a twenty-first century Peronism for a globalising world,[5] and is best understood through Pempel's Developmental Regime framework.

It is Peronist because of some of the key socio-economic bases for its support, maintained through Kirchner's rhetoric. It is Peronist also due to the key elements of continuity with 'traditional' forms of Peronism that have been identified in this chapter. It is 'twenty first century' in recognition of the changing nature of Peronism throughout Argentine history, and its ability to adapt to changing circumstances. This is represented partially through elements of continuity with *Menemismo*, but also through his adoption of key policies that originate from neither traditional *Peronismo* or from *Menemismo* (e.g. his SCRER). It is also twenty-first century in recognition of the changing circumstances in which *Kirchnerismo* operated. These changing circumstances are due to the context of both neoliberal restructuring in the 1990s under Menem, and the longer term impacts of the crisis of 2001–2. Finally, it is for a globalising world due to recognition of the important role of globalisation in shaping domestic political agendas and shaping the 'limits of the possible', which are the result of the imperatives of competitiveness and free markets. Such imperatives facilitate changes in the environment in which nation states operate, changes that lead to global processes of greater flexibility and informalisation of the labour market. Kirchner's harnessing of these forces in order to achieve domestic development reveal important characteristics of the existence of a clear *Kirchnerismo*, while also bringing into focus further differences with Peronism and Menemism.

This chapter has therefore both contributed to the analysis of *Kirchnerismo*, and to the Developmental Regime approach itself. Interpretation of the different components of *Kirchnerismo* through the lens of the Developmental Regime have shown the systematic way that the different elements of the relationships between all three developmental dichotomies have consistently been characterised within a developmentalist paradigm, or what (Grugel and Riggirozzi, 2007; Grugel, 2009) terms *neodesarrollismo*. The Developmental Regime approach has greatly helped to demonstrate that *Kirchnerismo* is a project that is necessarily rooted in all three of the developmental dichotomies, and can therefore only be wholly interpreted through such an approach. Pempel's investigation and integration of complex understandings of state–society and state–international relationships provides the analytical clarity necessary and appropriate for investigating *Kirchnerismo*.

After two chapters that conduct a similar exercise for Brazil, Part III of this book will move forward to analyse the wider regional and global implications of this analysis. If *Kirchnerismo* can be characterised within a Developmental Regime framework, then what about other regimes in Latin America that form part of the pink tide? Furthermore, can anything be learned from the developmental experience of East Asia, the continent where the concepts of Developmental State and Developmental Regime were first developed and applied? In addition, Part II of this book has shown that the Developmental Regime represented a particularly useful development for strategy for Argentina in the context of post-crisis political economy. Could such a strategy also be useful for other countries or regions experiencing post-crisis periods? How does a Developmental Regime approach compare to other strategies based more on neoliberal or SMC approaches? Or, what are the limitations to the Developmental Regime?

6
The Economic Policies of Lula's Regime in Brazil

The Lula administration in Brazil (2003–10) represents the second in-depth case study of this book, which will provide further evidence for the thesis that the Developmental Regime approach is the best meta-theory of political economy for interpreting the pink tide in Latin America as defined and analysed in Chapter 2. This chapter will therefore begin with an analysis of the Brazilian financial crisis of 1998, in order to provide the necessary background and contextualisation for subsequent consideration of Lula's regime. This consideration will encompass the economic policies of Lula, from efforts to stimulate growth to social policies such as *Bolsa Familia*. Once a complete analysis and understanding of Lula's policies has been achieved, Chapter 7 will be able to move forward and explore the implications of these policies for Brazilian development.

The chapter will therefore be split into four sections. The first will examine the crises of 1994 and 1998, thus outlining the necessary contextualisation. The second will outline the economic characteristics of the period – broadly considered to be steady, if unspectacular, economic growth, low inflation, decreasing debt, and rising social spending translating into lower poverty and inequality. The third section will then analyse the policies of the Lula administration's that facilitated these characteristics. Therefore, policy areas that will be examined are: growth and investment policy, exchange rate policy, industrial policy, fiscal policy, debt, employment, poverty and wages, and inflation. The analysis will address the issue of whether the economic fortunes of Brazil during this period were the result of domestic policy or favourable international circumstances. A final section offers conclusions, attempting to determine whether Lula's regime represented a break from the past administrations of FHC, or if there was essentially continuity.

The financial crises of 1994 and 1998

The election of Collor in 1989 marked a decisive shift towards neoliberalism and away from state-directed development in the form of ISI. After the return of inflation in the early 1990s, Collor resigned in 1992 and his Finance Minister FHC became president in the 1994 presidential elections. FHC continued the neoliberal reforms of Collor, although with less orthodoxy (Kingstone and Ponce, 2010: 102). These neoliberal reforms can be summarised into four broad categories: first, extensive regulatory reform; second, the closure of several government agencies and departments; third, privatisation of assets worth approximately US$100 billion (or 18.5 per cent of GDP in 1994); and fourth, liberalisation of domestic finance, foreign trade, exchange rate movements, and the capital account (Mollo and Saad-Filho, 2006: 101). The impacts of these shifts in policy were far reaching. One-third of all manufacturing jobs were lost during the 1990s. Unemployment and informal employment doubled, combined with a radical restructuring of manufacturing industry itself. The state retreated partially or completely from several strategic sectors, especially steel, telecommunications, electricity generation, transport, and finance. In addition, the civil service underwent a series of reforms that reduced the government's capacity to regulate the market and implement targeted industrial policies (Saad-Filho, 2007: 15).

This shift towards neoliberalism intensified and was pursued with increasing determination in the wake of the *Real* stabilisation plan of 1994 (Doctor and Paula, 2008: 146). The key economic strand of the plan was to eliminate persistent high inflation, in which it was successful and represented the most significant achievement of the neoliberal decade (Mollo and Saad-Filho, 2006: 103; Burges, 2009: 201). This was achieved through instituting a crawling peg, thus anchoring inflation expectations of the *Real* to the US dollar (Evangelist and Sathe, 2006: 2). However, the *Real* plan was more than an inflation policy as it included high interest rates, capital account and financial liberalisation, privatisation or closure of SOEs, fiscal and labour market reforms, currency overvaluation, and the closure of several government agencies and departments; that is, all in line with the broader direction of neoliberal reform that sought to dismantle the old ISI state (Mollo and Saad-Filho, 2006: 103; Saad-Filho, Iamini, and Molinari, 2007: 22).

The macroeconomic impacts of the *Real* plan can be determined by examination of Table 6.1. As can be seen, high interest rates successfully tamed inflation, bringing it down from 1093.9 per cent in

Table 6.1 Brazilian select economic indicators, 1990–2002

	Inflation Rate (%)	Real Interest Rate (%)	Exports (US$m)	Imports (US$m)	Trade Balance (US$m)	Current Account (US$m)	Foreign Debt (US$m)	International Reserves (US$m)
1990	1476.7	–5.6	35,166	28,010	7156	–3784	123,439	–8183
1991	480.2	8.6	34,917	28,136	6780	–1407	123,910	–13,035
1992	1157.8	37.9	39,873	27,818	12,055	6109	135,949	16,964
1993	2708.2	9.5	42,509	34,456	8053	–676	145,726	25,214
1994	1093.9	32.1	47,937	43,128	4809	–1811	148,295	37,887
1995	14.8	33.5	51,435	62,384	–10,949	–18,384	159,256	50,918
1996	9.3	16.8	52,785	67,065	–14,280	–23,502	179,935	60,059
1997	7.5	16.6	59,870	77,269	–17,399	–30,452	199,998	52,106
1998	1.7	26.5	59,037	75,722	–16,685	–33,416	241,644	34,362
1999	20.1	4.7	55,206	63,381	–8176	–25,335	241,468	23,861
2000	9.8	7.2	64,584	72,444	–7860	–24,225	236,156	31,541
2001	10.4	6.5	67,545	72,653	–5109	–23,215	227,689	27,797
2002	26.4	–7.1	69,913	61,749	8164	–7637	235,414	16,339

Source: BCB, 2010.

1994 (or a high of 2708.2 per cent in 1993) to 14.8 per cent in 1995. Furthermore, high interest rates (combined with liberalisation of the capital account) led to large inflows of foreign capital, and a subsequent overvaluation of the *Real*. This policy was deliberately pursued so as to boost the impact of the liberalisation of imports. Therefore, '[c]urrency overvaluation and import liberalisation, along with fiscal reforms and de-indexation, were the functioning core of the *Real* plan' (Mollo and Saad-Filho, 2006: 104). This led to significant resource inflows in FDI and portfolio investment, but correspondingly large capital outflows in debt service payments, profit remittances, divestment and capital flight (Mollo and Saad-Filho, 2006: 110). In addition, the overvaluation of the *Real* led to a relative stagnation of export growth and corresponding large import growth, which impacted on the trade balance and therefore the current account (see Table 6.1), and by 1998 the current account deficit had ballooned to 4.2 per cent of GDP. This led to both an increase in external liabilities and a reduction in international reserves in order to finance this deficit, which resulted in the need to maintain high interest rates to ensure a steady flow of portfolio capital to finance the economy's needs. This perpetuated problems of *Real* overvaluation and its continuing misalignment (Evangelist and Sathe, 2006: 3).

High interest rates depressed growth and investment, with economic growth averaging 2.7 per cent between 1994 and 2004, compared to 6.3 per cent between 1933 and 1980 (Mollo and Saad-Filho, 2006:110). Combined with the privatisation drive in the 1990s this led to high unemployment, which 'increased to 14 per cent in 1998 from a low of 6 per cent a decade earlier' (Evangelist and Sathe, 2006: 3). All of this limited the expansion of tax revenues (with the government deficit remaining in the 6–7 per cent range throughout the 1990s) and increased public debt even more, forcing new and higher taxes. 'In essence, under neoliberalism, the state budget was used to transfer income and assets – averaging 8.6 per cent of GDP over ten years – from the taxpayers to the holders of public securities via the financial system' (Mollo and Saad-Filho, 2006: 106). This exacerbated inequality and shifted economic and political power towards finance. However, the overvalued *Real*, combined with the liberalisation of imports, fuelled consumerism as a wide array of cheaper consumer goods became available in Brazilian markets. This ensured FHC's re-election in 1998, as he was widely seen as bringing modernisation to Brazil as well as the benefits of a new globalising economy.

The *Real* plan was therefore successful in eliminating inflation, but at the expense of a macroeconomic policy trap where the economy relied on high interest rates to continue functioning, high interest rates that increasingly exacerbated an overvalued *Real*, with subsequent detrimental effects on the balance of payments. It was this situation that eventually facilitated devaluation and crisis, and therefore it could be argued that the *Real* plan created the conditions for the 1998 crisis (Edwards, 2010: 209). Indeed, following the Asian financial crisis in 1997 and the collapse of the Russian economy in August 1998 foreign investors became increasingly skittish and, despite high interest rates in Brazil, began to withdraw their capital from Brazil. On 15 January 1999 sustained capital flight of several billion US dollars every couple of days forced the Central Bank to abandon the band system established by the *Real* plan and devalue the currency. Within a month the value of the *Real* fell by 35 per cent. While hyperinflation did not return, as many had feared, the government still had to scramble to face up to the underlying fiscal problems that continued to concern anxious investors and threaten the currency (Montero, 2005: 34). The devaluation did help to improve current account deficits (see Table 6.1) but, at the same time, it increased the value of Brazil's sizeable public debt held in US dollars. However, unlike the Asian financial crisis in 1997, a large amount of Brazilian debt was not held in foreign denominated paper and therefore was able to avoid a financial sector collapse (Evangelist and Sathe, 2006: 4).

Emerging from the crisis: 1999–2002

The FHC government introduced a new macroeconomic policy regime shortly after the currency crisis. This included a combination of inflation targeting, large fiscal surpluses, and the managed fluctuation of the *Real* (Doctor and Paula, 2008: 148). This combination of policies was to reproduce the successes of the *Real* plan (i.e. low inflation) without the macroeconomic imbalances of increasing public debt, persistently high interest rates, and current account deficits that contributed to the 1998 crisis as described in the preceding section. However, these policies were only partially successful. While manufacturing output expanded and there were substantial FDI inflows between 1998 and 2001, there were a number of negative aspects. The *Real* devaluation triggered temporary inflation, with bubbles in 1999 with a rate of 20.1 per cent, and in 2002 with 26.4 per cent (see Table 6.1). Due to this persistent inflation, and the continued prevalence of an inflation-targeting regime, real interest rates remained high (see Table 6.1). In turn, this made it difficult to stabilise public debt despite high primary fiscal surpluses post-1999 and the government had to issue a greater amount of dollar-linked securities, leading to persistently high levels of foreign debt (see Table 6.1) and overall debt, which increased from 27.3 per cent of GDP in 1994 to 47.2 per cent of GDP in 2003 (Mollo and Saad-Filho, 2006: 109). In addition there was periodic exchange rate instability, primarily due to fluctuations in the availability of foreign exchange or 'political uncertainty' in the opinion of the financial markets. This volatility hindered export growth and therefore a correspondingly slow reaction of the trade balance to the devaluation (see Table 6.1; Mollo and Saad-Filho, 2006: 109).

Social indicators during both the *Real* plan of FHC and in the post-crisis period did not fare well. 'Economic underperformance over long periods, high interest rates, rapid import liberalisation, and the structural transformation of Brazilian industry through mergers and acquisitions and the "flexibilisation" of the labour force led to a significant deterioration of the labour market' (Mollo and Saad-Filho, 2006: 110). This is evident across a range of indicators. Real wage income in the São Paulo metropolitan area declined from a base of 100 in Q1 1992 to 90 by Q1 2003 (Mollo and Saad-Filho, 2006: 112). Unemployment increased in the same area from just over 10 per cent in 1991 to just under 20 per cent by 2003 (Mollo and Saad-Filho, 2006: 112). The destabilisation of the Brazilian labour market was also evident in the rapid increase of irregular employment (*empregados sem carteira*) since the mid-1990s (Mollo and Saad-Filho, 2006: 111). Lower wages combined with higher unemployment and underemployment fed into the poverty figures with poverty peaking in 2003 at 38.7 per cent of the population and extreme poverty at 13.9 per cent (Kingstone and Ponce, 2010: 114).

The economic characteristics of Lula's regime, 2003–10

In 1999 Brazil's economic problems remained severe. After the Asian financial crisis of 1997 and the January 1999 devaluation of the *Real*, debt service payments rose significantly with total public debt (domestic and external combined) increased from 29 per cent of GDP in 1994 to 58.7 per cent of GDP in 2003. This fiscal situation remained grave, with interest payments on its debt totalling US$50 billion a year by 2004, or 8 per cent of GDP (Montero, 2005: 34). This was the fourth largest debt service to GDP ratio in the world. Foreign investors continued to doubt Brazil's ability to repay and capital flight perpetuated, reaching a high point in 2003 as US$6 billion exited Brazil. Thus, '[FHC's] inability to pass fiscal reform set in motion a worsening of public accounts, despite his *Real* Plan's initial success against inflation and its stabilisation following the 1999 crisis' (Montero, 2005: 35).

Luis Inácio Lula da Silva (from here on Lula) took office on 1 January 2003, after having won 46.4 per cent of the vote in the first round (double that of the next nearest candidate, José Serra), and 61.3 per cent in the second round. As a result of the crisis of 1998 and the subsequent turmoil in the markets as a result of their perception that Lula would at least partially declare a default on Brazilian debt after being elected president, Lula was forced to assure markets that he would continue the fiscal and monetary policies set in place by FHC through his 'Letter to the Brazilian People' on 22 June 2002 during the election campaign (Mollo and Saad-Filho, 2006: 113; Arestis, Paula, and Ferrari-Filho, 2007b: 39). In addition he set in motion policies that would institutionalise this promise, with a new IMF agreement on 4 September 2002 that would provide a framework for the continuity of core macroeconomic policies in 2003 (i.e. under the new administration). Furthermore, Lula agreed to submit a constitutional amendment granting independence to the Central Bank.

This section will examine first the trajectory of the Brazilian economy in the years 2003–10, examining macroeconomic patterns such as growth and investment, inflation, debt, and fiscal policy. In addition, the evolution of social indicators will also be examined such as wages, poverty, and inequality. Such an analysis will set the necessary quantitative backdrop for an analysis in the next section of the policies of the Lula administration(s) that facilitated these characteristics. The analysis will address the issue of whether the economic fortunes of Brazil during this period were the result of domestic policy or favourable international circumstances. A final section will offer some conclusions, which centre on the question of continuity or change?

The macroeconomic environment in Brazil, 2003–10

As can be seen from Figure 6.1 Brazilian GDP has grown at positive rates throughout Lula's first term (2003–6), with rather sluggish growth in 2003 of 2.2 per cent, which was the result of the turmoil in the financial markets preceding Lula's election (Tussie, 2009: 74). However, this picked up in the 2004–6 period with average year-on-year growth of 5.6 per cent. This growth was driven by industrial production, which rose sharply in 2004 by 8.3 per cent, the biggest growth since 1986 (Flynn, 2005: 1224). Indeed, industrial production continued to grow throughout Lula's administrations, developing from a base of 92.2 in

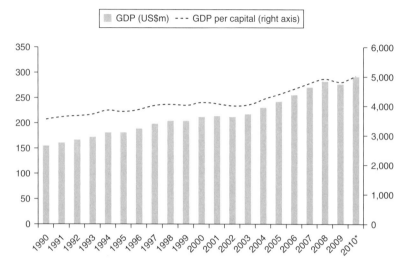

Figure 6.1 Brazilian GDP and GDP per capita in constant 2000 US$, 1990–2010
Source: CEPALSTAT, 2011.
Note: * only includes data up to 20 December.

January 2003 (where 2002 = 100) to 133.6 in July 2010 (latest available figures) (CEPALSTAT, 2011). Real per capita GDP growth recovered to about 2.25 per cent over the 2001–4 period, which was well above the rates experienced during the 1980s and 1990s (Adrogué, Cerisola, and Gelos, 2010: 258). Nevertheless, the GDP growth rates were consistently lower than those reached by most emerging economies due to the benign and buoyant nature of the international economy during this period (Carvalho, 2007: 30). Growth has also been driven by an expansion of consumer credit in Brazil. Consumer borrowing as a share of GDP doubled between 2001 and 2006, with the stock of outstanding credit increasing from R$137 billion to R$177 billion in the year before the election in 2006 (Hunter and Power, 2007: 15). During Lula's second administration (2007–10) the economy grew strongly until the effects of the global financial crisis in 2008 affected GDP growth. The economy was quick to recover however, certainly in terms of other economies, especially those in the OECD, and returned to positive growth in 2010.

Investment has also been growing, therefore suggesting that current GDP growth in Brazil can be sustained in the medium- and long-terms. Figure 6.2 shows that GFCF grew steadily during Lula's first term from

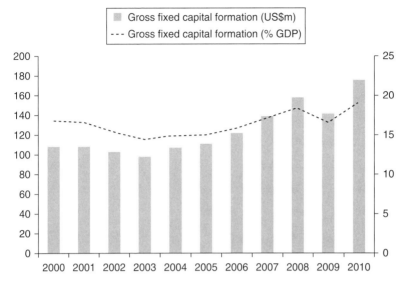

Figure 6.2 Brazilian gross fixed capital formation in constant 2000 US$, 2000–10
Source: CEPALSTAT, 2011.

a post-crisis low in 2003 of US$98,349.8 million (at constant 2000 prices) to US$122,056.3 million by 2006. Lula's second administration saw further investment growth, with a slight interruption in 2009 due to the impact of the global financial crisis. Furthermore, in the context of a growing economy, GFCF as a percentage of GDP grew across Lula's administrations from 14.5 per cent in 2003 to 19.1 per cent of GDP in 2010 (see Figure 6.2). CEPAL estimate that between 24 and 27 per cent of GDP would need to be achieved in investment in order to achieve an annual growth rate of 6 per cent (CEPAL, 2006: 18); therefore, by this calculation, while growing, levels of investment in Brazil are still too low to maintain high growth rates that it began to experience towards the end of Lula's second term. Commentators such as Kingstone and Ponce (2010: 123) have suggested that this can be explained at least partially by the policy of macroeconomic stability, which meant that the very mechanisms used to secure stability worked against increased levels of investment.

Part of this evolution of the growth record can also be explained by the pattern of trade experienced by Brazil during this period. In fact, as Figure 6.3 demonstrates Brazil began to show surpluses in the trade

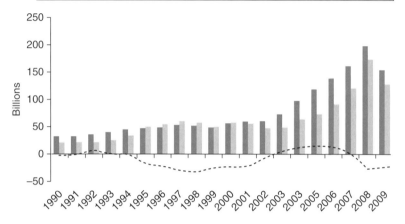

Figure 6.3 Imports and exports of goods and services in Brazil in current US$, 1990–2009
Source: World Bank, 2010b.

balance under FHC, the result of a change in the exchange rate regime after devaluation in January 1999. The increases in exports made it possible to reach significant surpluses in the current account, also shown by Figure 6.3 where the current account balance reached positive figures in 2003 and were maintained until the effects of the financial crisis began to take hold in 2007. Such a turnaround in the structure of trade in Brazil removed an important source of external vulnerability that makes Brazil so dependent upon international markets. However, 'one cannot forget that this performance was favoured by the intense growth of international trade [prior to the onset of the global financial crisis] and by the significant rise in the prices of commodities, including those exported by Brazil' (Carvalho, 2007: 27). These considerations will be examined in detail in the next section.

After reaching a historical peak of US$32.8 billion in 2000, annual FDI declined in the 2000–3 period, as illustrated in Figure 6.4. This decline was the result of several factors, including the decline in investment expenditures and demand in developed countries in 2001 as a result of the dot.com bubble, reduced investment opportunities as the result of the completion of major privatisations, and, in 2002–3, uncertainties associated with the transition to a new government. This last

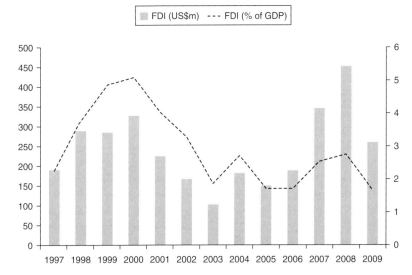

Figure 6.4 Foreign direct investment in Brazil, 1997–2009
Source: World Bank, 2010b.

factor caused delays in some investment decisions in 2003, particularly in sectors that have undergone a redefinition of the regulatory environment (e.g. electricity and telecoms). The decline of FDI over this period is not unique to Brazil, but has also occurred in other emerging economies (except for China). In 2004, FDI in Brazil reached US$18.2 billion, recovering from 2003, and proceeded to rise every year until 2009, due to the impacts of the global financial crisis (BCB, 2010: 12). This recovery in FDI aided the current account's return to surplus in these years, although by far the most important impact was the rise in exports, as shown in Figure 6.3.

In fiscal terms the Lula administrations saw significant consolidation of the government accounts. As Table 6.2 shows, the public sector registered a significant primary surplus throughout Lula's administrations. It is true that these had been achieved by FHC after the crisis of 1998, but nevertheless were continued by Lula. In 2009 the primary surplus decreased significantly to 2.05 per cent of GDP, which was the result of further resources being placed into the Programa de Aceleração do Crescimento (Growth Acceleration Program or PAC). This will be discussed further in the next section. However, Table 6.2 also shows that significant interest payments on outstanding debt stock has led to

Table 6.2 Select Brazilian central government statistics (as a percentage of GDP), 1998–2009

	1998	1999	2000	2001	2002	2003	2004	2005	2006	2007	2008	2009
Total revenue	18.74	19.65	19.89	20.74	21.63	20.92	21.55	22.68	22.87	23.20	23.78	23.45
Total expenditure	22.41	22.17	21.72	22.82	22.80	25.26	23.40	26.27	25.75	25.08	25.00	27.04
Consolidated primary result of the public sector	0.01	3.23	3.46	3.64	3.21	3.34	3.80	3.93	3.24	3.37	3.54	2.05
Nominal interest	–	–9.06	–7.08	–7.21	–7.63	–8.47	–6.59	–7.31	–6.78	–6.06	–5.45	–5.39
Nominal fiscal result	–	–5.84	–3.61	–3.57	–4.42	–5.13	–2.79	–3.38	–3.54	–2.69	–1.90	–3.33

Source: CEPASTAT, 2011 for total revenue and expenditures; BCB, 2010 for rest.

persistent nominal fiscal deficits that have fluctuated between 2 and 5 per cent of GDP. As a result, as Figure 6.5 demonstrates, total government debt has increased throughout the period despite consistent primary surpluses, showing that Brazilian debt is more a function of interest rates and exchange rates (Carvalho, 2007: 27).

The exchange rate depreciation in 2002 had a significant impact on the debt-to-GDP ratio, which reached a peak of 61.7 per cent in September 2002. In subsequent months, however, the upward trend was reversed as the nominal exchange rate appreciated. The ratio entered a downward trend in 2003, favoured by higher GDP growth and by increases in the consolidated primary surplus (BCB, 2010). This trend then continued throughout the 2004–8 period, until the global financial crisis in 2007 reversed the downward trend as a result of deficit spending and fiscal stimulus on the part of the Brazilian government. Nevertheless, foreign debt, which was at 45 per cent of GDP when Lula took office in 2003 represented a mere 15 per cent of GDP in 2010 (Sotero, 2010: 72).

In terms of expenditure Figure 6.6 shows that while spending increased in absolute terms quite significantly from 2003 onwards, as a percentage of GDP it has remained within a relatively narrow band of between 38 and 40 per cent. This shows that sound Brazilian finances

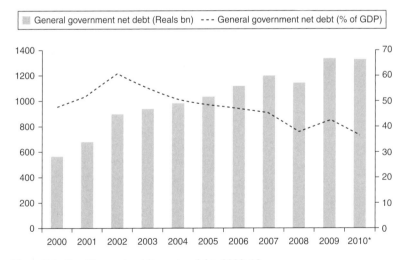

Figure 6.5   Brazilian net public sector debt, 2000–10
Source: IMF, 2010.
Note: * IMF staff estimate.

were the fundamental characteristic of the period, and further reinforces the conclusion that increases in Brazilian debt stock across the
period were the result of interest rate and exchange rate movements,
rather than extra discretionary spending on the part of the state.

As shown in Figure 6.7 the Brazilian RER was overvalued during the
1994–8 period, coinciding with FHC's *Real* plan. This helps explain the
relative stagnation of Brazilian exports during this period, the current
account deficit (see Figure 6.3), and the subsequent accrual of debt (see
Figure 6.6). With the floating exchange rate adopted in January 1999,
the RER depreciated significantly through the second half of 2002,
and then corrected in the following three years (BCB, 2010). Compared
to the average in the period from 1994 to June 2005, the graph shows
that the RER at the end of June 2005 was relatively depreciated, and
continued to depreciate into 2010, with a brief period of appreciation
in 2009 due to the effects of the global financial crisis.

The cycles of hyperinflation that had plagued Brazil's recent macroeconomic history seem to have been tamed. Dropping from the huge
levels of 2477.15 per cent in 1993 to 1.66 per cent by 1998 FHC's *Real*
plan succeeded in stabilising Brazilian prices. However, a 40 per cent
devaluation of the Real between 2000 and 2003 (see Figure 6.7) led
to increasingly high levels of inflation thereafter, peaking in 2002 at

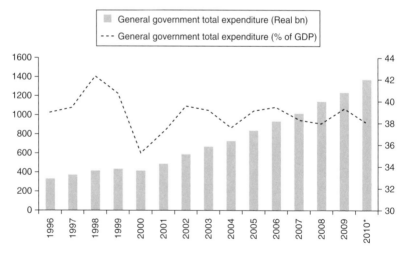

Figure 6.6   Brazilian government expenditure, 1996–2010
Source: IMF, 2010.
Note: * IMF staff estimates.

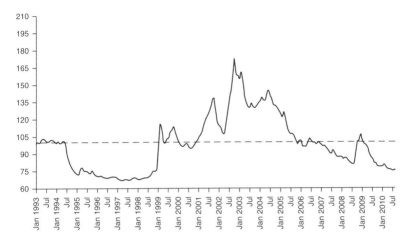

Figure 6.7   Brazilian real exchange rate index (June 1994 = 100)
Source: BCB, 2010.

12.53 per cent, although dropping off a little for the remainder of Lula's administration and, most importantly in the context of Brazil's history of hyperinflationary episodes, remaining stable. The main tool that has been used to control inflation rates in Brazil during this period has been very high interest rates (Flynn, 2005: 1224), which will be examined in greater detail in the next section.

Social indicators in Brazil have demonstrated mixed results. Between 2003 and 2009 approximately 20 million people have been lifted out of poverty, significantly reducing the percentage of Brazilians living below both the US$1.25/day and US$2/day poverty lines (see Figure 6.8). Between 2003 and 2008, the absolute poverty rate dropped from 39 to 25 per cent, while extreme poverty declined from 17.5 to 8.8 per cent of the population (World Bank, 2010a: 19). These reductions in poverty have also served to reduce inequality (see same figure). Brazil, a famously unequal society in terms of income distribution, had a Gini coefficient that was at 57 in 2003 when Lula started office, and had reduced to 54.8 by 2008. Although overall economic growth could be described as steady at best, this fall in inequality is indicative of where GDP growth is taking place. 'In percentage terms, the proportion of GDP going to the poorest deciles of the population is growing faster than it is for the richest' (Burges, 2009: 210). In addition, the government's flagship Conditional Cash Transfer (CCT) programme *Bolsa Familia*, has helped many of the poorest in Brazilian society (see later sections for

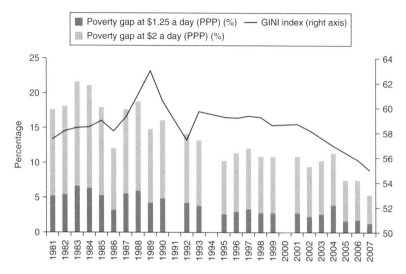

Figure 6.8   Poverty, extreme poverty, and Gini coefficient in Brazil, 1981–2007
Source: World Bank, 2010b.

a full discussion of this programme). These steady improvements in the poverty and inequality figures in Brazil throughout the 2002–10 period have reversed the continuingly worsening trends of previous decades, and represent one of the best achievements in reducing poverty and inequality in the Latin American and Caribbean (LAC) area, and indeed globally (World Bank, 2010a: 20).

   In the first five months of 2003 more than half a million jobs were lost, leading to an unemployment rate by the end of the year of 9.7 per cent. However, if the period is seen as a whole, 'total formal employment has grown monotonically, if not very quickly, since 2000 ... There is some evidence to suggest that the *net* expansion of employment has been much lower, with formal employment expanding at the expense of informal jobs, as a result of monitoring crackdowns on employers' [italics in original] (Carvalho, 2007: 28). However, by 2005 unemployment in the six major metropolitan areas fell to 9.6 per cent, the lowest figure in three years (Flynn, 2005: 1224). In the last few years of the Lula administration, however, there was a significant reduction in the unemployment rate from 9.3 per cent in 2007 to 5.7 per cent in 2010. This acceleration in the reduction of unemployment came in the period of the global financial crisis. Nevertheless, if one is to take a longer term perspective, unemployment remained high in comparison to the mid-1980s when Brazil had a much greater level of state direction and involvement in the economy through central planning and SOEs. While the level of state involvement in the economy has decreased significantly since this time, there was still a steady 2 per cent a year expansion in state employment from 2003 to 2008, especially in state enterprises such as Petrobras (17,000 new jobs or 25 per cent of the firm's workforce), *Banco do Brazil* and several others (Tussie, 2009: 74).

If employment growth has been sluggish in the 2003–10 period, then real wage growth has been a huge disappointment. Public sector wages remain significantly above private sector wages, although the private sector creates the vast majority of jobs, demonstrated by the fact that the overall average real wage is much closer to the private sector wage due to the greater impact that this sector has on the data. Although real wages have been on an upwards trend for the 2003 to 2009 period (with a slight dip in 2010), this increase has been almost insignificant from R\$1387 in 2003 to a peak R\$1753 in 2009, with a drop to R\$1518 in 2010. While the minimum wage has increased across the period, it has hardly been of major significance, and has barely kept pace with the general increase in real wages, despite the almost stagnant nature of the latter. Nevertheless, an average annual growth of 6.6 per cent under Lula was well above the 2.6 per cent that was achieved under FHC (Kingstone and Ponce, 2010: 116).

The economic policies of the Lula administration, 2003–10

The following section will now examine the policies of the Lula administration that facilitated the characteristics outlined in the previous section. Lula da Silva was elected on a leftist to LOC ticket, but has been accused of 'being unwilling to abandon orthodox or neoliberal economic policies once in office' (Tussie, 2009: 67). This section will therefore examine Lula's policies thematically, addressing issues that will include growth and investment, fiscal policy, monetary policy (interest rates and inflation), trade policy, and social policy. This will be conducted in a framework of attempting to address the central question of continuity or change: do Lula's policies represent a break from the neoliberal policies of FHC? Once complete, this will facilitate a discussion in Chapter 7 regarding the exact nature of Lula's political economy, or *Lulismo*, which will include discussions of the state–society and national–international relationships to complement the state–market discussions in this chapter.

Growth and investment policy

The first and most widespread criticism of Lula relates precisely to the perception that 'growth opportunities have been lost due to wrong-headed macroeconomic policies' (Carvalho, 2007: 30; see also Doctor and Paula, 2008: 165). Indeed, the inability to sustain a regular rhythm of growth for the economy does stand out, especially if one takes into consideration the highly favourable external environment (at least up until 2008), with expanding trade, rising commodity prices, and relatively benign financial markets. Therefore, for Carvalho (2007: 29), 'Brazil has actually missed an important opportunity to accelerate its growth rate'. This is a sentiment shared by others, especially from the left both inside and outside Brazil. Therefore, for Mollo and Saad-Filho (2006: 116), '[t]he administration's indefatigable pursuit of short-term "credibility" with the financial markets has undermined important potential sources of growth in the economy'. Or, for Paulani (2005: 42), 'the incoming [Lula] administration decided to continue the ortho-dox economic policies that were typical of the previous eight years under [FHC]'.

Carvalho (2007: 31) claims that a 'combination of monetary and fiscal policies exerts a strong regressive impact on income distribu-tion, redistributing income from workers and productive firms towards rentiers. Punishing, as it does, productive activities to favour purely financial investors and other rent-seeking groups that benefit from the inability of the government to change the profile of its expenditures'. Mollo and Saad-Filho (2006: 118) concur, 'the most important macro-economic limitations on growth in Brazil are the fiscal, financial, and balance of payments constraints'.

It is indeed true that the growth record under Lula has been less than impressive, especially when compared to the extremely robust growth of Argentina in the same period. This is especially true given the relatively benign international conditions present during most of the period and the reversal in the declining terms of trade for many of Brazil's core agricultural exports (see Chapter 4 for a full discussion of this). Much of this failure to grow at substantial rates can be explained through Lula's policies in fiscal, monetary, and balance-of-payments areas, policies that represent fundamental continuity with FHC's previ-ous administration. The 'Letter to the Brazilian People' by Lula in the 2003 presidential race effectively meant continuity of economic policy whatever the outcome of the election, a factor that was reinforced by the partial institutionalisation of the letter through a new IMF standby agreement and the promise of a constitutional amendment to facilitate the independence of the Central Bank.

Two points should be made to balance this appraisal. The first is that while growth has been unspectacular, it has been steady and it has been positive. The 2003 to 2008 period registered year-on-year growth in excess of any other period in recent Brazilian history (see Figure 6.1). This was only interrupted by 2009 and the advent of the global financial crisis, which leads to the second point that this was a crisis that Brazil was relatively quick to recover from, especially in comparison to many of the OECD economies. This comparison is something that will be addressed more completely in Part III of this book, but here one of the key policies that must be outlined, which can help explain Brazil's solid growth trend across the Lula administration, is the Programa de Aceleração do Crescimento (PAC). Launched in 2007, the PAC is an umbrella terms for thousands of infrastructural projects around Brazil. Lula announced an initial investment of US$4.2 billion in the PAC, with projects planned in areas such as sanitation, water, sewage, electricity, road and housing construction. The plan is to spend around US$250 billion over a four-year period (Branford, 2009: 158). The effects of this programme can be seen in the evolution of key macroeconomic indicators, with a strong return to growth in 2010 (Figure 6.1), a jump in GFCF in 2008 and 2009, as well as corresponding increases in investment as a percentage of GDP in a growing economy (Figure 6.2), and increases in expenditure with declines in the consolidated primary surplus of the public sector (Table 6.2). In addition, the PAC was specifically designed to target many of the poorest in Brazil. Therefore, the rebuilding of the *favelas* and the introduction of basic infrastructure to these areas was to act as a catalyst for social change. In Rio de Janeiro, for example, the work of the PAC in *favelas* such as Rocinha and Complexo do Alemão employs *favelados* (those who live in the slums) to work on projects that improve their own living spaces, and thus the project aims to temporarily address unemployment along with the promotion of growth and furthering the goal of greater social equality.

The PAC has also involved the exemption of taxes to encourage further investment, in order to help sustain long-term growth in Brazil. Therefore, 'the PAC provides for the reduction of taxes in semiconductor equipment applied to digital television, microcomputers, supplies and services used in infrastructure construction, and steel profiles. The plan also includes long-term fiscal measures, as is the case of control spending on payroll and upgrading of the tendering process [which are] fundamental to ensuring the balance of public-spending' (PAC, 2010).

Brazil has also maintained an active industrial policy, underscored by policies regarding organisation of SOEs, economic plans, large-scale subsidies, and the creation and development of basic national industries (Teixeira, 2007: 13). The overall vision was to foster a shift in industrial competitiveness through innovation and differentiated products and services, so as to move Brazil into greater value-added production. The institutionalisation of this policy came in the form of its Industrial, Technological, and Foreign Trade Policy (PITCE), which began in March 2004. Its purpose was to bring increased efficiency and competitiveness to Brazilian companies and place them in international markets, thereby creating jobs and raising incomes. Its institutional partner was the Brazilian Industrial Development Agency (ABDI), charged with promoting these policies through the input of government ministers and representatives from civil society (Teixeira, 2007: 18).

Brazil has therefore managed to achieve accelerated economic growth, improved and sustained investment to ensure the continuity of medium- and long-term growth trends, and a responsible fiscal environment with a reduced but nevertheless maintained primary surplus. While there are clearly some problems with implementation and maintaining the efficiency of investment (*A Folha de São Paulo*, 7 May 2008), this nevertheless represents a strong commitment to growth. Indeed, 'Lula's overriding priority was ... to get the economy growing strongly again' (Branford, 2009: 158).

Fiscal policy

Control of the public sector deficit is critically important for the formulation and implementation of macroeconomic policy in Brazil. In order to gain the confidence of international capital and markets Lula published his 'Letter to the Brazilian People' during his election campaign in 2002. In that letter he promised to maintain the fiscal responsibility of his predecessor FHC, thus committing the Brazilian government to the IMF-recommended primary fiscal surplus of 3.75 per cent of GDP. In fact, Lula took the initiative to increase that amount to 4.25 per cent, in order to dampen the growth of domestic debt and facilitate the reduction of the interest rate in the wake of the 2002 crisis (Mollo and Saad-Filho, 2006: 115). As Table 6.2 shows Lula found this promise difficult to keep, and while the consolidated primary surplus of the public sector remained above 3 per cent it never hit the target of 4.25 per cent. In 2009 the figure fell to 2.05 per cent, although this was as a direct result of Lula's growth policy, which allowed for this percentage to decrease with expenditures linked to the PAC (BCB, 2010: 9).

As a result of this fiscal conservatism management of the federal public debt can be counted among the successes of Lula's administration (Carvalho, 2007: 27). While the total amount of debt increased throughout the period as a percentage of GDP it decreased steadily throughout Lula's administration (see Figure 6.5). The fact that the outstanding debt stock increased, in spite of the consolidated primary surplus, was chiefly the result of interest payments on the outstanding debt stock – something that the administration had very little control over. What the government was able to do was to increase the percentage of fixed income bonds issued, and decrease the percentage of interest-rate linked bonds. Therefore, the interest rate risk was carried increasingly by the bondholders, thus reducing the long-term cost of debt (Sobreira and Gaya, 2005: 196). This has been reinforced by the steady increasing maturity of the external debt, where average interest has decreased from a high of 6.4 per cent in 1999 after the crisis in 1998, to 2.5 per cent in 2009. Furthermore, the average maturity on new external debt commitments increased from 7.8 years in 1999 to 15 years by 2009 (World Bank, 2010b). The consolidation of external debt in this manner has facilitated a steady decrease in interest payments on external debt, both as a percentage of exports and as a percentage of GNI (World Bank, 2010b).

This focus on fiscal conservatism and the rationalisation of the outstanding debt stock to make it more sustainable in the long term has facilitated an anti-growth bias. Due to the fact that the monetary authorities have sustained high interest rates throughout the period (see next section) the only way to maintain such fiscal conservatism, given that a large proportion of current expenditure is protected by legal dispositions, strong lobby groups, and the decentralised nature of the federal system in Brazil, is to raise taxes or curtail public investments (Carvalho, 2007: 31). Both of these serve to reduce the rate of growth in the economy. In order to fully understand this factor that has affected the ability of the Brazilian economy to experience robust growth such as that experienced in Argentina during the same period, monetary policy must be analysed, which will be done in the next section.

Monetary policy (interest rates and inflation)

The real interest rate in Brazil has rarely been below 10 per cent for several years (Vidotto and Sicsú, 2005: 180), with the Selic Rate not dropping below 15 per cent (Carvalho and Ferrari-Filho, 2007: 72). High interest rates are used to tame inflation and/or regulate the exchange rate. However, one might argue that high interest rates induce a permanent fiscal imbalance, because of the heavy burden of domestic debt, as well as not allowing the rate of unemployment to fall as a result of the constraining effect on demand (Vidotto and Sicsú, 2007: 180). Therefore, the interest rate in Brazil has had important consequences for inflation, the exchange rate, and for the fiscal administration, all of which must be analysed and understood in order to comprehend their collective impact on the growth pattern of the Brazilian economy in the 2003 to 2010 period.

The chief reason for such high interest rates in Brazil in the 2003 to 2010 period has been to control the rate of inflation. Indeed, inflation control has posed difficult challenges for the Lula government. However, he has managed to bring inflation down from over 14 per cent when he took office in 2003 to less than 5 per cent in 2009 (see Figure 6.8). Furthermore, there has been no return to the hyperinflationary episodes that have dogged Brazil's recent economic history (see Table 6.1). In order to achieve this, however, Lula has maintained very high interest rates that have brought profits accruing to the financial sector to record levels, while manufacturing and agricultural business have suffered from higher borrowing costs, thereby reducing incentives for further productive investment (Tussie, 2009: 74). However, it appears that interest rates must remain permanently high in order to maintain low inflation. Conventional thought suggests that high interest rates suppresses demand (refer to discussion of neoliberalism in Chapter 2). However, in the context of Brazil, which has a highly liberalised capital account, inflationary pressures are contained by preventing depreciation of the currency through maintaining capital inflows. Therefore, 'the fragility of the balance of payments situation in which inflows and outflows can lead to severe crises, which was created by external liberalisation, is the main cause of the permanently high rates of interest' (Neto and Vernengo, 2007: 88). As a result, interest rates must remain high, even in a low inflationary environment, so as to prevent depreciation of the Brazilian Real that could facilitate a balance-of-payments crisis and potential default on external debt.

The liberalisation of the capital account during the presidencies of Collor de Mello, Franco, and FHC, combined with the adoption of a floating exchange rate regime in the aftermath of the 1998 currency crisis, has established a strong link between the exchange rate and interest rate in the Brazilian economy (Vidotto and Sicsú, 2007: 180). If Table 6.1 and Figure 6.7 are examined in conjunction, it can be seen that as interest rates increase there is a strong response in the RER as the currency becomes increasingly overvalued, and vice versa. As analysed at the start of this chapter, the high interest rates that formed an integral part of FHC's Real plan, while successful at eliminating inflation, increasingly exacerbated an overvalued Real, facilitated an unsustainable current account deficit due to the suppression of exports, and eventually facilitated devaluation and crisis. The actions of the BCB (Central Bank of Brazil) during the time of the crisis were to massively increase the interest rate in response to huge capital flight. As Table 6.1 shows, real interest rates reached 26.5 per cent in 1998, due to the fact that the BCB's reaction to the abrupt devaluation of the Real was to increase nominal interest rates from 19 per cent in November 1998 to 45 per cent in March 1999 (Vidotto and Sicsú, 2007: 181). This suggests that interest rates were the tool by which the BCB was targeting the exchange rate: whenever the exchange rate declined, interest rates were raised. 'Capital flows, so to speak, *drove* the interest rate. The interest rate was an endogenous variable, determined by the exchange rate, while the exchange rate was determined by capital movements' [italics in original] (Vidotto and Sicsú, 2007: 181).

The conservative fiscal policy pursued by the Lula administration, as demonstrated by the consistent consolidated primary surpluses outlined in the previous section, was the result of an overarching goal of stabilising the debt/GDP ratio, and thus generating credibility in the markets and with international capital that Brazil could continue to service its debt stock. 'As a consequence, the possibility of implementing an activist fiscal policy, which could stabilise the rate of GDP growth at high levels, [was] discarded' (Vidotto and Sicsú, 2007: 184). Therefore, some have argued (Saad-Filho, 2007; Carvalho, 2007; Vidotto and Sicsú, 2007) that this policy is self-defeating. First, high interest rates inflate the financial burden of the public debt; and secondly, the suppression of aggregate demand that higher interest rates facilitates sacrifices full employment, which makes a sustainable adjustment to long-term fiscal policy less likely as this is something more achievable in an expanding economy with growing public revenues and lower public spending on social programmes.

To summarise, 'the monetary policy changes associated with the introduction of the inflation targeting regime, the floating exchange rate regime, and the liberalisation of the capital account of the balance of payments have consolidated a political hierarchy. At the top stands monetary policy and fiscal policy is slotted in a subordinate position' (Vidotto and Sicsú, 2007: 188). This has resulted in a stable macroeconomic environment, defined in terms of consistent and low inflation, but at the expense of high economic growth due to the suppression of aggregate demand though lower consumption and lower investment.

Trade policy

Throughout Lula's administration Brazil pursued a reasonably successful effort to become a leader of a regional South American bloc. Indeed, these ambitions have moved beyond regional considerations and into the global arena. Therefore, not only has Brazil spearheaded MERCOSUR's interaction with Europe, China, and the US but also taken the lead in WTO negotiations, weakening that organisation's attempts to embed a neoliberal agenda though trade policy. 'At the core of its regional and foreign policy, therefore, is a developmentalist reaction that seeks to avoid or compensate for adjustment costs and a concern with global redistribution that accepts the inevitability of some trade liberalisation while trying to manage its worst aspects through producing continuous counterproposals across all negotiating fronts' (Tussie, 2009: 83). This occurred through attempts to expand existing regional mechanisms, such as MERCOSUR, by proposing the accession of Venezuela, as well as promoting the creation of new regional blocs such as the Union of South American Nations, the South American Defence Council, and the Community of Latin America and the Caribbean States (Sotero, 2010: 76). Furthermore, in 2003 Lula introduced a new 'South–South strategy', thus strengthening its embassies across the world – most notably in Latin America and Africa – in order to boost sales growth abroad (Boschi and Gaitán, 2009: 15). This can be also seen in the September 2003 WTO negotiations at Cancún, where Brazil, India, and Argentina resisted broadening the Doha Round agenda despite the opposition of the United States, the EU, Japan, and Canada. Therefore, Brazil emerged as a key player in international trade talks, and demonstrated the administration's desire to forge closer links with other emerging economies though a South–South cooperation agenda (Sotero, 2010: 74).

In combination with an increasingly competitive Real in the 2003 to 2006 period especially (see Figure 6.7), exports almost tripled from mid-2003 (US$66 billion) to mid-2010 (US$169 billion) (Sotero, 2010: 72). In addition international reserves increased substantially from US$37.6 billion in January 2003 to US$252.5 billion in June 2010. In February 2008 the Central Bank announced that, 'for the first time in our economic history' Brazil's international reserves and other foreign assets were greater than the country's net foreign debt (cited in Branford,

2009: 160), a situation that only improved in subsequent years despite the international economic turmoil of the global financial crisis.

Social policy

The package of CCTs, known collectively as *Bolsa Familia*, represent the government's flagship social programme in support of Lula's *Fome Zero* (Zero Hunger) initiative. At his inauguration Lula famously pledged: 'if by the end of my term in office every Brazilian has food to eat three times a day, I shall have fulfilled my mission in life' (Lula cited in Hall, 2006: 690). In October 2003 Lula launched his programme, although the package of CCTs that were used to realise that promise were essentially a continuation and amalgamation of previous policies: *Bolsa Escola* (school grant), *Bolsa Alimentatação* (maternal nutrition), *Auxílio Gás* (cooking gas subsidy), and added *Cartao Alimentaçãa* (special credit card to purchase select food items).

This collection of schemes is targeted at two social groups: the 'very poor' (defined as households with incomes up to R$50 per month), and the 'poor' (defined as household incomes of R$51–100 per month). The definition of poor was changed to R$51–120 in April 2006 to expand coverage. 'Very poor' families received a fixed sum of R$50 a month, while both 'poor' and 'very poor' families received R$15 per child of school age (six–15 years under *Bolsa Escola* and up to six years of age under *Bolsa Alimentatação*) to a maximum of three children. The maximum benefit per household was set at R$95 (World Bank, 2010a; Hall, 2006: 698). These transfers were conditional upon families keeping their children in school, under regular medical supervision, and gaining vaccinations. This was the means by which the programme sought to reduce both immediate and future poverty (World Bank, 2010a). The *Auxílio Gás* (cooking gas subsidy) provided R$15 every two months for the same social groups, and the *Cartao Alimentaçãa* gives families earning up to half the minimum wage a monthly cash supplement of R$50 for food purchases.

Hall (2006: 695) argues that while these policies did represent a continuation and rationalisation of various schemes introduced under the FHC administration (see also Almeida, 2005), Lula did introduce some major changes to previous policy: 'Firstly ... a clear and vociferous political commitment to benefit the very poorest sectors of Brazilian society. Secondly, to bypass local political interests to create an alternative distribution network ... Third, appeals were made to companies such as Ford and Unilever, as well as to supermarket chains, for contributions towards *Fome Zero* that would signify a new sense of corporate social responsibility and alliance between public and private sectors'. On this first point Neto and Vernengo (2007: 73) suggest that the rate of expansion of the *Bolsa Familia* programme represents a break with the past, even if the details of the schemes are 'new wine in old bottles'.

This renewed emphasis was certainly backed up by funds, as well as rhetoric. The Brazilian government spent over US$24 billion as of 30 June 2009 (World Bank, 2009: 31), which was complemented by a World Bank loan in 2004 of US$572 million and a further loan of US$200 million in September 2010 – combined with staff technical assistance. Therefore, between 2004 and 2008 Brazil's social spending grew from 12.28 per cent to 13.1 per cent of GDP (World Bank, 2009: 46). This has meant that since Lula took office in 2003 the state now provides minimum income levels through the *Bolsa Familia* programme to around 44 million people, or one-quarter of the population (Tussie, 2009: 74). In addition, the Lula administration has complemented its *Bolsa Familia* programme through the PAC (see earlier section of this chapter). Infrastructural projects such as the provision of running water and new school buildings in the most impoverished areas of the Northeast, or road and house building in the city *favelas* represent developmental policy targeted specifically at the very poorest and most vulnerable in Brazilian society. However, 'it should be remembered that *Bolsa Familia* accounts for just 2.3 per cent of direct monetary transfers in Brazil, far outweighed by pensions at 82 per cent, which are far more regressive' (Hall, 2006: 694). Whereas pensions in OECD countries account on average for 33 per cent of total spending, this figure rises to 44 per cent in the case of Brazil, surpassed only by Italy and Mexico (Hall, 2006: 692). Social assistance targeted at the poorest groups therefore remains a relatively small proportion of the total social budget, 'although it is one that has expanded steadily under the administrations of both [FHC] (1995–2002) and, especially, Lula (2003–2010)' (Hall, 2006: 692).

Despite this massive increase in emphasis and money, some scholars have highlighted serious problems of implementation (*see*, for example, Hall, 2006; Carvalho, 2007). Widespread reports of clientelism as political criteria were adopted for selecting beneficiary families led to investigations where 10 per cent of municipalities sampled showed signs of political manipulation (Hall, 2006: 702). In addition, an overly centralised system of management, the duplication of benefits, and a lack of proper household-level data have all become apparent as the programme expanded. However, others (see, for example, Fenwick, 2009: 125) have highlighted the relative success of the programme due to the fact that the Federal government was able to directly bypass powerful municipal governors and thus better and more efficiently direct the flow of funds.

More fundamental criticisms, beyond operational effectiveness, have also been aired. The whole concept of CCTs and the use of safety nets, a broad label to describe short-term, targeted interventions for vulnerable households to mitigate the immediate effects of poverty, represents a major ideological shift towards a more selective and means-tested approach for addressing mass poverty (Hall, 2006: 691). Indeed, this shift has reflected a global change of emphasis since the 1990s where, apart from Brazil, major CCT programmes have been introduced in Mexico (*Progreas,* now *Opportunidades*), Colombia (*Familias en Acción*), Chile (*Subsidio Unitario Familiar*), Nicaragua (*Red de Protección*), Argentina (*Jefas de Hogar*) and Ecuador (*Bono de Desarrollo Humano*) (Rawlings, 2004). These CCT programmes concur more with the neoliberal concept of welfare and the safety net approach (see Chapter 2), 'encouraging human capital formation and family responsibility [as well as being] easier to target than other social assistance programmes' (Hall, 2006: 692). However, Hall (2006: 700) continues his analysis by saying that 'sweeping assumptions are being made that safety net programmes such as these can reduce inequalities, strengthen human capital and improve people's well being'. In addition, Hall expresses doubts concerning the ability of these safety nets to 'mount a serious challenge to poverty in the context of highly unequal societies such as Brazil' (Hall, 2006: 703). With the seventh-most unequal income distribution in the world, the top 20 per cent in Brazil earn almost 64 per cent of personal income and the bottom quintile just 2.3 per cent, frustration is sometimes expressed over the seeming inability of *Bolsa Familia* to bring about any redistribution of wealth (Hall, 2006: 704).

The social indicators during the years 2003 to 2010 seem to support this analysis (see also Figure 6.8). The number of Brazilians living in absolute poverty (per capita family income below US$80 a year) has fallen from 50 million in 2003 to 29 million in 2010, and is predicted to be cut in half by 2014 to 14.5 million, or 8.5 per cent of the population (Sotero, 2010: 73). However, while there has been improvement in the poverty figures, there has been little effect on income distribution. While the gap between the rich and the poor has declined under Lula's administration, and about 15 per cent of that decline between 2003 and 2008 has been put down to the effects of *Bolsa Familia* (World Bank, 2010a: 19), this decline has been limited and certainly less than was expected of Lula's administration (Neto and Vernengo, 2007: 73–4; Almeida, no year). However, other studies (see, for example, Haddad, 2008: 665) conclude that *Bolsa Familia* has contributed towards greater social equality if the criteria are based on increases in public school enrolment, which represents a key input in the production of social equity (Haddad, 2008: 654; see also Santos, Vieira, and Reis, 2009: 615).

Other areas of social policy have been less impressive, and have not created synergies with *Bolsa Familia* in order to facilitate a more substantial impact on the poverty and inequality figures. Social security reform, for example, was minimal. Accounting for approximately half of all social spending and taking up around 36 per cent of total public expenditures, social security in Brazil constitutes the single most expensive and regressive form of social spending (Hunter and Sugiyama, 2009: 34). This is because financing of social security benefits, which includes disability severance payments, unemployment insurance, and pension provision (which accounts for the vast majority of the spending), is contribution-based and formal sector workers on average earn higher incomes. In 2003 Lula was able to pass limited reforms: raising the effective minimum retirement age, placing tighter limits on benefit ceilings, reducing survivor benefits, and instituting a tax on the benefits of the most affluent (Hunter and Sugiyama, 2009: 36), but these reforms did not address the core problem of the fact that the vast majority of Brazilian social spending went on the middle classes, which arguably contributes to the high levels of inequality in Brazilian society.

Real wages have either declined or grown only modestly during the last decade and unemployment and underemployment have remained high, with Lula's promise of ten million new jobs disappearing rapidly from his presidential discourse (Saad-Filho, 2007: 7). Therefore, this employment and real wage data 'makes it difficult to defend any claims that the Worker's Party is committed to reducing social exclusion as a central element of its agenda' (Neto and Vernengo, 2007: 84). In addition, commentators such as Carvalho (2007: 34), or Neto and Vernengo (2007: 73) suggest that the inconsistency between economic policies that prevent the economy from growing at its true potential and social policies means that impacts on the social indicators are limited, as high levels of unemployment and suppressed demand limit the impacts on poverty and inequality. However, these analyses underestimate the contribution of consistently low inflation that Lula's macroeconomic regime has facilitated (Burges, 2009: 210; Sotero, 2010: 73). In the context of Brazil's recent history, the maintenance of sound money, a traditionally neoliberal priority (see Chapter 2) has been key to allow families to save, increase real lower wages, expand credit, and prompt stores to offer payment for basic durable goods on a layaway basis, all of which facilitate the expansion of the domestic economy and markets, which have become an increasingly important driver of Brazil's economic growth (Sotero, 2010: 73).

Conclusions: Continuity or change?

By way of conclusion, this section will consider the central theme of continuity or change in the economic policies of Brazil during the Lula administration, continuity being defined largely in terms of the previous FHC administration that can be broadly characterised as neoliberal. This will set the stage for the next chapter, which will consider the project of *Lulismo* as a whole. Such a consideration will allow for an attempt to place this project within the Developmental Regime concept, a concept that has been developing throughout the book. Once complete, Part III of the book will move forward by considering the implications of the Developmental Regime for wider regional and global contexts.

Under FHC economic reforms such as privatisation and trade liberalisation were the primary tools of the recovery, which facilitated monetary stability and fiscal adjustment. Those goals were pursued through a variety of policies that changed in time but included: monetary and exchange rate policies, inflation target rules, increases in taxes and other compulsory contributions, and limiting rules for expenditures at different levels of government (Almeida, no year; see previous sections). Both the goals, and the means by which they were pursued, were labelled as neoliberal by a number of commentators (see, for example, Saad-Filho, 2007; Mollo and Saad-Filho, 2006; Carvalho, 2007).

It has been suggested that Lula's policies did not fundamentally differ from those of FHC (*see*, for example, Arestis, Paula, and Ferrari-Filho, 2007b: 51–7). In the first years of his administration some argued that it was necessary in order to placate the markets whose concerns over the incoming Lula administration had precipitated the 2002 financial crisis (Carvalho, 2007: 24). However, this mode seemed to perpetuate long after the crisis had passed, leading Burges (2009: 195) to conclude that 'the process has been one of continuity of central features of the national political economy, with changes primarily limited to the mode of application'. Carvalho (2007: 33) has said that '[i]n the absence of well-defined strategies, Lula's policies seemed to have consisted mostly of surfing on the favourable winds of the international economy that preserved the Brazilian economy from suffering any significant adverse shock'. Or, Almeida (no year), who suggests that 'Lula's government did not bring any significant change regarding economic policies, which have been in clear continuity to those implemented in the four previous years: inflation targets, high interest rates, free exchange rates, high tax burdens, and compliance to international finance compromises and agreements'. Almeida (no year) even concludes that this is the case with regard to Lula's social agenda, 'in spite of the strong symbolic association between Lula and the PT and the promise of social reform their government did not have an innovative approach to the issue. Rather than change, Lula's social policies show significant continuity with those of the previous government and an unexpected affinity to the neoliberal agenda'. Therefore, in summary, '[d]espite internal dissent and critics (sic) from its allies, continuity rather than change has been the hallmark of the PT government's economic policies' (Almeida, no year).

These interpretations, however, do not tell the whole story. Especially in the context of the ISI of Brazil's past, Lula's regime demonstrates important areas of change from Brazil's economic history. Therefore, the transformation of the national political economy that began in the late 1980s means that the market is now the driver of economic growth. However, this has led to a new challenge for the state, one which Lula has provided a different answer to than his predecessors. That challenge is 'how to strategically direct the economy without dominating it, while simultaneously engaging in the social spending needed to support the country's legion of poor and allow them to develop future opportunities for an improved quality of life' (Burges, 2009: 213–14). Lula's answer has been to use the state to implement national development policies, only now by 'recruiting and seducing' markets (Burges, 2009: 196). This stands in contrast to the state-directed methods of ISI and to the laissez-faire attitude of the 1990s and FHC (among others). This recruiting and seducing is exemplified by Lula's PAC, but also by his maintenance of a stable macroeconomic environment facilitated by low inflation, a stable exchange rate, and controlled public finances. Furthermore, Lula has opposed any further privatisations (Carvalho, 2007: 25). This has been complemented by social policy that has brought poverty and hunger to the forefront of the national agenda. While some of the details of the programmes used to help achieve this policy have remained the same, the renewed emphasis and centralisation of this objective in Brazilian policy, combined with this initiation of complementary policies such as the PAC, have all served to create change in Brazilian economic policy. Therefore, it is not a simple question of continuity but, and rather similar to the conclusions in Chapter 4 of this book concerning Argentina, continuity *and* change in Brazilian economic policy under Lula 2003–10. These changes in economic policy have been part of a much broader change in Brazilian political economy, and it is to this wider consideration that the next chapter now turns.

7
Neoliberalism or Developmentalism? The Political Economy of Brazil 2003–10

This chapter aims to expand the analysis carried out in the previous chapter, as economic reform in Brazil has been about far more than macroeconomic accounts. Rather, 'it has been an integral part of a long-term program of socio-political change accepted by vast swathes of the Brazilian political landscape' (Burges, 2009: 196). The task of this chapter is twofold. Firstly, to analyse the broader political economy themes of *Lulismo* and expand the analysis into the realm of political economy, based on the evidence presented in the previous chapter. Second, to contextualise this political economy within the Developmental Regime framework, thus synergising with the evidence presented in Chapters 4 and 5 on Argentina, and providing a deeper empirical base for the main thesis of this book, that the political economy of the pink tide can be best framed and characterised within a Developmental Regime framework. Once complete, Part III will then consider the wider regional and global implications for the experiences of Latin America in a post-crisis context.

The political economy of *Lulismo*

There is much contestation in the literature regarding the political economy of *Lulismo*, or indeed, if it is even valid to talk of a *Lulismo* at all. As analysed in the concluding section of the previous chapter, many commentators have suggested that there was strong continuity with the preceding neoliberal regime of FHC. While areas of continuity exist within the policy mix, important areas of change are present which are the results of a distinct new form of political economy present in Brazil during the 2003 to 2010 period. The four main policy areas that represent the core of this political economy are inflation (or monetary policy), promotion of economic growth, poverty reduction or anti-poverty programmes, and labour policy. It is clear that not all these areas represented areas of change from the previous regime of FHC, however this chapter will demonstrate that the particular blend of these policies, and the way in which each mutually reinforced the overall agenda of *Lulismo*, facilitated a change in Brazilian political economy. The interaction of these four factors is key, and each will be considered in this chapter in detail in order to demonstrate how each generated key bases of support for Lula's regime, as well as how the particular policy mix facilitated a successful *Lulismo* in terms of stable, long-term growth for Brazil. Once complete, this chapter will expand the analysis to consider Brazilian political economy in an international context, analysing how global imperatives helped shape the domestic agenda. This exercise will further reinforce the analysis of *Lulismo*, as in an era of globalisation no single state's policy can be considered in isolation of international pressures. Having established the specific political economy of *Lulismo* in an appropriate international context, this chapter will then finish with a consideration of the Developmental Regime framework developed in Part I of this book. This analysis will conclude that this framework provides sufficient analytical leverage to aid in the interpretation of this period of Argentine political economy, much in the same way as it did in the previous case study on Argentina in the 2003–7 post-crisis period.

Monetary policy

The previous chapter showed that Brazil ran a very conservative, tight monetary policy throughout the 2003 to 2010 period. Interest rates were high, and inflation kept low after a small spike in the first year of the administration. Such a policy represents a clear continuity from FHC ever since the adoption of the *Real* plan. In order to understand the political economy behind this prioritisation of low inflation, one must examine the institution of the *Real* plan more closely. Burges' (2009: 202) contribution to this area demonstrates that there was a clear 'democratising imperative' embedded in FHC's plan of 1994. This is due to the fact that the success of the plan was contingent on the population understanding the logic behind the programme, and that this logic would work. Therefore, the Brazilian people became more actively involved in the economic policy, facilitating a 'critical electoral constituency for future political power ... the anti-inflation poor that had previously been marginalised' (Burges, 2009: 202). Combined with the general retreat of the state from the economy in the form of dismantling the legacy of ISI (privatisation of SOEs, reduction of bureaucratic capacity for state direction of firm behaviour for example) this 'created a self-sustaining process of transformative economic, political, and social democratisation ... [that] efficiently capture[d] and channelle[d] the interests of important emerging political and economic actors' (Burges, 2009: 197). Therefore, economic policy in the 1990s under FHC simultaneously transformed both the nature of the economy and the nature of policies required for political success. The extension of the vote in the 1998 constitution, combined with these policies, gave a voice to the 'masses of informal workers and poor who were not protected from inflation through the sorts of carefully crafted union negotiations that [FHC's] presidential predecessor undertook in the 1980s' (Burges, 2009: 198). The subsequent prioritisation of a low-inflation regime, as analysed in the previous chapter, can therefore be seen as a product of the 'average voter's obsession with prices', a fact that subsequently constrained the left from pursing unfettered statism in all policy areas while in power (Baker, 2009: 15, 192). Indeed, this reflects a broader trend in Brazil (and across Latin America more widely) towards consumerism, with one of the major concerns thus being price levels (Baker, 2009: 258; see also Fortes, 2009: 114). During the dictatorship period inflation was acceptable as the elites were politically powerful, and these sectors could mitigate inflation effects through greater access to financial intermediation.

As Edwards (2010: 210) analyses, 'inflation is a tax that affects the poor in a disproportionate way. It is a tax that falls mostly on those that cannot move their savings abroad.' As a result, 'the poor of non-unionised, informal sectors are effectively pro-liberal economic policies because it removes one of the greatest strains on their economic welfare: inflation' (Burges, 2009: 199). This shift in the political calculus is critical for understanding why this anti-inflationary bias of Lula's macroeconomic policy conforms so closely to supposedly neoliberal economic policies (Kingstone and Ponce, 2010: 109). This policy also possessed other, more obvious supporters. International capital was a natural ally of this policy (see later section on global imperatives for a detailed discussion of this). Furthermore, domestic exporting businesses were natural allies as they benefited from the international credibility that came with the macroeconomic stability that this economic regime facilitated. Therefore, one can discern a new coalition of interests in Brazilian society that emerged as a result of FHC's *Real* plan, a coalition that was harnessed by *Lulismo* through the maintenance of a low-inflation regime (Burges, 2009: 198).

Exchange rate policy has also been used as a supplementary tool for inflation control (Vidotto and Sicsú, 2007: 183). This is because, unlike many Asian countries (e.g. China, Malaysia, and India) or indeed Argentina (see Chapter 4), Brazil has not employed the exchange rate as an instrument for regulating international competitiveness. Instead, rather than intervention in the foreign exchange markets to maintain an undervalued currency, Brazil has allowed its exchange rate to float and therefore appreciate as demand for Brazilian exports (especially those of agricultural origin) has increased (see Chapter 6). This floating exchange rate regime and the subsequent rise of the Real has dampened the expansion of exports in order to restrict domestic demand, and encouraged competition between imports and domestically produced goods – both of which supplement high interest rates in reducing the rate of inflation (Vidotto and Sicsú, 2007: 184).

Economic growth

Intrinsically linked to this low-inflation regime has been the promotion of economic growth (Kingstone and Ponce, 2010: 106). Edwards (2010: 210) observes that 'in an inflationary environment it is very difficult for consumer credit to develop, and the poor are forced to live in a strictly cash economy. Without credit small businesses cannot develop and prosper, and employment suffers accordingly. And in the absence of credit, the middle classes and the poor have limited access to housing and the durable goods such as refrigerators and cars are beyond their reach'. Furthermore, inflation can lead to a reduction in growth by reducing time horizons and increasing the risk of potential investors, leading to a drop in the rate of investment. Inflation also has serious consequences for the distribution of income, transferring income from agents with fixed incomes to agents who can operate within an environment of increasing prices (Roxborough, 1992: 641). Therefore, the underlying argument of this analysis is that there is a fundamental link between sustainability of a fully functioning democracy in Brazil, economic stability (defined as low inflation), and growth (Burges, 2009: 202). This is a conclusion complemented by the analysis of Tavolaro and Tavolaro (2007: 429), 'monetary orthodoxy prevailed under the argument that it was a condition *sino qua non* for higher rates of economic growth'. This conclusion is of course contested, as there is a natural tension between the mechanisms by which a low-inflation regime is maintained, and the stimulation of economic growth. The high interest rate level impacts both on employment generation, due to suppression of private investment, and also squeezes social spending, as government expenditures increasingly go on higher levels of debt servicing (Neto and Vernengo, 2007: 85). Furthermore, higher interest rates targets demand side inflation, therefore their very success is the result of dampening consumption levels, suppressing real wages, and limiting the expansion of employment – all of which suppress GDP growth (Mollo and Saad-Filho, 2006: 114).

Lula's fiscal policy can also be interpreted in the same vein. In the words of the *Carta ao Pavo Brasileiro* the broad fiscal programme would include tax reforms and reforms in social security based on a 'clear and sensible transition … the fruit of a new social contract. The contract is naturally premised on respecting the country's contracts and obligations. We want to preserve the primary surplus as much as possible to prevent the internal debt from growing and destroying the government's capacity to honour its commitments' (*Carta ao Pavo Brasileiro* cited in Flynn, 2005: 1247). Lula's debt policy thus forged a social base among middle-class voters, centrist, and even conservative political forces that did not endorse a left-wing programme yet were unwilling to tolerate further neoliberal fallout (Robinson, 2004: 148). Fiscal constraint can therefore be interpreted as part of a wider effort towards promoting growth as well as facilitating the low-inflation regime (Neto and Vernengo, 2005: 78). Such constraint is also reflected in areas other than debt policy. Reform of the pension system was seen as a prerequisite for establishing appropriate conditions for renewed economic growth, although it was branded as simply adhering to the neoliberal recipe of FHC (Tavolaro and Tavolaro, 2007: 429). Nevertheless, as demonstrated in the previous chapter, pension provision is far more regressive than other forms of monetary transfer and reform of the huge liabilities of the Brazilian system was seen as both necessary to maintain fiscal health as well as rebalance social spending towards the poorest sections of Brazilian society. However, it is clear that tensions exist between fiscal conservatism and the pursuit of economic growth. As Carvalho (2007: 29) analyses, 'public investments … have been continuously sacrificed in favour of financial transfers (servicing public debt) and current expenditures … [therefore] expenditure cuts are entirely *ad hoc*, actually reducing the growth potential of the economy'.

The PAC represents a further cornerstone policy of the Lula regime to promote economic growth, and can be interpreted within this emerging developmentalist political economy. As analysed in the previous chapter, the PAC was a government infrastructural investment programme designed to promote growth, especially among the poorer sections of Brazilian society. This once again demonstrates well the interconnected nature of the core elements of *Lulismo*, showing that the projects of the regime must be considered holistically in order for a complete understanding to be developed. Growth was pursued by the regime, particularly in the second of Lula's two terms, but policies were designed attempting to direct the proceeds of that growth to the poorer sections of society. This served not only to cement support for his regime among the poorer sections of society, but also sought to facilitate growth of the domestic market. The large population of Brazil means that there is enormous potential for sources of economic growth within its own borders, but the general lack of infrastructure combined with the high levels of absolute poverty have served to suppress domestic demand and consumption. The PAC sought to address these problems, promoting growth through investing in infrastructure in some of the poorest areas of Brazil in order to not only provide a boost to growth through increasing the investment component of aggregate demand but also facilitate long-term growth through removing barriers to increases in private consumption and private investment components.

A further component of this strategy has been Brazilian industrial policy. Carvalho (2007: 26) suggests that these policies have often been implemented erratically, 'in which some good ideas were advanced but are seldom consistently implemented'. Furthermore, Mollo and Saad-Filho (2006: 116) claim that the Lula government failed to promote the integrated development of the country's manufacturing base and to pursue an aggressive policy of export promotion. However, in many respects, government action was strong: loans and grants, tax subsidies for research and development, and governmental procurement especially in areas where Brazil already has comparative advantages – agribusiness, mining, petroleum, construction, and some industrial sectors – all represent active areas of industrial policy (Menezes, 2011: 6). In addition, there have been a number of institutional changes adopted, thus reconstituting the relationship between government and sectors of civil society with the goal of fostering the coordination of strategies and plans for promoting economic development and industrial and technology changes (Teixeira, 2007: 19; Menezes, 2011: 5). As outlined in the previous chapter, since 2003 Brazil has implemented some plans and programmes of industrialisation and rebuilding its national innovation system (The PITCE, PDP and PACTI are the most expressive examples). The PITCE (in English the Industrial, Technological and Foreign Trade Program) in particular has been successful in promoting Brazilian exports, which grew by 100 per cent in the 2003 to 2005 period alone (Boschi and Gaitán, 2009: 15; Menezes, 2011).

Government policy towards privatisation has complemented this active industrial policy. From 1991 to 2001, 68 enterprises owned by the Federal government were privatised (Almeida, no year). This included steel, chemical, and petrochemical companies, as well as the largest mining corporation, the railway system, telecommunications, and electricity companies. Lula and the Workers' Party (Partido dos Trabalhadores – PT) government did not attempt in any way to reverse this sweeping programme of privatisation implemented in the 1990s. However, he did not proceed with the process, and maintained what was left of the Brazilian public sector. On the other hand, Lula did pursue a policy of public–private partnerships, facilitating contracts with private companies in public service sectors such as utilities that were designed to attract private investment in Brazil's infrastructure systems (Almeida, no year). Once again, this can clearly be linked to his other policy areas in respect of promoting growth; the PAC, monetary policy, and fiscal policy were all used in conjunction to create an atmosphere in which sustainable growth could be fostered that would benefit the poorer sections of society. This represents a clear difference with both the previous neoliberal administrations of the 1990s, as well as the dictatorship period, which may have been concerned with economic growth, but not necessarily equitable growth that would be shared by all sections of Brazilian society (Amann, 2005: 151–3).

Lula's political economy as outlined thus far conforms to a 'modern left' model, or pink tide as defined in Chapter 2 of this book. While some authors see this as a surrender to the current domination of markets that characterises contemporary international political economy (see, for example Mollo and Saad-Filho, 2006; Saad-Filho, 2007; Carvalho, 2007), the argument of this chapter suggests that orthodox economic policies have been combined with the goal of protecting the more vulnerable social groups. As concluded in the previous chapter, Lula's answer has been to use the state to implement national development policies through 'recruiting and seducing' markets (Burges, 2009: 196). There are, of course, tensions in this policy. Maintaining fiscal surplus through tight control of government expenditure conflicts with the objective of increasing social protection is one example. Maintaining low-inflation conflicts with expansion of aggregate demand through consumption and investment due to the high interest rates necessary for this orthodox monetary policy is another. In addition, the subsequent dampening of economic activity that this facilitates keeps unemployment high. Nevertheless, Lula's government has maintained orthodox macroeconomic policy while at the same time having an interventionist streak, characterised by industrial policy as outlined previously, with programmes such as the PAC, and social policies supporting the most vulnerable groups being extended and intensified. It is to these social policies that this chapter now turns.

Social policy

Conservative fiscal policy under Lula has resulted in relatively scarce sources of funding for Federal government social spending. Therefore, the solution for maximising both economic and political returns from the distribution of this scarce social funding has been to target the poorest and most vulnerable groups through the use of specific instruments such as social funds implemented by a range of institutions including government, civil society, international donors, and, indeed, poor communities themselves (Hall, 2006: 691). As analysed in the previous chapter, the *Bolsa Familia* programme that represented the central element of Brazilian social policy was designed around the safety-net model of welfare, and while it has had an important impact on poverty levels its impact on inequality has been questionable. This safety-net model is based on neoliberal theory (see Chapter 2), and a more fundamental reform addressing long-term structural inequality in Brazilian society would require a more radical political economy. Instead, Lula's political economy 'takes a results-orientated and pragmatic stance, focusing on social policy within a market orientated framework to create sustainable, equitable, and widespread economic, political and social development' (Burges, 2009: 208).

More comprehensive and radical social policies were simply not part of the make-up of *Lulismo*, which utilised specific tools to pursue defined goals in response to the voice of the inflation-hating poor (see, for example, Almeida, 2005). Again, this model of political economy conforms to the 'recruiting and seducing' of market forces thesis. The absolute poor in Brazil formed a large part of Lula's base of support, and he forged a new social contract that would ensure these elements would receive state help. However, those other elements of his support base, middle-classes, domestic bourgeoisie and industrialists, would not support a social contract that would oversee massive transfers of wealth to these groups. Furthermore, this meant that Lula was only willing to engage in modest pension reform, the main beneficiaries of which were middle-class elements including formal sector workers, civil servants, and the military (Hunter and Sugiyama, 2009: 34). Therefore, absolute poverty was addressed through *Bolsa Familia*, some longer term problems were tackled – such as education reform – but the core of the model remained within the logic of the market and therefore inequality was not tackled in any systematic way. It is true that inequality did drop slightly over the 2003 to 2010 period (see previous chapter), but this was the result of complementary growth policies (such as the PAC) that ensured the proceeds from new growth were distributed evenly across Brazilian society, as well as a residual impact as a result of social policy (Santos, Vieira, and Reis, 2009: 615). More fundamental redistribution of wealth would have required a model of political economy that was simply not part of *Lulismo*.

Lula was widely criticised as a result of adopting this form of model (Neto and Vernengo, 2007; Carvalho, 2007; Saad-Filho, 2007), claiming that Lula simply offered a paternalistic form of social programme that did nothing to address the fundamental structural nature of poverty in one of the most unequal societies in the world. Furthermore, others such as Hall (2006: 707; 2008: 816) suggested that another consequence of choosing this model was that key areas of social infrastructure such as schools and hospitals were starved of resources, which arguably is where long-term investment is required to build up the human capital necessary as the basis for sustained and long-term reductions in inequality. This model of social welfare can be explained within a developmentalist form of political economy, addressing absolute poverty as a result of key areas of Lula's electoral base but maintaining policy within a market-orientated approach to encourage a wider agenda of economic growth. The poor were further protected through this wider agenda in a complementary fashion, with the maintenance of a low-inflation regime representing the core of this agenda, as well as the fact that economic growth was pursued in a balanced fashion in order to ensure that the wealth generated from this growth would not disproportionately end up in the hands of the wealthy as often happened in previous models of political economy: for example, during the dictatorship period. However, the extent to which this is an appropriate model to address the specific nature of Brazilian inequality and long-term structural poverty is questionable.

Labour policy

In Brazil labour policy and industrial relations from the 1930s until the 1980s was classified as state corporatist (Doctor, 2007b: 132). Defined elsewhere in this book, in Brazil it manifested itself in a classical sense, as a socio-political process in which functional interests in society engaged in political exchange with state agencies over policy output (Doctor, 2007a: 109). Therefore, the state granted a monopoly of representation to designated corporatist bodies, and voluntary associations had much less opportunity to influence the formulation and implementation of policy (Doctor, 2007b: 133). This system was codified in the Consolidation of Labour Laws (CLT) in 1943 (although its origins dated back to the 1930s) which created a 'fragmented, often clientelistic, sectoral corporatism that limited a group's vision and reduced the goals of interaction with state actors to narrow short-term objectives' (Doctor, 2007a: 109). In other words, the Brazilian state monopolised power in labour relations, and was able to manipulate labour-representing bodies to suppress the political ambitions of these bodies, thus being able to grant few concessions. This structure helps explain the final (limited) outcomes of the series of strikes in the automotive sector in May 1978 (see Humphrey, 1979), to use but one example.

In the 1980s, democratisation and economic crisis generated growing pressures for institutional modernisation and structural reforms, with state corporatist institutions gradually shifting towards corporate pluralism (Doctor, 2007a: 110). In turn, business interest intermediation with the state was typically fragmented, particularistic, clientelist, and sector-orientated, with no peak level association (Doctor, 2007a: 113). This new type of corporatism, with an emphasis on contention and growing interdependence between the state and private interests was referred to as 'neocorporatism' in the literature (Doctor, 2007a: 110). Wilson (2003: 102) provides a useful definition of neocorporatism as 'a form of governance in which organisations representing major economic interests, usually unions and employer's organisations, are given major, privileged opportunities to participate in policy-making in return for accepting responsibilities to assist the state in the governance of society'. Neocorporatism thus emphasises the value of structured, long-term relationships in tripartite negotiations over adjustments to global and national economic processes and the interdependence of the state and societal actors in policy formulation and enforcement (Doctor, 2007b: 134). Doctor (2007a: 111) provides a further refinement of this concept when he identifies three different models of neocorporatism: 'micro', 'meso', and 'macro'. Macro neocorporatism is related to the state's interaction with peak associations of both capital and labour; Meso neocorporatism is related to the state's interaction with specific sectors or professions that may or may not involve labour; Micro neocorporatism is related to the state's special relationship with a single large private enterprise.

This growing pressure in the 1980s led Collor to set up 'sectoral chambers' in 1991. These were the institutional manifestation of interaction between government officials, business associations, and labour unions, which were expected to coordinate reform implementation and encourage productive investment to boost economic growth (Doctor, 2007a: 106). This form of social pact was new to the history of Brazilian industrial relations, and represented a marked shift from the classic corporatist and clientelistic structures of the 1930s to 1980s period. Critics highlighted the fact that Collor engaged in a closed decision-making style, used executive decree powers regularly, shut out collective articulation of business interests, and encouraged personalistic access and clientelistic ties. The state effectively controlled choices and determined to what extent business influenced policy outcomes (Doctor, 2007a: 127). Nevertheless, he extended and institutionalised these sectoral chambers so that specific policy areas benefited from the inclusion of societal input, via tripartite negotiation between business, labour, and state actors (Doctor, 2007a: 114). Within the theoretical framework outlined by Doctor, Collor's sectoral chambers could be described as 'a meso [neo]corporatist experiment *par excellence*' (Doctor, 2007a: 111).

This experiment in meso neocorporatism was, however, short-lived. In the first half of the 1990s Brazil experienced severe macroeconomic dislocation and instability in the form of hyperinflation and stagnation, which was only brought under control after FHC's *Real* plan (see previous chapter). This overriding concern with macroeconomics led to a loss of interest in industrial and labour policy. As a result, these proto meso neocorporatist arrangements, institutionalised through the sectoral chambers, lost their voice and influence and by 1996 entirely disappeared from the policymaking stage (Doctor, 2007a: 114). However, industrial relations were still markedly different from the pre-1980s era. The government did not punitively intervene to fire directorates that organised strikes, nor did it freeze the bank accounts of combative unions as Murillo Macedo (minister of Labour under Genreal João Batista Figueiredo) used to. Strikes were no longer prohibited, and the formation of labour federations that unified unions horizontally were no longer banned. The *pelegos*, or government-supported trade unionists, who monopolised leadership posts in official Brazilian unions under the military regime had been dislodged and their posts passed into the hands of directorates composed of anti-government labour figures tied to the CUT (Central Geral dos Trabalhadores or General Labour Federation) (Boito Jr, 1994: 87–9). Nevertheless, the overall union structure maintained a general characteristic of dependency of the labour hierarchy on the state.

When Lula took office in 2003 there was a renewed interest in understanding the functional structure of, and lessons learned from, the short-lived Collor experiment at improving government communication with business and labour. As Doctor (2007a: 116) summarises, he promised to: (i) engage civil society in a dialogue over reform, (ii) give business a voice in the formulation of economic policy, and (iii) revive Brazil's pre-crisis economic growth trajectory. Therefore, the sectoral chambers had not been forgotten, and Lula created the 'Development Council' (Conselho de Desenvolvimento Econômico e Social – CDES – or Council for Economic and Social Development to give it its full name) in February 2003 (Panizza, 2005: 723). However, while modelled on the sectoral chambers of Collor, Lula modified the institutional design away from meso neocorporatist logic towards a wider macro-level negotiation between state and society, therefore removing one potential source of rent-seeking behaviour. Therefore, 'it was clear that the government was concerned with more than simply getting the policy right. It saw long-term benefits from engaging in a process of consultation that was not just a means to an end but an end in itself' (Doctor, 2007b: 139).

In many ways the CDES can be seen as an evolution of the meso neocorporatist sectoral chamber into a fully fledged macro neocorporatist institutional structure in Brazil (Doctor, 2007b: 136). Its basic aim was clear: to provide a mechanism for greater dialogue and improved governance in order to better implement the government's reform agenda. Furthermore, the CDES was not only 'the locus where streams of problems, policies, and politics converged into a "primeval soup" but also the source of viable proposals ready to be processed whenever a policy window appeared' (Doctor, 2007b: 139). It is true that many of these changes were incremental, seeking to overlap rather than replace old corporatist institutions, based on a typically Brazilian attitude towards change that could be described as 'sedimentation rather than metamorphosis' (Doctor, 2007b: 135). Therefore, Lula sought to update and adapt Brazil's (neo)corporatist institutions to make them more capable of responding to the demands of democratisation, economic liberalisation, and globalisation (Doctor, 2007b: 137).

As well as attempting to shape institutions that managed the relationship between state and society, and thus transformed that relationship to one that was more inclusive than seen under the neoliberal regime of FHC for example, Lula also sought to shape these institutions to synergise with his wider political economy. Labour relations are therefore a large part of the complex puzzle of *Lulismo*, where the attempts at institutionalising macro neocorporatism can be understood as part of a wider goal of facilitating social inclusion and stimulating economic development (Doctor, 2007b: 141). The aims of the CDES were therefore part of the whole political economy of *Lulismo*, which sought to ameliorate social injustice and facilitate economic growth. The overwhelming policy focus of the CDES remained on economic issues and the methods by which the *Conselhão* operated were as inclusive as possible.

Global imperatives and the international political economy of *Lulismo*

The previous chapter outlined the events surrounding Lula's first election in 2002, focusing on the fact that Lula found it necessary to assure international capital that he would continue the fiscal and monetary policies of his predecessor FHC through his 'Letter to the Brazilian People' on 22nd June 2002. In addition he set in motion policies that would institutionalise this promise, with a new IMF agreement on 4 September 2002 that would provide a framework for the continuity of core macroeconomic policies in 2003 (i.e. under the new administration). Furthermore, Lula agreed to submit a constitutional amendment granting independence to the Central Bank. Many (see, for example, Saad-Filho, 2007: 18; Carvalho, 2007: 37) have suggested that these events demonstrate the extent to which domestic Brazilian political economy, and its leaders, are subject to the constraints of international capital. Therefore, Brazilian monetary policy and fiscal policy, as outlined in Chapter 6 and analysed in the previous section, could be argued to be the product of international pressure, which is the result of imperatives derived from global capital.

As analysed in Chapter 5 concerning Argentina the contemporary character of globalisation leads domestic economies, and subsequently domestic policy, to operate within the 'limits of the possible' (Santizo, 2006). Furthermore, there is evidence to suggest that this is even truer for Brazil than it is for Argentina and other developing economies. This is due to the key role played by Brazil's highly liberalised capital account, a policy promoted in the 1990s. The key element of these liberalising reforms was to allow residents in Brazil to make financial investments abroad, and the Central Bank removed almost all barriers to outflows of domestic financial capital. The events of 2002 during the election campaign demonstrate that a policy or government decision that does not meet the approval of wealth-holders results in capital flight, causing significant economic instability. In addition, the ever-present possibility of similar events taking place in the future acts as a continuing check on government behaviour through the potential for the imposition of market discipline that would take the form of further capital flight. Thus, this thesis concludes, the Lula government was forced to adopt its monetary and fiscal policies under the duress of international capital, and continues to maintain these policies due to the continuing possibility of further economic upheaval should it deviate from the set path.

This is a thesis outlined by William Robinson (2004: 147–8), who suggests that these dynamics reveal the real power of transnational finance capital. The emergence of an elected leftist populist bloc in Brazil, and the region more widely (see Chapter 2), was 'unwilling or simply unable to challenge the global capitalist order' (Robinson, 2004: 148). Therefore, once elected, Lula promised not to default on the country's foreign debt, to maintain the previous government's adjustment policies, comply with IMF dictates in health and education and therefore slash spending on these programmes in order to create a fiscal surplus. A similar explanation, but with a different emphasis, is advocated by Francisco Panizza (2005: 727). He suggests that the 'economic policies of the PT's administration reflect a pragmatic understanding of the political and economic constraints under which all national economies operate'. Therefore, he is suggesting that there is no inevitability behind the PT's decision to accept IMF tutelage on key areas of macroeconomic policy, but accepted them nevertheless due to the practical nature of the government and its understanding of the realities of contemporary globalisation.

This hypothesis of Brazil entering the economic abyss should it choose to ignore the imperatives of global capital has been disputed (see especially Paulani, 2007: 44). The behaviour of three variables linked to the influence of global capital have been used to support the pessimistic proposal of economic doom. Those are: the exchange rate, the value of the C-bond (the main public debt bond negotiated in the international market), and the country risk indicator (Paulani, 2007: 43). Three points related to these factors suggests the idea that Brazil was under intolerable international pressure is simply not the case. First, Figure 6.3 in the previous chapter shows that at this time (2002–3) Brazil had a high trade balance with an associated current account surplus. In addition, the presence of reserves demonstrates that capital flight at this time was simply not happening at the kind of scale suggested (see Table 6.1). Second, while problems with the external accounts did exist, these were of a 'structural nature' (Paulani, 2007: 43). Therefore, there was a rise in import dependence due to a very open economy, a rise in the liquid external liabilities due to the internationalisation of productive capital promoted under the FHC privatisation drive, and rises in expenditures associated with a massive influx in portfolio investment once again due to the liberalised capital account. Paulani concludes that '[t]his kind of problem is far from the worsening economic *conjuncture* which was the argument used by the new government' [italics in original] (Paulani, 2007: 44). Third, high interest rates were justified by a declining Real and subsequent inflation. However, delays in the transition mechanism between raising interest rates and the subsequent drop in inflation lead Paulani to conclude that, 'with or without a tighter monetary policy, the price indices would continue to rise until all the impact had been incorporated … [therefore] there was no significant risk of inflation running out of control. And how could there be, if the economy had been moving sideways, and had been almost stagnant in the long-term?' (Paulani, 2007: 44).

Paulani's contribution suggests that perhaps the international pressures on domestic Brazilian policy were not as strong as has been proposed by others. The context of Paulani's work is that therefore the government must take responsibility for its own actions, and therefore judged from a traditional leftist position Lula can be charged with betraying his roots in radical leftist politics once having obtained power. However, this chapter has suggested that such a charge is inappropriate for Lula's regime (2003–10). Speaking at the G8 summit, President Lula spoke about the need to forge a new development paradigm that combines financial stability with economic growth and social justice (Panizza, 2005: 730–1). The analysis of the previous section has attempted to show how Lula has attempted to achieve this new development model, and the support base he has constructed behind this agenda. Part of that support base can very much be located in within fractions of international capital. As Panizza suggests, the practical acceptance of contemporary globalisation has led Lula to attempt to harness these forces to work for his model, rather than struggle against them, hence his attempt to bridge the gap between rival groups through his shuffling between Porto Alegre and Davos.

Practical acceptance of the contemporary character of neoliberal globalisation has not meant total 'surrender' to its principles. Rather, he has attempted to 'recruit and seduce' (Burges, 2009: 196), or 'bend and mould' (Panizza, 2005: 15), markets to fit his own agenda. This can be seen domestically, and the previous section outlined ways in which he attempted to do this. This has also been done internationally. Therefore, renegotiation of Brazil's debts in the market through extending the average maturity and reducing the average rate of interest rate (see Figure 6.11) on new external debt has been one way in which he achieved this. Furthermore, and at significant cost to current expenditure levels, he has relatively stabilised general government net debt, and even reduced it as a percentage of GDP (see Figure 6.5). In addition, on 13 December 2005 Lula paid off its outstanding US$15.5 billion IMF debt facility early (*The Economist,* 20 December 2005).

All these achievements have served to reduce the influence of international capital on Brazilian domestic policy through removing the mechanisms by which it can cause economic turbulence. For example, reducing and rationalising the foreign debt burden means it is less likely to default if investors begin pulling money out of Brazil, or become less willing to lend. Paying off the IMF means that the IMF can no longer exert direct influence over domestic Brazilian policy through conditionality. While it is true that Lula could have done more to reduce external vulnerability, imposing capital account restrictions for example, this would have been against his wider model of political economy and could have served to alienate important bases of support for his regime both among domestic conservative elements and fractions of international capital.

Lula's relations with international capital, and his policies that serve to renegotiate Brazil's relationship with it, can therefore be interpreted within the wider political economy of *Lulismo*. Arguably Brazil is limited by international interests more than other countries (although this is by no means undisputed), and Lula has implemented a number of policies that have served to reduce this external vulnerability while, at the same time, being careful not to adopt too radical measures that might alienate important economic actors and sources of support for his regime. The final section of this chapter will now, in a similar exercise to that conducted in Chapter 5, demonstrate that the political economy of *Lulismo* cannot be easily explained within traditional theories of political economy (as outlined in Chapter 2 and the first part of Chapter 3), rather one must look to the 'Developmental Regime'.

Lula's Brazil as a Developmental Regime?

The central thesis of this book is that the pink tide in contemporary Latin America can be best characterised by and analysed within a Developmental Regime framework. Chapter 3 outlined this framework, tracing its intellectual origins from Developmental State theory. Within the analysis of Chapter 5 this framework was applied to the political economy of *Kirchnerismo* in the first case study. This exercise will now be repeated here for Lula's Brazil. Once again, this will provide both analytical clarity to the characterisation of Lula's Brazil 2003–10, and further develop and enrich the Developmental Regime approach.

Lula's administration can be better understood as a regime, due to its specific blend of socio-economic alliances, political–economic institutions, and its public policy profile. The socio-economic alliances forged by Lula were arguably unique to Brazilian history. Paulani (2005: 52) suggests that '[p]olitically, Lula's government was very smart, since it promoted an association between the very poor, who were turned into clients of the state through social and compensatory income programmes, and the extremely rich, who figure among the largest *rentier* groups' [italics in original]. The glue of a low-inflation regime further bound the interests of these normally disparate socio-economic groups together further. As well as this coalition of interests, Lula and the PT were able to enhance their party's electoral appeal to the moderate middle classes through approval of its managerial capacity at the local level (Saad-Filho, 2007: 11). Over the longer term, Lula was able to cement this socio-economic group's support through his ideology and blend of policies that delivered benefits to them over time.

Within the political left itself Lula and the PT had traditionally forged an alliance between the 'political' (i.e. middle-class) and the 'trade-unionist' (i.e. working class) wings. 'This coalition included Lula's metalworkers' union and ... other influential trade unions in the manufacturing and service sectors. It also included the liberation theology sector of the Catholic Church, many student organisations, a large assortment of urban and rural social movements and NGOs, prestigious intellectuals, clandestine left parties, and a wide range of progressive organisations, from small newspapers to theatre groups' (Saad-Filho, 2007: 11). The creation of a coalition of interests based on these socio-economic groups formed a strong power base for Lula, who won over 65 per cent of the votes in 2003 in an entirely legitimate election, and who entered power with 'public opinion on its side, sympathy in military circles, ample support from the church, and a well organised party with experience of government across the country' (Flynn, 2005: 1248).

Lula and the PT's coalition was therefore structured around four main socio-economic groups, or what Morais and Saad-Filho (2003: 17) calls the 'alliance of losers' (see also Saad-Filho, 2007: 18) – due to the fact these were the four groups that had lost out during neoliberal restructuring: first, the unionised urban and rural working classes who were the backbone of the Brazilian left who had lost out to neoliberalism; second, the unorganised and unskilled working classes; third, prominent capitalists who had become disillusioned by the growth record of the neoliberal governments, enhanced TNC activity in their markets, and pressures from competing imports; fourth, several right-wing oligarchs, landowners, and influential politicians from the poor regions as the result of 'shrewd political calculation' (Saad-Filho, 2007: 19). In addition to this elements of international capital were very much part of the alliance, after initial doubts in 2002–3 during the election campaign and the first few months of Lula's first term.

These state–society relations forged through the socio-economic alliances of *Lulismo* were underpinned by an institutional structure that formed the basis of Lula's public policy profile. The core elements of that profile were stability through a low-inflation regime, poverty reduction strategies, macro neocorporatism, and growth stimulation through industrial policy and infrastructural investment. These policies have been examined in detail in previous sections but here it would be useful to recall how each has been institutionalised, in order to specifically address the nature of Lula's regime. Low inflation was aided by monetary policy that was set by an independent Central Bank, specifically responsible for low inflation through inflation targets. Therefore, expectations could be anchored to a target whose achievement was the responsibility of a technocratic institution, free from political interference. It is true that low inflation is also achieved through control of the supply side of the economy as well as the demand side, and therefore fiscal policy always plays its role. The 'Letter to the Brazilian people' from Lula anchored this supply side through commitment to persistent primary fiscal surpluses, although the relative weakness of this institutionalisation of fiscal policy was made clear in later years when this commitment to surpluses made way for infrastructural spending and state largesse prior to the election of 2010. As a result, as this book is being written (mid 2011), Dilma Rousseff is overseeing a recommitment to fiscal probity through her negotiations with trade unions, linking increases in the minimum wage to inflation and resisting further increases in order to help suppress supply-side pressures on the inflation rate. This effort is matched on the demand side, with the Central Bank increasing interest rates.

Poverty reduction strategies are centred upon *Bolsa Familia*. Large-scale state commitment to this set of policies, combined with greater involvement of the private sector through a corporate social responsibility agenda have served to embed and institutionalise these arrangements in Brazilian society. Furthermore, efforts to limit the practice of clientelism through bypassing local political interests as much as possible in the allocation and distribution of payments have attempted to increase the efficiency of the system, although the success of this institutional reform has been debatable. This has been complemented by the minimum wage policy, which has seen steady increases throughout the 2003 to 2010 period, thus further institutionalising state policies towards reducing levels of poverty in Brazilian society. Other complementary policies include Lula's growth strategy, grounded in a limited amount of industrial policy and infrastructural investment that has been institutionalised in the PAC (see Chapter 6 and previous sections). Focusing on infrastructure in the poorest regions helps both tackle poverty and unlock Brazil's huge domestic markets and therefore reduce (and potentially remove in the long run) one of Brazil's key barriers to sustained growth.

The institutionalisation of macro neocorporatism has been achieved through the creation of the Development Council (see previous section on Lula's labour policy). The practice of macro neocorporatism represents a fundamental change to the political economy of Brazil, fostering a more inclusive state–society relationship than has hitherto been present. Such a fundamental change has reshaped labour relations in Brazil, and is a legacy that should be long lasting given the strong institutions left in place to help guide this new state–society relationship. It is this long-lasting legacy not only in labour policy but also all the areas of Lula's public policy profile just analysed earlier that calls for the labelling of Lula's administrations as a 'regime'.

If Lula's administration is best labelled as a regime, defined through Pempel's theoretical analysis, why is it also developmental? Again, the same exercise conducted in Chapter 5 with Néstor Kirchner's Argentina will now be repeated here, with the key aspects of Developmental Regime applied to Lula's Brazil 2003–10.

The socio-economic support coalition that has underpinned *Lulismo* was outlined in previous paragraphs and need not be repeated again, although they can be referred to when examining the other three key aspects of a Developmental Regime: the definition of the central issue in politics, the legitimisation of a central ideology, and in delivering benefits through policy to the different elements of this support coalition. Therefore, the central issue in Brazilian political economy has been defined by *Lulismo* as economic development defined in terms of more equitable growth, with the benefits and proceeds of that growth going to the poorer elements of Brazilian society. This equitable development agenda has formed the core ideology of *Lulismo*, and has delivered benefits to the different elements of his socio-economic support base. While it is true that in the context of scandals in 2005 (prior to the election) it became more difficult for the PT to control the agenda and carry through its business (Flynn, 2005: 1227), the subsequent re-election of Lula and the PT reinvigorated his regime, facilitating further reform of Brazilian political economy.

This reform agenda has often been gauged according to traditional LOC principles such as the integration of universal social policies tied with full employment and the search for a more equalitarian income distribution (Neto and Vernengo, 2007: 89–90). However, judging *Lulismo* according to these criteria is inappropriate, as his regime is *not* a traditional LOC government, rather it is a Developmental Regime. Therefore, the ideology by which Lula's regime's policies are legitimised is grounded in different principles. More equitable distribution of income is part of that agenda, but not through the traditional LOC method, rather in the form of generating new growth through a developmentalist agenda and ensuring that the proceeds from this new growth are equitably shared across different sections of Brazilian society. Therefore, economic stability, underwritten by fiscal and monetary discipline serves the interests of both international investors and Brazil's poorest citizens, who have the fewest defences against runaway inflation (Sola, 2008: 37). In addition, the multiple goals of *Bolsa Familia* include the immediate alleviation of poverty as well as the promotion of citizenship among the most excluded sectors of Brazilian society (Tavolaro and Tavolaro, 2007: 431).

This articulation of an alternative legitimate ideology, through the definition of the central issue in politics, has accrued benefits to the different elements of *Lulismo*'s support base. Therefore, as mentioned before, economic stability through a tight monetary and fiscal regime benefits international capital, domestic bourgeoisie, and the poorest elements of Brazil's society when combined with progressive anti-poverty measures such as the package of *Bolsa Familia*. Critiquing *Bolsa Familia* from a LOC perspective through suggesting that a social safety-net approach to poverty reduction is inadequate and inappropriate may be valid, but it is not an appropriate criteria by which to judge *Lulismo*, as it is not based on such principles. His Developmental Regime is more interested in facilitating economic growth, partially achieved by drawing poorer elements into the social contract through social safety-net measures such as *Bolsa Familia*. Therefore, unionised urban and rural working classes benefited from new and sustained growth in the economy; unorganised and unskilled working classes benefited from CCT programmes such as *Bolsa Familia*; domestic capitalists benefited from growth promotion as they were those individuals that would facilitate a large proportion of that new growth; oligarchs and landowners benefited from the promotion of growth through stimulating agricultural exports; and international capital benefited from the continuing payment of outstanding debt. All these groups benefited from, and saw gains from, growth consolidated by the low-inflation regime.

Groups such as the unskilled poor could have benefited further perhaps from greater fiscal largesse on the part of Lula's regime but ran the risk of seeing those gains eroded through inflation, as well as by the fact that such a coalition would not have been possible as the support of key elements of Lula's regime would have become more difficult to maintain. Therefore, a more leftist agenda would have split the coalition of interests that got Lula into power in the first place, as these policies would not have delivered benefits to all his elements of support. Rather, Lula chose to pursue a different agenda, one that can best be encapsulated by the term Developmental Regime. Use of this term and its associated theoretical analysis reveals the true nature of *Lulismo* and facilitates deeper understanding of its goals and political orientation.

Conclusion: The legacy of Lula and *Lulismo*

The Lula administration can be seen as a case of 'leftism' without an actual leftist project (Tavolaro and Tavolaro, 2007: 428). Leftism can be defined as a type of political practice that puts forward a set of populist-like (in the sense of having considerable popular appeal) measures aimed at alleviating poverty and socio-economic inequality. This is as opposed to a left-wing government, which in a developing country would normally pursue at least four goals: full employment, economic growth, income and wealth distribution, and the empowerment of dispossessed groups through spreading out citizenship rights (Carvalho, 2007: 30). As Kingstone and Ponce (2010: 99) conclude, the policies of Lula 'reflect the triumph of a pragmatic market orientation that has come to occupy a kind of consensus centrist position in the Brazilian polity'. Lula was not elected on a platform of rupture and his victory should not be seen as 'a definitive historical transition in Brazilian history, but only as an open door to a possibly different future' (Fortes, 2009: 116).

Lulismo's core strategy for achieving alleviation of poverty and socio-economic inequality has been through the stimulation of economic growth in a stable macroeconomic environment so such proceeds from growth are not eroded from inflation. Some studies have seen these objectives as contradictory or conflicting. For example, Arestis, Paula, and Ferrari-Filho (2007b: 63) talk of the need for an economic growth regime rather than an inflation-targeting regime. However, this book suggests that this is a false dichotomy, as while a low-inflation regime may sacrifice some of Brazil's growth potential, it is in order to ensure concrete gains for the poorer classes who are most vulnerable to inflation. Lula has thus been a pragmatist, adapting quickly to new circumstances and operating within the 'limits of the possible' due to the imperatives imposed on any developing country in the context of globalisation characterised and shaped by the principles of neoliberalism. While Edwards (2010: 213) suggests that his goal has been to transform Brazil into a modern European-style social democracy along the principles of political economy as outlined in Chapter 2 with reference to SMC, it is the thesis of this book that a more suitable characterisation and interpretation of *Lulismo* is to be found within the Developmental Regime literature.

Lula's political economy has been grounded in a developmental bias. From a low-inflation regime, to a tight fiscal policy and the controlling of national debt, macroeconomic policy has been anchored by the need to pursue sustainable and stable growth. Many commentators have suggested that higher growth rates could have been achieved by Lula, especially in his first term, through different measures. However, these analyses fail to appreciate a number of factors in the political economy of *Lulismo*. First, the restrictive environment in which any developing country must operate given the nature of the 'limits of the possible' in terms of neoliberal globalisation, thus the need to maintain the confidence of international investors to maintain stability of the Brazilian economy, especially given its high levels of debt and very open capital account. Second, the domestic socio-economic alliance that formed the political base of *Lulismo* contained a number of disparate groups that required a mix of policies which could not appear to be too radical; thus there were a number of domestic political realities as well as international ones. Third, the genuine belief that a low-inflation regime was imperative to providing stability and security of any gains made by Brazil's poor. Inflation had been seen in the past in Brazil as one of the principle drivers of massive social inequalities, and therefore its eradication was imperative.

In addition to this developmental bias *Lulismo* also involved a genuine attempt to distribute the proceeds from growth in a way that would reduce absolute poverty and inequalities in Brazil, both of which were achieved with some (limited) success. This was not only to bring in these previously marginalised groups into Brazilian society but also to help unlock the potential of Brazil's large domestic market as a source of growth in the future, and thus provide more balanced growth through stimulation of domestic consumption and investment as well as exports and government spending. Other methods to empower previously marginalised groups included a move towards macro neocorporatism through the introduction of the Development Council. This was not only to give sectors of Brazilian society a greater say in the running of the country and its policy direction, but also, in line with the wider goals of *Lulismo*, to stimulate and promote economic growth.

A Developmental Regime is therefore more than just an administration that stimulates economic growth. It is a regime because it has a specific public policy profile that offers benefits to its alliance of socio-economic interests that elected it into power. This public policy profile must be institutionalised over time so as to provide longevity to the project, thus offering a greater chance for success as development occurs over the *long dureé* rather than simply in the lifetime of one or two administrations. Furthermore, to be developmental means much more than the presence of economic growth. It implies that the growth achieved delivers benefits to the socio-economic base of the regime. Therefore, in the case of *Lulismo* this meant attempts to redistribute wealth generated from growth to poorer elements of Brazilian society. However, this was not to be at the expense of other parts of its coalition of interests: domestic bourgeoisie and rural oligarchs. Therefore, the policies were not radical in nature, or overtly 'of the left'. In addition, *Lulismo* was offered up as a legitimate ideology that would define the central issue in Brazilian politics: the alleviation of poverty and the reduction of inequality in Brazilian society through economic growth characterised by stability and pragmatism given the nature of global imperatives placed on a developing country like Brazil. The success of this model remains open to question, and the election of a new President, Dilma Rousseff, signals the start of a new era, one which could lead to the extension of Brazil's Developmental Regime, its transmutation into something different, or its complete rejection. This issue will be discussed further in the concluding Chapter 9 of this book.

Part III
Post-Crisis Political Economy in Latin America: Global Lessons?

8
Crisis and Post-Crisis States in a Regional and Global Comparative Perspective

Part II demonstrated that the economic crises in Argentina and Brazil inflicted pain (in the case of Argentina severe pain) on the less well-off in society, with the lower and middle classes bearing the brunt of restructuring. Indeed, this conclusion can be extrapolated across time and space, and therefore be said to be true for all economic crises in all countries or regions. It is also true for the recent global financial crisis, or the 'Great Recession'. However, while the social costs of crisis demand our full attention, crises are also particularly important events for the larger debates over economic ideas that they set in motion. Moments of crisis show economic paradigms in clear view and the ensuing contest of models opens up the possibility of economic change (Robertson, 2008a: 1). Indeed, the repetition of currency, sovereign debt, and/or banking crises in Latin America, and their appearance also in Asia and in almost every other region in the developing world at some point, as well as most recently in the developed world in the form of the 'Great Recession', has spawned a voluminous academic, policy-orientated, and even journalistic literature, especially in the last decade (Porzecanski, 2009: 8).

In the context of Latin America one universally emerging trend is realisation of an increased reliance on and role for the state in ways unthinkable only a few years ago (Cox, 2009: 145). The analysis of this book is no exception to this trend, showing in Part I that Latin America as a continent has taken a 'left turn' – dubbed the pink tide – ever since 1998 and the rise of Hugo Chavez in Venezuela, and that this phenomena can be partially interpreted as an increasing role for the state in development. This conclusion was further cemented in Part II through the examination of two detailed case studies: Argentina and Brazil. Furthermore, the book has suggested that these shifts of paradigm witnessed in Latin America can be interpreted within a Developmental Regime framework, thus adding a layer of analytical rigour that facilitates an understanding that moves beyond simply 'more state involvement in the development process' and into more nuanced analyses of state–market, state–society, and national–international dichotomies.

The purpose of this chapter is to analyse these new Developmental Regimes in Latin America in the context of the most recent global financial crisis, and to draw normative conclusions with regard to crisis and post-crisis performance, thus scrutinising the efficacy of such regimes as compared to other models and strategies of development. While the previous section looked in depth at how both Argentina and Brazil were able to emerge from their respective domestic crises in a robust and dynamic fashion, this section will examine how Brazil, Argentina, and Latin America as a whole has dealt with the global financial crisis of 2007–8 and the post-crisis recovery. After this analysis, further discussion will assess how that performance compares with other countries affected by the crisis, most notably those that represent the more traditional models of political economy: the neoliberalism of the US and UK, and the SMC model of Continental Europe. This will allow for a conclusion to be drawn regarding the relative effectiveness and potency of these models of capital accumulation in comparison to the Developmental Regimes of Argentina, Brazil, and Latin America more widely.

A series of crises: Mexico–Asia–Russia–Brazil–Argentina – the global crisis

The academic discourse on globalisation has proliferated ever since the 1980s. With some notable exceptions (Hirst and Thompson, 1999) this literature has concluded that contemporary society is evolving in the direction of an ever-increasingly integrated world, and one of the important manifestations of this is the transmission of market cycles across the globe (Porzecanski, 2009: 7). While in the good times this could have strong beneficial effects for those markets that are more open, thus facilitating strong growth in these countries, in bad times restrictive monetary policies, credit crunches, market downturns, and generalised risk aversion in the United States, Europe, and Japan likewise reverberate most powerfully in those developing countries. Indeed, many markets are so integrated that even crises or imbalances that form in other developing countries can contaminate markets that are linked to them either regionally or globally, precipitating what Williamson (2004) labelled 'the years of emerging market crises' – based on a thesis of contagion from one crisis to the next (see also Arestis, Paula, and Ferrari-Filho, 2007b: 47).

In general, there are three major reasons as to why this is the case. Porzecanski (2009: 7) identifies these three transmission mechanisms as the credit channel, international trade, and investor and lender herd behaviour through contagion effects. As a result of these transmission mechanisms growth in Latin America has been constantly interrupted: the Tequila Effect in 1994, the Asian Crisis in 1997, the Vodka Effect in 1998, the Samba Effect in 1999, and the Tango Crisis of 2001–2 have all served to facilitate torpor rather than dynamism in the Latin American region. The region of Latin America is therefore no stranger to aggregate economic shocks triggered by financial crises (IDB, 2009: 1).

The Tequila Effect was the impact of the Mexican economic crisis in 1994 on the rest of Latin America. After a forced devaluation of the Mexican Peso many Latin American countries found their own currencies had significantly appreciated relative to Mexico's. Combined with general recession in Mexico and the subsequent falls in consumer demand this meant that exports from Latin America to Mexico dropped significantly. Furthermore, in the medium term, businesses in other Latin American countries found it more difficult to compete with Mexican exports due to the relative strength of their own national currencies relative to the Mexican Peso. These trade effects were compounded by investor behaviour, as spreads on Latin American bonds in general rose, making new credit more expensive to obtain in the market. Similar dynamics occurred after similar crises in Asia, Russia, Brazil, and Argentina throughout the decade. As a result, existing debt levels were affected by the host of currency devaluations associated with this series of crisis.

The effects of these crises were therefore greater than the sum of their parts, resulting in economies throughout the region in the 1995 to 2002 period lurching from one crisis to the next, buffeted by the economic and financial waves that were left in their wake. A mild recovery in the first half of the 1990s, after the 'lost decade' of the 1980s, had given way to yet another period of volatility, sluggish growth, and recurrent crisis (Petras and Veltmeyer, 2009: 201). This process led to a search for alternatives. Neoliberalism had failed economies and societies across the continent time and again, and led to the rise of the pink tide. Chapter 2 examined this process in detail, but for the purposes of this chapter what this meant was that when the Global Financial Crisis of 2007–8 hit, unlike the national or regional crises of the preceding decade, many economies across Latin America were structurally very different, and operated according to different principles than neoliberalism. This book has shown that such principles can be characterised within a Developmental Regime framework, and the rest of this chapter will examine how Brazil, Argentina, and Latin America more broadly has dealt with this crisis – both in isolation and relative to the developed world, culminating in a conclusion that suggests such a model of capital accumulation represents a more dynamic form of political economy in terms of post-crisis development.

The global financial crisis, Brazil, Argentina, and Latin America

The global financial crisis of 2007–8 led to the Great Recession as it impacted the real economy in the form of overproduction and demand contraction. This resulted in a number of different policy responses across the world. Many of the initial responses in the developed world led to selective public interventions that were squarely against neoliberal principles. Bankrupt banks were placed under public control and massive investments to stimulate the economy were made. A new wave of Keynesianism thus emerged as a reaction to the crisis in the developed world in the immediate aftermath of the collapse of Lehman brothers and the associated economic fallout. As the dust settled neoliberalism seemed to be reasserting itself once again as the modus operandi of developed economies, with the UK especially embracing the logic of balanced budgets and fiscal retrenchment. Both neoliberalism and (neo)Keynesianism are based on the market as the principal production, distribution, and consumption mechanism, although the latter aims at regulating it. Both are technocratic proposals devoid of social participation. Both strengthen the private control of the means of production, deriving profits from the exploitative extraction of surplus value from labour and from nature (de la Barra, 2010: 640). However, the sluggish recovery of much of the developed world in the aftermath of the crisis – the potential default of the PIG (Portugal, Ireland, and Greece) countries, the ballooning US debt and deficit combined with the rating agencies warnings and downgrades, and the flatlining of UK growth well into 2011 – has meant that the financial crisis has become much more than this: it has become a social, environmental, and energy crisis, a crisis of democracy, of multilateralism, of neoliberalism, and ultimately a crisis of capitalism (de la Barra, 2010: 635).

In the developing world, however, the story has been different. In Latin America, the principal subject of this book, the crisis was initially felt through a slowdown in capital flows, large declines in stock price indices, significant currency adjustments, and an increase in debt spreads (Bustillo and Velloso, 2009: 35). Nevertheless, the Great Recession was different from the preceding crises of the twentieth century in Latin America. Jara, Moreno, and Tovar (2009: 53–4) outline four main areas of difference: first, the shock originated in the financial sector of advanced economies rather than in Latin America or another emerging market region; second, the significant reduction of Latin American public external debt gave governments more leeway for playing a stabilising role for private markets; third, new kinds of vulnerabilities surfaced associated with financial innovation and integration rather than with macroeconomic imbalances or banking sector weaknesses; fourth, policy responses differed as central banks provided liquidity in foreign exchange and domestic money markets to facilitate expansion of credit as well as adopting a countercyclical monetary policy stance alongside government countercyclical fiscal policy. These areas of difference will be explored in greater detail in the following sections, which will break down the impact of the global crisis on Latin America into three distinct time periods: Phase I (Q3 2007 to Q3 2008), Phase II (Q4 2008 to Q1 2009), and Phase III (Q2 2009 to present day). In their totality, these sections will demonstrate that capitalism in Latin America has weathered the storm better than capitalism in the core. Such an analysis will provide the empirical foundation for a subsequent examination of the different models of capitalism present in Latin America and those in the developed countries in Europe and the US, an analysis that will demonstrate the advantages of Argentine, Brazilian, and Latin American Developmental Regimes over the neoliberalism and (neo)Keynesianism of the core with respect to post-crisis development strategy.

Phase I, Q3 2007–Q3 2008: The crisis comes late to Latin America

The crisis began in the summer of 2007, as global inter-bank credit markets dried up in response to the growing awareness of massive overlending, most famously the so-called sub-prime household mortgage market in the US (Radice, 2011: 21). The economic impact of this hit the United States and Europe before spreading to Latin America. As Figure 8.1 shows, in 2007 real GDP growth declined in the advanced economies to 2.7 per cent, while in Argentina, Brazil, and Latin America more widely it grew by 8.6, 6.1, and 6.7 per cent respectively. Therefore, in contrast to past recessions (discussed in the previous section) the Great Recession hit the advanced economies first, and it initially looked as if Latin America would escape the effects of the collapse of sub-prime

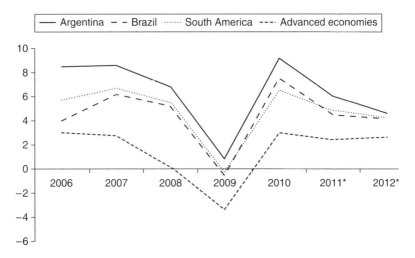

Figure 8.1   Real GDP growth (percentage change) 2007–12
Source: IMF, 2011a.
Note: * indicates IMF staff predictions.

markets. The fact that Latin America at this time was not feeling the impact of the crisis was due to the fact that the 1999–2002 period had destroyed many of the 'toxic assets' in the regional banking system, as well as links to the speculative heartlands of New York and London has been lessened (Petras, 2009: 203). In addition, Latin America had diversified its markets in the first half of the 2000s and its new Asian markets retained their resiliency longer. Therefore, the loss of demand for key Latin American commodities and manufactures from the US and Europe had much less of an impact that in the past (with the exception of more Central American states – especially Mexico – due to their higher reliance on US domestic demand for their exports). This experience led some to hypothesise about a 'decoupling effect', where the rise of countries like China meant that alternative locomotives outside of the ACCs would drive the global economy forward (Valadão and Gico Jr, 2009:2).

However, despite initial signs of this decoupling effect, Latin America was strongly affected after the Lehman Brothers Bankruptcy in September 2008, as were other emerging market regions. Figure 8.1 shows dips in Argentine, Brazilian, and Latin American growth trajectories, which were the result of particularly bad fourth-quarter results; the advanced economies of the Western world were also hit badly, with growth barely registering at 0.2 per cent for the year. The reasons why the crisis hit Latin America at this time will be explored in detail in the next section. Furthermore, as Figure 8.1 also shows, the slowdown that began in Q4 2008 for Latin America was significantly less severe than that registered in the advanced economies (primarily represented by the United States and Europe). The next section will also explore the dynamics behind why when the crisis did eventually reach Latin America, it was significantly milder than in the core industrialised world.

Phase II, Q4 2008–Q4 2009: The crisis hits

After the collapse of Lehman the crisis hit Latin America, driving most economies in the region into recession. As Figure 8.1 shows South America dipped into recession in 2009 as a result of –0.2 per cent GDP growth. This recession was driven by the reversal of external factors that had helped facilitate the 2003–7 economic boom (see Part II), which were now working in the opposite direction (Ocampo, 2009a: 721). Therefore, a collapse in commodity prices (see Figure 8.2), a collapse in demand for manufactured goods from the advanced capitalist countries (Porzecanski, 2009: 12), and a fall in remittances as employment fell in those same countries. While remittances were especially important for a number of Central American countries, the severity of the shock that Latin America as a whole experienced can only be fully explained by

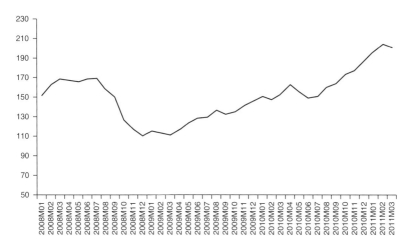

Figure 8.2 General commodities price index (excluding fuels)
Source: IMF, 2011b.

the strength of the trade shock (Ocampo, 2009a: 722). The transmission of recessionary forces via the international trade channel led to a more than 45 per cent year-on-year collapse in the export earnings of emerging and developing countries from the fourth-quarter 2008 to the first-quarter 2009 (Porzecanski, 2009: 12).

A further mechanism at play was the wave of risk aversion post-Lehman that led to herding and contagion selling in stock, bond, currency, and commodity markets around the world. This facilitated a de facto shutdown of the international capital markets, thus affecting the availability of international bank loans and cross-border portfolio investments. This sudden stop of the international credit channel led to nearly US$270 billion drop in cross-border bank loans to emerging and developing countries during the period October 2008 to March 2009 (Porzecanski, 2009: 13, 15; Jara, Moreno, and Tovar, 2009: 53). Therefore, for Latin America the main problem with the crisis was that it affected foreign demand for its products and services, while drastically reducing the excess international liquidity that had financed a substantial part of the investments and expansion of those markets in previous years (Valadão and Gico Jr, 2009: 3). One notable exception to this was Argentina, which as a result of its own 2001–2 crisis had been frozen out of international capital markets for some time, and therefore its banks had very limited exposure to them and the government had no reliance on the credit channels to fund debt or budget deficits.

This collapse in commodity prices and volume of both primary and manufactured goods led many to foretell the end of Latin America's long boom of the twenty-first century. James Petras (2009: 196) summarised the mood at the time most eloquently: 'Latin America's economies are feeling the full brunt of the world recession; every country in the region is experiencing a major decline in trade, domestic production, investment, employment, state revenues, and income … The precipitous decline in commodity prices, reflecting an abrupt drop in world demand, is sharply reducing government revenues dependent on export taxes.' This spiral was compounded by the fact that as commodity prices fell so did Latin America's terms of trade, thus making imports more expensive and threatening to turn trade surpluses into trade deficits (Petras, 2009: 197). Others shared this gloom; de la Barra (2010: 647) concluded that as Latin American economies were fundamentally based upon the export of natural resources, the combination of factors outlined in this section spelt the end of the boom.

Relative to other regions, however, Latin American was not uniformly hit the hardest blows (Porzecanski, 2009: 15). The ACCs aside, the Baltic countries have been ravaged, Eastern Europe was hit badly, and Central Europe did not fare much better. 2008–9 thus marked the first time in decades that a sharp economic slowdown and major financial disturbance emanating in the industrialised world had not hit Latin America the hardest (Porzecanski, 2009: 16).

Phase III, Q1 2010–current: Recovery and growth

Latin America was to witness a remarkable recovery, sooner and stronger than many expected in 2009. Figure 8.1 shows that Latin America as a whole grew 6.5 per cent in 2010, bouncing back from the 2009 slump. Argentina and Brazil, the two largest economies in South America, grew at an even more impressive 7.5 and 9.2 per cent respectively. These figures were considerably better than the recovery in the ACCs, which grew on average by only 3 per cent in 2010 – a figure that was considerably lower in countries like the UK, USA, and the PIG countries in the Eurozone. If the region maintains this momentum, it will double its income per person by 2025 to an average of US$22,000 a year (PPP). By then, Brazil may be the fifth-largest economy in the world, behind China, the US, India, and Japan. In addition, half-a-dozen countries in the region may have achieved developed-country status, with an income equivalent to Spain's today (*The Economist*, 11 September 2011: 4).

Figures 8.3 and 8.4 show the quarterly breakdown of GDP by expenditure in Brazil and Argentina. They show that the recovery was driven primarily by increases in trade. In Brazil, imports and exports increased by 36 per cent and 12 per cent respectively from 2009 to 2010, and in Argentina by 33 per cent and 15 per cent. However, trade was not the only source of the recovery, as GFCF played an important role; in Brazil GFCF increased by 22 per cent between 2009 and 2010, which was partly the result of a large increase in inventories that had been run down during the downturn in 2009. In Argentina, GFCF increased by 20 per cent.

Consumption also played a role, although not as large as trade and investment. Private consumption increased by 7 per cent between 2009 and 2010 in Brazil, and 9 per cent in Argentina, but as a result of government measures (see next section) private consumption had not really been hit during the downturn in 2009 and therefore did not have a lower base from which to recover. Government consumption increased by 3 per cent and 8 per cent in Brazil and Argentina respectively, the result of some of the fiscal measures adopted by both governments during this period. In Argentina, for example, the government launched a US$21 billion plan for public works (later expanded to US$32 billion), credit

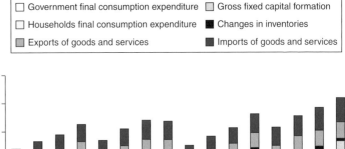

Figure 8.3   Quarterly GDP in Brazil by type of expenditure at constant prices (base year 2000)
Source: CEPALSTAT, 2011.

lines of US$3.8 billion to stimulate consumption, investment, labour and production – which included consumption credit of US$2 billion to electrodomestic goods and vehicles, US$360 million for pre-financing exports and loans for labour capital, and US$864 million for SMEs – and finally US$500 million for the agricultural sector (Bustillo and Velloso, 2009: 40; see also Petras, 2009: 196). In Brazil impacts on employment were dampened by CCTs, increasing the minimum wage, fiscal incentives for employers who made fewer workers redundant, and the protection of social expenditure from budget cuts (de la Barra, 2010: 644).

In summary, the breakdown of the effects of the crisis and subsequent recovery in Latin America highlight a number of important points. First, the crisis came relatively late to the continent due to a financial sector that was generally shielded from the more exotic and ultimately toxic financial instruments that resulted in the collapse of so many Western-based institutions. Furthermore, the diversification of export markets away from the US and Europe meant that when demand from these countries dried up Latin American countries had alternative markets in Asia

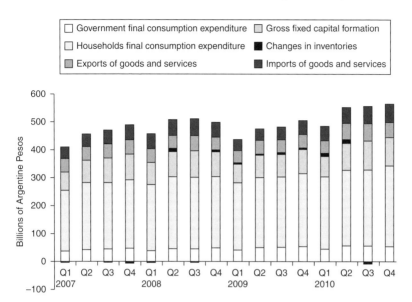

Figure 8.4   Quarterly GDP in Argentina by type of expenditure at constant prices (base year 1993)
Source: CEPALSTAT, 2011.

to which they could export their goods and services. When the crisis did reach Latin America, it was partly the result of a fall in global commodity prices – the result of a general decline in global demand that also hit volume of sales despite continuing demand in Asia. This downturn, however, was relatively shallow when compared to ACCs and some regions in the developing world. In addition, it lasted a relatively short period of time, as recovery was both swift and robust. This was in contrast to other parts of the global economy, especially those markets in the UK, the US, and parts of the Eurozone. While the recovery in 2010 was grounded in trade, there were other important elements to it. The next section will explore in detail the political economy of the crisis and post-crisis recovery in Brazil, Argentina, and Latin America as a whole, outlining the factors behind the trajectory of the crisis and subsequent recovery.

The political economy of the global financial crisis in Latin America

The literature outlines a number of reasons behind the relatively shallow nature of the downturn in 2009 and subsequent recovery in 2010. For

Llaudes, Salman, and Chivakul (2010) these were the result of stronger fundamentals, which can be expressed as five core areas of strength: reduced currency mismatches, exchange rate flexibility, banking resilience, development of local capital markets, and fiscal and monetary policy (see, for example, Porzecanski, 2009: 19; Bustillo and Velloso, 2009: 35; Jara, Moreno, and Tovar, 2009; Cox, 2009). This section will examine these five areas in detail, examining how they served to produce the crisis and post-crisis dynamics present in Brazil, Argentina, and Latin America in general.

The first core area is reduced currency mismatches. These are said to exist when a change in the exchange rate leads to major capital losses of gains among debtors because of a disparity in the currencies in which the assets and liabilities are denominated. One classic example of this was the Argentine situation in 2001–2, where due to the system of *Convertibilidad* many liabilities were denominated in US dollars while assets were in Argentine pesos (see Chapter 4). One indicator of this situation is the level of foreign-denominated debt held within a country or region. In Latin America 40 per cent of all debt was denominated in foreign currency in 2000, a figure that by 2007 had reduced to 20 per cent (Porzecanski, 2009: 20). The rise of the pink tide, as discussed in Chapter 2 in general and in Chapters 4 and 6 for Argentina and Brazil respectively, led to an alternative political economy that both facilitated and prioritised debt reduction and rationalisation. Argentina in particular, as a result of its debt default in the 2001–2 Tango crisis, significantly reduced its overall debt levels, as well as gaining favourable extensions in maturity and reductions in interest. Both Argentina and Brazil repaid outstanding IMF loans in December 2005, with Argentina in particular using a large portion of new debt (denominated in local currency) to make the payment. While *The Economist* newspaper at the time suggested that the higher interest rates attached to the new debt made the decision of questionable value (*The Economist*, 20 December 2005: 65), these short-run costs were more than justified in the face of reducing currency mismatch risks in the long run and therefore reducing exposure to exactly the kind of problems that emerged in the 2007–8 global financial crisis.

A second useful indicator of currency mismatches is a country's net foreign-currency asset position. As governments, banks, and corporations in Latin America were switching away from liabilities denominated in foreign currencies, they were also building up a substantial stock of assets denominated in foreign currencies. In terms of governments, one easily measurable indicator is the level of official international reserves.

By 2006, Latin America as a whole had a net foreign asset position of US$150 billion (Porzecanski, 2009: 21), increasing to US$180 billion by end of 2007 (Jara, Moreno, and Tovar, 2009: 55). In Brazil official international reserves reached US$85 billion by 2006, and then skyrocketed to US$252 billion, or 86 per cent of total external debt, by 2010 (see Table 6.1). In Argentina, reserves increased substantially from a crisis low of US$10 billion to over US$50 billion by 2010, or around 100 per cent of government-held foreign debt (Porzecanski, 2010: 7). These reserves represented a healthy cushion that could be used, and was used in 2008, to help stabilise the external financing position of the region during the crisis. As most of the region's currencies came under downward pressure in August–September 2008, in the aggregate, the public and private sectors in Latin America experienced a balance sheet windfall – quite a contrast with the enormous balance sheet losses that currency devaluations used to impose on many of the region's banks, corporations, and governments in prior decades (Porzecanski, 2009: 21).

The second core area that explains the short and shallow nature of the impact of the global financial crisis on Latin America is that of exchange rate flexibility. External shocks that involve sudden increases or decreases in trade or capital flows will result in a change in the equilibrium RER. If the nominal exchange rate is fixed then adjustments in the country's balance of payments is inevitable, which will take place through changes in domestic nominal prices (wages, profits, and rents) and in domestic demand – consumption and investment spending (Porzecanski, 2009: 23). Indeed, this was the underlying cause of the Argentine crisis of 2001–2 as the system of *Convertibilidad* led to a growing trade imbalance throughout the 1990s that was funded through debt financing, leading to a steadily appreciating RER and ultimately sovereign default (see Chapter 4). The economic theory of exchange rate regimes generally agrees that in a world of free trade and high capital mobility fixed exchange rate regimes are more prone to crisis (for a summary of the literature, see Willett, 2007: 711–13). Given traditional analysis of the unholy (or impossible) trinity (Fleming, 1962), in the absence of capital controls and a policy of a fixed exchange rate regime, governments give up sovereignty of monetary policy. Starting with Mexico after its 1994–5 crisis and ending with the spectacular collapse of Argentina's currency board in 2002, a significant number of countries in Latin America shifted from rigid to flexible exchange rate regimes. Therefore, they were able to move from monetary policies focused on exchange rate targets to monetary policies anchored on inflation targeting.

In response to the most recent trade shock due to the global financial crisis, central banks across Latin America were both willing and able to let their exchange rates depreciate and serve as natural shock absorbers. For example, the local currency price of the US dollar was allowed to increase by as much as 50 per cent in Brazil, Chile, Colombia, and Mexico from March 2008 to March 2009, and by nearly 20 per cent in Argentina and Peru (Porzecanski, 2009: 23). This helps explain why the crisis came late to Latin America when compared to many other parts of the world; the depreciation of domestic exchange rates against the US dollar allowed Latin American economies to initially offset the slowdown in capital flows and decreasing demand for their exports. However, as the crisis deepened, especially in the advanced capitalist counties, depreciation of the exchange rate ceased to be sufficient and the continent tipped into a light recession.

The third core area that aided Latin America during the global financial crisis was the degree of banking resistance across the region. Many Latin American countries had banking collapses in the 1980–2002 period, and had therefore undergone restructuring during these periods. This meant that many domestic banking systems across Latin America were much more robust (*The Economist*, 11 September 2011: 3), especially in terms of capital ratios when the crisis hit. On average, tier one capital ratios for Latin American banks were 14 per cent, much higher than even projected post-crisis Basel III stipulations of 10 per cent. One of the particular ways in which the global financial crisis manifested itself was through the freezing of the inter-bank loan market, forcing certain banks that relied heavily on this market for wholesale financing of its operations to seek government help (most famously Northern Rock in the UK). Given Latin American banks capital buffers, such reliance on these markets was not so much of a factor and therefore no countries in Latin America saw any major banking collapses. In Argentina especially, the lack of gearing to fund the local economy meant many investments remained unaffected. Furthermore, the large absence of mortgages in the retail sector resulted in very little exposure for local banks whose operations therefore remained largely unaffected (Interview with Dujovne, 2011). In addition, the major international banks that operate across the continent are Santander and HSBC. Both of these banks were less affected by the global crisis than others – for example, Barclays, Lloyds, or CitiGroup. They were less exposed to the hardest-hit regions such as Eastern Europe, and although clearly exposed to core markets in the US and Europe were sufficiently large, diversified, and capitalised to avoid government help like so many of their global competitors. Furthermore, these and other foreign banks operated a model whereby a higher percentage of local lending was backed by local deposits (80 per cent in 2008), thereby relying less on the volatile wholesale markets.

All of these factors led to much stronger banks and banking system in general in Latin America. This meant that the governments of the region were not burdened with hugely expensive bailouts such as in the UK and US, reflected in the fiscal accounts of governments. This gave many governments the freedom to adopt counter-cyclical fiscal expenditure, which will be discussed later in this section. It also meant that the banks continued to operate in a normal manner, providing credit to businesses and thus allowing for levels of investment fundamental to long-term GDP growth. Again, this stands in contrast to the experience of many ACCs, especially the UK and US, where hamstrung banks reeling from massive losses due to bad loans and defaults found it difficult, despite cajoling from national governments (e.g. Project Merlin in the UK), to maintain their usual operations of providing credit to the economy, especially SME operations.

The fourth core area was the development of local capital markets (Jara, Moreno, and Tovar, 2009: 66; Porzecanski, 2009: 27). Domestic bond markets were slow to sprout in Latin America. This was due to a decade-long track record of macroeconomic instability, the absence of a diversified investor base with a long planning horizon, the lack of transparency and accountability on the part of private and government issuers, a high degree of judicial uncertainty, and, in many cases, a history of balance-of-payments arrears and outright defaults on the part of some governments (Porzecanski, 2009: 27). Since 2003, however, this has changed. In the region's larger countries domestic bonds markets constitute a growing source of financing for Latin American governments and top-tier local corporations, demonstrated by an increase in the stock of government bonds from US$320 billion in 2002 to US$800 billion by 2008 (Porzecanski, 2009: 27). Such a change has also been mirrored in the decline of foreign currency-denominated debt stock. In Brazil, for example, this has dropped from 35 per cent in 2002 to 10 per cent in 2008 (Bustillo and Velloso, 2009: 38). This has also been true in Argentina (see Chapter 4). This allowed many governments to endure the economic contraction and sudden stop of external capital flows of late 2008 to early 2009. While these markets were not sufficiently developed to provide shelter for most private companies in most countries (Porzecanski, 2009: 28), the region's financial vulnerabilities would have been much greater and corporate financing woes would surely have been much more critical, resulting in more adverse macroeconomic repercussions more common of the past in Latin America.

The fifth and final core area was that of domestic fiscal and monetary policy in Latin American countries (see, for example, Bustillo and Velloso, 2009: 35; Porzecanski, 2009: 19). In terms of fiscal policy many Latin American countries were able to adopt counter-cyclical measures to confront the crisis. In addition to policies adopted in Argentina and Brazil (detailed in the previous section), 16 other Latin American countries also enacted fiscal strategies to counter the effects of the global slowdown. The recent years of fiscal discipline have allowed these countries the budgetary space to fund these expenditures (Cox, 2009: 150). This was in stark contrast to previous domestic or regional crises that affected Latin America in the past, particularly in the 1980s and 1990s. This temporary financing was crucial to avoid cuts to spending on social protection, health, education, and vital infrastructure. For example, multibillion-dollar stimulus packages were set into motion in Argentina, Brazil, Mexico, and Chile to invest in infrastructure, protect jobs, provide credit, and promote consumer spending. In addition, other countries throughout the region were able to implement initiatives to create jobs through public works projects, programmes boosting microcredit, self-employment initiatives, and small enterprise development – all of which were critical to the relatively shallow nature of the downturn and the speedy recovery of the region's economic fortunes (Cox, 2009: 150).

In terms of monetary policy, the much more sustainable debt burdens of many countries (see Chapters 4 and 6 for discussion of these measures for Argentina and Brazil respectively) gave the room for the fiscal measures described earlier (de la Barra, 2010: 657). Improved macroeconomic conditions were not only the result of inflation-targeting-cum-exchange-rate-flexibility; they were also a function of the interventions in the foreign exchange markets as discussed earlier in this section. Indeed, this break with the orthodoxy perhaps represents one of the fundamental strengths of Latin American Developmental Regimes: as Ocampo (2009a: 722) concludes, 'pragmatism rather than orthodox management has therefore been one of the major sources of current macroeconomic strength'. Furthermore, as analysed in this section, prudent macroeconomic and financial policies, including stronger financial regulation, softened the impacts of the crisis on the region. In addition, currency policy supported this with more flexible exchange rate regimes softening the blow of the sudden stop in capital flows, and the accumulation of foreign reserves acting as an important buffer for many states (Jara, Moreno, and Tovar, 2009: 63).

In summary, the significant reversal in capital flows and the collapse in commodity prices that pushed Latin America into an economic downturn in 2009 was both relatively shallow and short lived because of the characteristics outlined in this section. Widespread use of flexible exchange rate regimes, limited exchange rate pass through to inflation, lower currency mismatches and lower dollarization, and the greater credibility of central banks all helped when international trade was affected (Jara, Moreno, and Tovar, 2009: 58). The effect of the sudden stop in capital flows did not adversely affect the economies of the region due to resilient banking sectors, relatively developed local bond markets, and government fiscal policy designed to offset the worst of the effects.

The next section will now examine these policies in the context of the theoretical framework outlined in Part I of this book. It will suggest that many of these characteristics just examined can be traced to reform by pink tide governments. The section will examine these in detail with regard to Argentina and Brazil, cross-referencing those reforms outlined in Part II with the analysis of this chapter to suggest that the Developmental Regimes in Latin America facilitated significant change to the political economy of those countries such that they were able to weather the economic storm of the global financial crisis. A following section will then suggest that this was in contrast to alternative forms of political economy that led to different (less successful) strategies and policies in the developed world.

Post-crisis Developmental Regimes in Argentina, Brazil, and Latin America

The political economy of post (global) crisis Argentina and Brazil specifically, and more broadly large areas of Latin America, can be characterised within the Developmental Regime framework. While there are clear exceptions to this generalisation, such as Colombia, large swathes of the continent have been swept by the rise of the pink tide, and as Chapter 2 demonstrated this tide is resistant to characterisation and classification within the mainstream theories and strategies of the political economy of development. Part II of this book set out in detail the policies of Argentina and Brazil, and there are a number of ways in which those policies helped facilitate the characteristics that helped those countries through the most recent global financial crisis, allowing it to emerge from a relatively shallow downturn strongly and quickly. These policies can be grouped under two main themes: first, currency regimes, and second, monetary and fiscal policy.

First is the political economy of exchange rate regimes. In Argentina, the crisis of 2001–2 ended the decade-long system of *Convertibilidad*, which was replaced by a coherent policy of an SCRER by Néstor Kirchner. This policy was one of the lynchpins of his Developmental Regime, a domestic industrial policy designed to stimulate manufacturing was coupled with a currency policy designed to help foster a new export economy (see Chapter 4). This new export economy has not only helped to stimulate GDP growth, but also to rebalance the economy towards production of industrial manufactures and thus moving the Argentine economy up the value chain. As the previous section showed, the move away from a fixed exchange rate allowed the currency to act as a natural shock absorber when the initial wave of the global financial crisis hit the Argentine economy. It is true that this policy of an SCRER means that the Argentine peso is not a fully free-floating currency but in terms of the global financial crisis the trend was for the currency to depreciate, and the Kirchner government policy was set in this direction and therefore was not working against the trend.

Some of the economics literature suggests that this form of narrow band adjustable peg exchange rate regime makes the domestic economy more prone to crisis (Obstfeld and Rogoff, 1995; Meltzer, 2000). However, Frankel (2004) has shown that there is no solid theoretical understanding as to why this is the case, and Willett (2007) is able to demonstrate that there is no a priori reason as to why a policy such as Kirchner's SCRER should be more prone to crisis. For Willet the key is the 'extent to which political and institutional conditions allow decision makers to base exchange rate policy on long-run economic considerations rather than short-run political ones' (Wilett, 2007: 710). The long-term developmentalist view of *Kirchnerismo*, combined with his specific forging of a new social contract in Argentina (see Chapter 5), has helped facilitate this belief that strong, stable government is helping to foster a newly institutionalised regime in the country, and therefore aiding the stability of the exchange rate policy.

In Brazil the crawling peg regime that formed the basis of the *Real Plan* led to a medium term overvaluation of the currency that precipitated the crisis of 1998–9. After the collapse of the *Real Plan* a managed flotation of the currency emerged, leading to steady depreciation of the RER until the end of June 2005 when the currency switched direction and started to steadily appreciate into 2010. This appreciation was interrupted by a period of depreciation in 2009 as the effects of the global financial crisis reached Brazil, showing how – like in Argentina – the currency was able to act as a natural shock absorber during the crisis period. Lula's policy was therefore to allow the currency to float, with its value driven by capital flows that in turn were determined by the interest rate (Hiroi, 2009: 13–14). The interest rate was the prime monetary variable that was used to control inflation with a low-inflation regime representing one of the cornerstone policies of the Lula regime (see Chapter 6). As capital flows dried up in 2009, the currency depreciated in response, which helped investment to continue to flow – albeit at reduced levels – into the country thus helping keep the downturn relatively subdued. As the economy began to recover once again in 2010 the currency began to appreciate once more as capital flows returned to Brazil in the context of low interest rates in the developed countries.

Across much of the rest of Latin America similar dynamics can be seen (*The Economist*, 11 September 2010: 3). Ricardo Lagos and Michelle Bachelet's administrations in Chile pushed for the currency to devalue through arguing against the monetarist approach of Chile's central bankers, who were bent on increasing interest rates to contain inflation (Heidrich and Tussie, 2009: 47). Tabaré Vázquez in Uruguay stimulated strong flows of foreign capital into Montevideo through freeing up the capital account and allowing the currency to float – the effect of which was to lead to appreciation in the first part of the decade but, as in the other examples, allowed depreciation to occur in the face of a reversal in these flows, which helped to stabilise the Uruguayan economy in the face of the effects of the global crisis in 2009 (Heidrich and Tussie, 2009: 47).

These exchange rate policies stand in contrast to those of the 1990s, where many economies across the continent relied on some form of exchange rate anchor. While many of these policies were successful in ending the history of chronic high inflation, they showed, nonetheless, that local currency appreciation as a result of favourable differentials between domestic and foreign prices was causing balance-of-payments disequilibria (Arestis, Paula, and Ferrari-Filho, 2007a: 121). The appreciation of RERs increased public debt profiles, which deteriorated economic performance and fiscal balances. In addition, this left many Latin American countries vulnerable to speculative attacks and thus subjected them to currency crises. The currency crises in Mexico (1994), in Brazil (1998 and 2002), and in Argentina (2001–2) are examples of this dynamic process (Arestis, Paula, and Ferrari-Filho, 2007a: 121).

In addition to the floating of many exchange rate regimes across the continent the policies adopted also helped many of the countries in Latin America to accrue substantial foreign exchange reserves. As stated previously, Argentine reserves increased substantially to over

US$50 billion by 2010; in Brazil growth accelerated at high velocity and reserves reached US$252 billion by 2010. Across Latin America as a whole, reserves were US$180 billion by end of 2007. These reserves not only provided stability to domestic economies as they could be used to help stabilise currency fluctuations but they also sent a strong signal to international capital and currency markets, thus helping protect against speculative attacks. These factors were another aspect of the policies of the Developmental Regimes across the continent, strongly associated with currency regimes that were designed to stimulate development and economic growth.

The second core area of Developmental Regime policy in Argentina, Brazil, and Latin America that helped protect the continent against the most egregious aspects of the global financial crisis were monetary and fiscal policies (*The Economist*, 11 September 2010: 3). Furthermore, these policies were often complementary with the exchange rate policies outlined before. In Argentina, the economic growth that was stimulated as a result of the SCRER policy facilitated large increases in fiscal revenue, especially in foreign currency due to high growth in export sectors. Combined with a general policy of fiscal conservatism (see Chapter 4) these policies put the economy on a sound, sustainable fiscal path and helped to draw down or rationalise debt. For example, the total debt to GDP ratio was substantially decreased, and interest and maturity of much of the rest was lowered and extended (see Chapter 4). In addition, the conservatism of much of the decade paid dividends when the crisis hit as there was enough room for manoeuvre to implement counter-cyclical fiscal measures, and therefore increase spending in the face of crisis rather than cut government budgets as had so often been the case in the past, especially so in 2001–2 with such dramatic social consequences in terms of unemployment, poverty, and general disillusionment with the political system.

In Brazil Lula too adopted fiscally conservative policies (see Chapter 6). The institutionalisation of a policy of a significant primary surplus kept spending in check, although absolute spending was able to substantially increase due to the context of a growing economy. While total debt increased despite this fiscal conservatism, as a percentage of GDP it declined and the stock itself was rationalised. Therefore, maturity was extended, interest rates paid were reduced, and, most importantly, the level of foreign-denominated paper was substantially reduced. This served to reduce exchange rate risk associated with ballooning debt profiles after currency depreciation, and thus made Brazil's debt profile much more sustainable in the long run.

Similar trends can be seen across Latin America as a whole. In Chile, for example, low outstanding debt in the country at the start of the leftist administrations of Lagos and Bachelet meant that there was no need to enact a policy of debt reduction, but general fiscal conservatism meant that the leeway was there in the government accounts to adopt counter-cyclical fiscal measures when the crisis did hit the country in 2009. In Uruguay, careful management of the fiscal and trade accounts allowed for investment in public infrastructure to stimulate growth, reduce unemployment, and increase social services to help lower poverty levels. Once again, this gave the country headroom to enact fiscal measures in the face of crisis, and also meant that the country was well placed in terms of investment levels when the sudden stop and reversal of capital flows hit the region, dampening the impact on GDP. In Ecuador and Bolivia, government revenues have been significantly increased through nationalisation schemes of the hydrocarbon and mining sectors. This has helped facilitate an active role for state-sponsored programmes to correct historical marginalisation and inequality (Kenmore and Weeks, 2011: 268).

In summary, the characteristics and policies that made Argentina, Brazil, and Latin America in general resistant to the effects of the global financial crisis outlined in the previous section can be attributed directly to key planks of the Developmental Regimes. Currency regimes and associated monetary policy, as well as fiscal policies, all helped facilitate characteristics that meant the crisis came late to Latin America, when it did arrive it was relatively shallow, and the continent was able to emerge from a downturn quickly and strongly relative to other economies. The next section will look at how Latin America as a continent emerged from the crisis in respect to other parts of the world, which followed qualitatively different strategies that can be characterised under different theories of political economy. It will conclude that the Developmental Regime can be shown as a more robust method of capital accumulation due to its strength in the face of global downward pressures and ability to deliver strong growth despite an adverse international economic climate.

Post-crisis development strategy in global perspective

If an eye is cast across the world as a whole, it can be seen that other areas of the globe have not fared as well as Latin American in the face of the largest systemic crisis of capitalism since the Great Depression in the 1930s. Prevailing neoliberal policies are limiting European capabilities to weather the crises and jeopardising the welfare of its peoples, especially in the newly integrated countries of Eastern Europe (de la Barra, 2010: 642). In the UK growth can be described as anaemic at best, and this is before the full effects of severe fiscal retrenchment due to take place in April 2011. The PIG countries have all required bailout from the European Union to keep their economies afloat and the spectre of default hangs in the air. Spain is teetering on the brink, and now even Italy is in the firing line. Across the Atlantic the US economy is moribund. A longer fiscal stimulus period has helped growth reach levels higher than that seen in the UK, but the impact on the budget deficit and outstanding debt stock has serious long-term consequences for both the country and the global economy given the central position of the US in the global economy.

As important has been the rise of privately held consumer debt. In the US this peaked at $2.6 trillion in July 2008, with total household debt approaching 100 per cent of GDP in 2007. Nor was the US alone. In Britain household debt rose from 105 per cent of disposable income in 2000 to 160 per cent in 2008, and in Spain the ratio rose from 69 per cent to 130 per cent over the same period (*The Economist*, 26 June 2010: 7). While consumption was held up temporarily through stimulus spending, the long-term impact is still unknown. As a whole, tax and budget reductions, labour flexibility, high credit costs, and fiscal deficit curtailment (ex-US for the moment) bring increased unemployment, worsening labour conditions, squeezes on real income levels, and sluggish growth; in short, the recovery across Europe and the US has been long and hard and many economies are not out of the woods yet (*The Economist*, 18 September 2010, 30 April 2011, 18 June 2011). One notable exception to this general trend has been Germany. Although affected by the initial financial crisis due to contagion of its banking system as a result of exposure to less-well performing EU countries (especially in Eastern Europe), it was able to swiftly recover and in 2011 is witnessing strong GDP growth driven by its vibrant export sector. However, Germany represents the exception rather than the rule.

While much of the developed world's response to the first wave of the crisis was Keynesian in terms of fiscal policy, the medium-term post-crisis response has been an overwhelming return to neoliberalism. Hugely expensive bank bailouts across the ACCs, the pumping of money into the automobile industry in the US, and general counter-cyclical fiscal pump priming in the general economy (coordinated at the G20 level) can be seen as classic planks of Keynesian policy in the face of economic crisis. Whether such policies staved off an even greater disaster is debatable, and can never be known, but what these policies did achieve was a legacy of severe fiscal deficit and devastated developed world balance sheets (*The Economist*, 20 June 2010). The uniform response has been fiscal discipline and retrenchment along classic neoliberal lines. Although this has yet to take place in the US, the contemporary political agenda is dominated by the issue of the deficit and the 2010 midterms saw the election of a number of fiscal hawks and the rise of the 'Tea Party' movement whose main focus was deficit reduction in Federal government.

Neoliberal fiscal retrenchment has had a predictable impact on growth in many countries (*The Economist*, 9 October 2010). Greece is still mired in a deep recession; Ireland is undergoing extremely painful reforms and the Celtic miracle has turned out to be a paper tiger; Portugal has slipped back into recession in 2011; UK growth flatlined in Q4 2010 and Q1 2011 and this is before fiscal contraction has even taken hold; Spain has a general unemployment level of over 20 per cent (a figure that is significantly higher in the 18–24 age bracket) and is next in line for the markets as a target for speculative attack – will the PIG acronym become PIGS (or indeed PIIGS given the current worries over Italy)?

In summary, Keynesianism best characterises much of the crisis strategy that took place in the developed world, and a return to neoliberalism has been the response of many in the face of overwhelming budget deficits and debt-GDP ratios that resulted. Many countries forgot that Keynesianism wasn't just about spending when times are bad; it was also about saving when times were good. Failure to do this meant that the fiscal outlays necessary to rescue the system from collapse destroyed the balance sheets of many developed countries (*The Economist*, 26 June 2010). This has resulted in a return to neoliberalism and fiscal retrenchment. In the UK a conservative-led coalition has put spending cuts at the centre of its agenda. In the US, the Tea Party movement has called for major fiscal retrenchment, and through its gains in the 2010 midterm elections has placed this concept firmly onto the agenda. In essence, much of the developed world has become embroiled in a highly charged debate over the proper size and role of the state in the economy (Kingstone, 2011: 2). This chapter has argued that this neoliberal/Keynesian policy nexus in response to the crisis and post-crisis scenarios has produced inferior results when compared to the Latin American experience of the same events – an experience that was met with the tools of the Developmental Regime, rather than the neoliberal or Keynesian regime.

Conclusions: The efficacy of the Developmental Regime in comparative perspective

This state of affairs in the developed world is in contrast to the Latin American experience. Indeed, the countries better positioned to withstand the global crisis are those with regulated economies and fewer links to the US economy. Combined with the growing awareness that poverty and exclusion levels in Latin America prove that hegemonic alliance with the US has not been favourable, there has been a growing recognition that a new development model that is totally different from neoliberal capitalism is needed. The rise of the pink tide has meant that Latin America has been at the forefront of resistance to neoliberalism, but the global financial crisis posed a new challenge: the need to confront capitalism and imperialism. This book has shown that Latin America is once again leading the way in this challenge, with the Developmental Regimes across the continent showing more dynamism in the face of the global financial crisis than the developed world.

As previous sections have shown, a relatively light downturn, followed by swift and strong recovery characterised the region. Such a trajectory can be attributed to the policies that have broadly characterised the pink tide in Latin America, and has examined this claim in detail with regard to Argentina and Brazil. Furthermore, the policies implemented can collectively be characterised within a Developmental Regime framework. Not just developmentalist in terms of economic policy but also encompassing renegotiation of the social contract in the affected states, a renegotiation that is different for each country concerned due to the specific and idiosyncratic ways in which politics manifests itself across political communities. The Developmental Regime concept is flexible enough to accommodate such differences, while at the same time maintaining theoretical rigour so as to add value in so much as the analysis facilitates a holistic understanding of the patterns of production, consumption, and distribution across twenty-first century Latin America.

Latin America was not the only continent to fare well in the face of the global financial crisis; Asia especially performed very well and in aggregate outperformed Latin America in terms of GDP growth, growing 5.5 per cent in 2009 (IMF, 2010) when much of the rest of the world was mired in torpid growth or in outright recession. However, these aggregate figures are dominated by the success of China, and must therefore be treated with some caution as they mask subregional trends. However, Asia is not the subject of this book, although its success in post-crisis economic recovery and development certainly merits a future research agenda. Can the concept of Developmental Regime be applied to a country or countries in this region? One of the tasks of this book has been to help develop and further construct the Developmental Regime concept so that it can be transposed across time and space. Therefore, a further measure of success would be complementary research agendas that seek to do such an exercise in the context of countries such as China, those in South East Asia such as Malaysia, and also Pacific Asia.

The final chapter of this book will now seek to examine the impact of these conclusions in terms of future trajectories. A full summary of the arguments presented throughout the book will determine if the study has been successful in terms of what it aimed to achieve as stated in the introduction. This will then be followed by a consideration of the limitations of any conclusions that have been drawn during such an analysis. The chapter will finish with an investigation into the sustainability of Developmental Regimes in Latin America, thus considering the prospect of the rise of a Latin American century, or, if the Developmental Regime approach can be used to help determine the question 'who will be next'?

9
Conclusion: Continuity and Change in Post-Crisis Political Economy – The Rise of Latin America?

The paths that countries tread on the road to development are different. Indeed, countries should not necessarily follow one path, as development is not a universal end point to be achieved via a linear model as envisioned by the modernisation school. Rather, development is an historical change process, and studies into its dynamics should be mapped around this understanding. However, while the paths of individual countries are different en route to idiosyncratic ends, broad trends can still be discerned. This book has demonstrated what these broad trends are in the context of contemporary Latin America and its response to both domestic crises and the global financial crisis. Furthermore, it has suggested that the concept of a Developmental Regime helps to best capture these trends on a theoretical level, thus giving the academic hermeneutical devices by which greater analytical clarity can be gained and future research agendas can be constructed.

Cardoso (2008) claims that Latin American countries opt to follow different paths, that the choice of paths has consequences, and that the politically responsible choice in the current context is to opt for the path of 'globalised social democracy' over the 'anti-globalisation' alternative. This study agrees with the first two points, but not with the third. It has shown that alternative paths exists to Cardoso's dichotomous categories and, furthermore, that these paths has been proved to be successful. While the paths are different, common trends can be discerned and these trends can be captured through the application of Developmental Regime analysis. This analysis looks at models of capital accumulation from three levels: state–market, state–society, and state–international. It suggests that broad principles such as industrial policy, macroeconomic stability, and the provision of a stable investment environment are essential characteristics of a developmentalist state–market relationship.

However, the way in which these policies manifest themselves are different across cases due to the different social contracts, or state–society relationships that are forged as the basis for the support of the political regimes that govern the state apparatus and institutions in any given country. Difference is also present through the national–international relationship. As Cardoso (2008: 5) articulates, countries have varying degrees of national autonomy, or state autonomy, vis-á-vis the global economy, and that the determinants of national autonomy include not only a country's resource endowment but also the nature of the social contract forged at the domestic level, which shapes alliances made between local classes and foreign interests, state structures, and the state's capacity to negotiate with external actors, as well as ideologies and strategies (Cardoso and Faletto, 1979: xvii). Therefore, while globalisation imposes 'structural limits' on developing countries, these countries still retain 'a certain margin of autonomy' (Cardoso, 2008: 25–6). In short, the international arena and domestic society constrain political choices but they do not fully determine them (Munck, 2009: 354).

The political economy of the pink tide

This book has examined detailed case studies of Néstor Kirchner's Argentina and Lula's Brazil. Under Kirchner, Argentina emerged from its devastating crisis of 2001–2 at a surprisingly brisk pace. This recovery was rooted in specific policies of Kirchner's administration, which were the function of a new form of social contract between the state and the people. Previous social contracts under Perón (1946–55) were based on the provision of economic rights and social inclusion, grounded in a form of developmentalism based on ISI. Under Menem (1989–99), the dismantling of social safety nets and the deregulation of the labour market ushered in a new era of state–society relations that can be characterised as neoliberal. The post-crisis administration of Kirchner saw a further redefinition of the social contract, containing important elements of not only both of these historical forms of political economy but also some characteristics unique to the history of Argentine political economy. Elements of populism and elements of neoliberalism were interwoven to create a form of *neodesarrollismo* (Grugel and Riggirozzi, 2007; Grugel, 2009). This relationships represent a 'bending and moulding' (Panizza, 2005: 15) of previous social contracts in Argentina, based on neoliberal social-safety nets and subsequent policies towards tackling poverty, segmented neo-corporatism, the genuine participation of business, and the construction of a consensus around the principles of nationalist/statist development.

Brazil under Lula can be seen as a regime based on the stimulation of economic growth through a stable macroeconomic environment. This in turn was complemented by its social policy, based partially on the control of inflation so as not to erode the real income of workers, and partly on the flagship CCT programme *Bolsa Familia*. Lula's political economy has therefore been grounded in a developmentalist bias. Low inflation through tight monetary policy and conservative fiscal policy, combined with an activist industrial policy (especially in his second term through programmes such as the PITCE, PDP and PACTI), were the platform for the pursuit of sustainable and stable economic growth. This developmentalism was supplemented by a desire to distribute the proceeds of growth so as to reduce poverty and inequality. The reduction of poverty was an important success in his administration, and inequality has come down – albeit marginally. Lula therefore, like Kirchner, also sought to redefine the social contract. Social groups and class fractions different from those in Argentina formed the basis of that contract, thus leading to different policies. However, while the domestic politics translated into different alliances, mediated through institutions, the broad principles that can be discerned can be understood as a developmentalist form of political economy.

In the wider context of Latin America, there were (and still are) a number of regimes that came to power in the same timeframe as Kirchner and Lula with similar agendas. From Hugo Chávez in Venezuela and Evo Morales of Bolivia, to Tabaré Vazquez in Uruguay, Lula in Brazil and Bachelet in Chile, Latin America has experienced the rise of a pink tide (Lievesley and Ludlam, 2009b). Such a rise prompted Castañeda (2006) to group these regimes into two distinct camps: the 'good left' and the 'bad left'. This distinction, however, represents a crude dichotomy between a good reformist left and a bad populist left that has dominated English language treatments of this subject. By placing Kirchner's Argentina into the populist bad left Castañeda reduces the explanation of the social contract in Argentina during these years as simply an expression of traditional Peronist populism. By placing Lula's Brazil into the 'good left' he also reduces *Lulismo* to an expression of a form of social democracy, or SMC. This is not sufficiently sensitive to the important differences between both Kirchner's particular brand of Peronism and those of the past in Argentina, and Lula's blend of continuity and change from the previous neoliberal administration of Cardoso. This is also true of other so-called contemporary 'bad left' or 'good left' regimes in Latin America, as their 'expressions of resistance to market liberalisation' (Roberts, 2007: 14) are also inadequately captured by the simple models of social democracy or populism.

The pink tide and the Developmental Regime

The multiple paths with common threads that this situation facilitates in the context of twenty-first century Latin America can best be captured within a Developmental Regime framework. The pink tide that has swept the Latin American continent cannot be interpreted through traditional models of political economy. Rather, the specific set of state–market, state–society, and national–international relationships present common threads outside of neoliberalism and SMC. While Developmental State theory offers closer synergies, especially in the state–market relationship, the pink tide offers enough points of departure to suggest that this model of political economy is also inadequate. Instead, the Developmental Regime is able to capture these relationships more accurately, and therefore offers analytical clarity when capturing the salient common threads of the pink tide. The public policy profiles of states across the Latin American continent offer benefits to a range of class fractions which form the basis of the social contract in Latin American states. Thus, it is objective economic consequences of policy and reform that matter for the subsequent popularity of a regime (Baker, 2009: 15). These benefits share a common thread of sustainable economic growth through developmentalist principles but represent different paths to this goal dependent upon the idiosyncrasies of individual countries socio-economic alliances and institutions. Thus, different countries in Latin America have experimented to varying degrees with pro-market reforms versus pro-state reforms – with the public's propensities to accept them partially a function of the benefits that these policies deliver, and partially on elitist discourse and the ability to dominate the policy agenda (Baker, 2009: 25). These idiosyncrasies are further manifested in the different ways that Latin American states intersect with global capital. Such developmentalist goals form the basis of a legitimate ideology that has defined the central issue in Latin American politics: equitable growth characterised by stability and pragmatism.

The key to understanding these differences in policy therefore lie in the role of institutions. As Boschi and Gaitán (2009: 11) suggest, '[p]olitical and institutional factors shaping production regimes generally make a difference in terms of economic performance'. Indeed, institutions also offer the key to development. It is not simply a question of states versus markets; policies matter but the institutional framework in which policies are designed, implemented, and enforced matter more (Kingstone, 2011: 149). In other words, it is not the amount of state involvement in the market per se, rather the character and nature of that involvement, which is fostered and shaped by institutions. Therefore, Kirchner in Argentina represented a more homogenous government, structured on the hegemonic position of the PJ in a post-crisis context. On the other hand, Lula's coalition government was fragmented and made up of parties both on the right and left of the ideological spectrum. This made the task of defining and obtaining support for a long-term development project more difficult, though nevertheless the government managed some success in this area. Part of this success has been through redefining key institutions. In Brazil this involved, for example, the introduction of the development council, which helped articulate a new corporatist relationship, or the institutionalisation of a primary fiscal surplus thus ensuring fiscal responsibility and aiding the low-inflation policy. Argentina also witnessed an institutionalisation of a new corporatist relationship, and also in other areas such as his SCRER. This exchange rate policy was institutionalised through the role of the central bank associated monetary and fiscal policies. Indeed, Willett (2007) suggests that although this kind of exchange rate regime is potentially prone to instability, such instability can be largely mitigated by appropriate and effective institutions. Nevertheless, the degree of institutionalisation has been relatively limited. This represents one of the key challenges for the longevity of this bold developmentalist project in Argentina, Brazil, and Latin America more widely, and will be discussed in more detail in following sections of this conclusion.

Post-crisis recovery in Developmental Regimes versus Neoliberal States

This book has shown that the recent global financial crisis had a more subdued impact on Latin America compared to previous regional and global crises. The relative robustness of Latin American economies can be traced to many of the policy changes that came from the institutionalisation of Developmental Regimes across the continent. Changes in the exchange rate regimes, coupled with different monetary and fiscal policies helped Latin American economies both reduce the impact of the crisis and emerge strongly from it at the end of 2009. Contemporary Argentina, Brazil, and other states throughout Latin America have resumed growth trajectories that were in place before the crisis of 2007–8, pointing to a promising post-crisis scenario. This stands in contrast to much of the developed world, with the UK struggling to emerge from anaemic growth, the US stalling under a heavy fiscal deficit, and the Eurozone reeling from continuing crises in peripheral (and some less peripheral) countries.

The post-crisis scenarios in Latin America look strong by comparison. The changes that helped facilitate this situation can be largely situated through examination of the internal changes in the political economy of individual states. Existing literature often focuses on external pressures for change in a post-crisis scenario, seeking to explain changes through examination of foreign economic and commercial power (Robertson, 2008a: 3). Robertson (2008b: 252) goes on to suggest that this can be too simplified a way of looking at this dynamic, and closer attention should be given to the changing external orientation of domestic economies, which can be characterised as increasingly favourable to domestic capital.

One way in which this has manifested is the theme of 'decoupling'. This is the thesis that due to changes in domestic policy, as well as changes in the external dynamics of the global economy, the fortunes of Latin American economies are no longer dependent upon the fortunes of the global economy more widely. The reason for this has been the fact that when compared to previous crises the disruption to domestic Latin American economies has been less severe. 'Phase I', as analysed in the previous chapter, can therefore be seen as evidence for this decoupling theory. Because Latin America diversified its markets and because its new Asian markets retained their resiliency longer, it appeared as if Latin America had escaped the severe downturns that characterised US and European economies. Furthermore, the subsequent recovery has been more robust than the economic recovery in large parts of the rest of the world (Jara, Moreno, and Tovar, 2009: 63). As Cox (2009: 146) analyses, 'Latin America did not experience the same declines in trade, stock markets, and currencies as other regions … While the subprime crisis roiled the economies of the industrialised world, the economic outlook for Latin America and the Caribbean was strong. Currencies were strengthening, the central banks continued to accumulate reserves, and levels of foreign direct investment were maintained while portfolio capital inflows rose.'

Increasing regional integration has also helped Latin America decouple from larger global markets. The plethora of regional projects from MERCOSUR, MILA, CAFTA, ALBA, and UNASUR has led to a regional integration movement that encourages the expansion, consolidation, and sustainability of emergent developmental processes (de la Barra, 2010: 651). As Ocampo (2009b) suggests regional markets offer a diversification opportunity as 'import substitutions' in the region as a whole rather than in countries individually. Therefore, regional integration, based on a growing affinity between a set of countries all betting on market economies, foreign investment, and trade with China to help achieve development, also offers a source of decoupling from wider international markets (*The Economist*, 9 April 2011).

This thesis was challenged from two main angles. The first concerns the role of China. Eva Paus (2009: 440) demonstrates that trade between Latin America and China has actually exacerbated the dilemma of the 'middle income trap' for many countries across the South American continent – where wages are too high to compete with low-wage countries in the production of labour-intensive commodities and productivity relatively too low to compete with more advanced countries in the production of higher-tech and skill-intensive products and services. Therefore, an influx of relatively high-tech Chinese imports has squeezed domestic producers, while much of Latin American exports to China have been in the form of primary and natural resources. Therefore, the qualitative nature of this supposed decoupling has brought into relief its relative efficacy. Although, Paus (2009: 445–7) also balances this assessment by suggesting how China also offers potential opportunities: first, China's proactive development strategy provides lessons on how to develop a domestic technological base;[1] second, using the income generated from these exports to fund such activities; and third, using Chinese FDI to help contribute to the regional integration that helps sustain and enhance the movement towards decoupling.

The second, more quantitative, challenge to decoupling theory concerns subsequent events. By mid-2008 commodity prices began to collapse and the decoupling theory melted away, represented by 'Phase II' of the crisis in Latin America as analysed in the previous chapter. Commodity prices were moving adversely for Latin America, reinforcing rather than offsetting the trend coming from the global slowdown and subsequent financial turmoil. This led Cordova and Selingson (2009: 674) to suggest that macroeconomic stabilisation in Latin America is still dependent upon how quickly recovery will occur in the ACCs. As Petras (2009: 138) suggests, Latin America cannot 'build capitalism on one continent'; indeed, the link between a fall in commodity prices and the fortunes of Latin American economies in the face of global crisis suggests that the real explanation for the Latin American 'oasis in the midst of crisis' (Cox, 2009: 146) was the boom in commodity prices. This is reinforced by the fact that when commodity prices recovered due to the recovery of demand in Asia (especially China) so did the economic fortunes of Latin America. This is represented by 'Phase III' of the crisis, as analysed in the previous chapter, which can be seen as a phase of 're-decoupling' (Llaudes, Salman, and Chivakul, 2010: 8).

This book has suggested that while commodity prices have certainly had a large role to play in the dynamics of Latin America's economic fortunes, reform under the Developmental Regimes across the continent have also had a role to play, and thus reduced the link between commodity prices and the fortunes of the continent. In other words, development in the region is still ongoing, but it is a process that is moving in positive directions. Therefore, in Argentina exchange rate policy has helped stimulate exports of a manufacturing origin, which represent an increasing component of total exports. While agriculture clearly represents the largest contributor to GDP, manufacturing has become the most dynamic sector in the economy. In Brazil directed industrial policy has had a similar effect. Across Latin America regional integration has helped unlock wider markets for domestic companies.

In summary, there has been a limited decoupling of Latin American economies from the wider fortunes of the global economy and the trajectory of global commodity prices. However, the limited nature of this decoupling should be stressed. Commodities continue to contribute the largest share of Latin American exports, and the lack of developed domestic markets as well as limited development of regional markets means that demand in other parts of the world represent an important contribution to growth in Latin American economies. This situation is changing, with regional projects proliferating, domestic markets developing (especially in Brazil) through infrastructure projects and industrial policy at the state level, and the increasingly important contribution of manufacturing to the export profile.

Petras (2009: 193) suggests that the 'reprimarisation' of Latin American economies in the 2003 to 2008 period accounts for its economic fortunes during the crisis. However, this book suggests that the strength of Latin America's recovery from the global financial crisis can therefore be traced to domestic policy and subsequent ways in which the domestic economies intersect with the wider global economy. This has served to produce a more robust recovery than many parts of the developed world, which have followed neoliberal or SMC responses to the crisis in contrast to Latin America's Developmental Regime approach. This leads to a conclusion that a Developmental Regime model represents a superior choice of political economy for Latin America than any previous models – namely neoliberalism or dependency and populism.

This picture is not uniformly superior, with *The Economist* pointing to three areas of concern for Latin America in the future. These are productivity, income distribution, and widespread crime and violence (*The Economist*, 11 September 2010: 4). All of the makeshift mechanisms that the poor invest for survival and interacting, both with each other and with the formal sector, are costly in and of themselves and constitute a drag on productivity (Kingstone, 2011: 146). This is a problem that could be solved through fostering better institutions, thus reducing the costs of legality and enhancing productivity growth. Productivity growth in Latin America has been the slowest of any region in the world since 1960, with the largest contributory factor being the role of the informal economy. If Total Factor Productivity (TFP) in Latin America had grown at the same rate it did in the US since 1960, per capita income would be 54 per cent higher – or one-quarter of the US – rather than one-sixth as it typically is today (Lora and Pagés, 2011: 16). Recent moves in Brazil and Argentina, for example, have sought to overcome this problem, with decent productivity growth in Argentina in particular (see Chapter 4) but there is still a long way to go. Much of the reason for this slow growth in productivity can be traced to the size and scope of the informal sector in economies across the continent. Previous chapters in Part II have demonstrated that income distribution has also been improving, although Latin America remains the most unequal region anywhere, with Brazil being one of the most unequal countries in the world. Finally, widespread crime and violence have long been an issue in Latin America, much of it perpetrated by organised drug gangs. This can become a drag on development and deter investment, factors that only increase in likelihood if the problem is not addressed (*The Economist*, 11 September 2010: 15).

The trajectory that Latin America is on has facilitated greater economic robustness in the face of crisis internationally and has generated impressive growth records across the past ten years: both in contrast to history. The application of a Developmental Regime model provides interesting insights to the region's political economy, and also offers potentially interesting insights into predicting the future of the developing world. Indeed, the specific nature of state intervention as the basis for breaking with long-prevailing negative complementarities stemming from endemic structural inequalities has been overlooked by many traditional theories of political economy. Traditional varieties of capitalism literature provide an analysis of the transformation of the capitalist system based on developed countries' point of view. In this vein, the state is treated as an epiphenomenon in terms of financing, research and development, labour force training and others. The capacities of peripheral and semi-peripheral states to meet social demands that precede the generation of such complementarities, as well as their capacity to face adverse conditions in the international system, would represent a turning point regarding future trends (Boschi and Gaitán, 2009: 25).

Who next? BRIC(S), VISTA, N-11, EMNCs, and the BCG emerging 100

One of the more fashionable exercises of the contemporary period has been to try and predict the next country or countries that will break through the glass ceiling and attain developed status. In this vein a number of agencies, corporations, and individuals have all proposed who they believe will be next, with by far the most popular acronym being that of the so-called BRIC (Brazil, Russia, India, and China) countries.[2] This phrase was coined in 2003 by Goldman Sachs (Wilson and Purushothaman, 2003), who suggested that in less than 40 years these BRIC countries would catch up with the ACCs of the United States, Japan, UK, France, Italy, and Germany, thus becoming the world's new engine of growth and demand in the context of declining populations and stagnating growth in the contemporary ACCs.

The grouping of these countries does not at first glance seem an obvious choice. As Armijo (2007) analyses, they are very different countries across a range of criteria, ranging from nature of domestic political systems to culture, and to nature of their economies. Even their choice as the next developed economies poised to challenge the hegemony of the United States in particular and the European–US axis in general can be brought into question. The growth record of these four countries varies widely, China and Russia in particular are heavily trade-dependent, and militarily none come even close to challenging the hegemony of the US. The core argument of Wilson and Purushothaman seems to be that the significance of the BRICs can be seen in their relative size, and the implicit assumption that large size implies dynamism (Armijo, 2007: 12). Indeed, why is Nigeria (a very large and fastest growing nation in the world in terms of population) not included? What about Mexico? However, the category begins to make more sense if one applies a more international *political* economy framework, and through an institutionalist lens one can discern that large size confers ability to rise as a major military power, or exert soft power (Sotero and Armijo, 2007) within the international system. The category of BRIC is therefore useful in providing insight into the implications that this set of countries holds for the larger system within which they are embedded, rather than necessarily as an accurate predictor for where the next set of ACCs will rise (Armijo, 2007: 38).

Other acronyms have been coined that, while less popular, nevertheless have added to the debate over the issue of who is next. VISTA[3] or the N-11[4] are two popular analytical groups, while others concentrate on the rise of Emerging Multi-National Corporations (EMNCs) such as Goldstein (2007) or BCG's '100 New Global Challengers'.[5] While many of these acronyms may capture the imagination of the investment markets, there is often a dominance of rhetoric over analytical clarity. One issue that this book raises as a result of the application of a Developmental Regime approach is this question of who will be next and whether the theoretical framework outlined and applied in this volume provides for some much-needed conceptual enhancement of the speculation in this area. Accurate prediction is, of course, several (methodological) bridges too far. As the nineteenth-century Danish philosopher Soren Kierkegaard once observed, 'we live forwards but understand backwards'. Not only does the full complexity of the global political economy defy scientific explanation, but also, attempts to gaze into the future can only in part be informed by an analysis of present processes.

Nevertheless, the Developmental Regime approach does offer some interesting insights. The generally positive tenor of this book with regard to the future prospects of Latin America as a continent suggests that the future is bright. Many caveats must be added to this statement, which have been elaborated throughout the volume. Furthermore, the sustainability of the current path can also be brought into question and will be the topic of the next section. However, this book has attempted to show that the contemporary path of Latin American political economy is facilitating the conditions necessary for Latin America to emerge as an important player in the global economy, facilitating a shift in its traditional role in the global division of labour. The policies of the pink tide governments have set into motion strong, balanced growth with stable macroeconomic fundamentals. Interpreted through a Developmental Regime lens the possibility is opened for applying the same framework to other parts of the world to help determine if other countries or regions are on the same path as Latin America and could therefore form part of the next wave of development. This is a task for future research and such an agenda will be outlined in the final section of this chapter.

Sustainability of Latin American Developmental Regimes

One of the main issues that must be addressed in order to justify labelling Latin America as potentially being at the forefront of the next wave of development is that of sustainability. A successful Developmental Regime must operate over more than one administration (i.e. a regime that facilitates sustained development in the context of forging a stable and accepted set of relationships between the state and society, while accommodating changing international conditions). The main method by which this is achieved is the institutionalisation of the set of relationships (defined through analysis of state–market, state–society, and national–international dichotomies) that facilitated the Developmental Regime in the first place. This is a conclusion shared by the Inter-American Development Bank (IDB, 2006) in their Annual Report, which suggests that good policy ultimately rests on the capacity of the system to facilitate 'inter-temporal' cooperation. Indeed, well-functioning institutions are the *sine qua non* of democracy and market economies (Kingstone, 2011: 130).

The institutionalisation of the Developmental Regimes that form the pink tide in Latin America has been patchy at best. In Argentina, the expanded role of the government in directing the economy that existed during Néstor Kirchner's regime relied very much on Néstor Kirchner himself, through his top-down and centralised decision-making processes. In instituting a strategy for economic growth based on selective protectionism and targeted state intervention and with the state taking on responsibility for that growth, Kirchner served to introduce a new version of the state–market relationship in Argentina 2003–7. This new state–market relationship must be founded on institutions rather than individuals in order to facilitate the continuation of this new set of relationships.

Néstor Kirchner's *Kirchnerismo* has also precipitated a new relationship between the state and society than that which had existed under previous forms of political economy in Argentina, a new relationship that must also be institutionalised. Social rights and access to welfare remain associated with employment, as has been the case in Argentina's Peronist past. However, due to the changing rules of the game (the result of neoliberal globalisation, *Menemismo*, and *El Argentinazo*), employment was no longer guaranteed in the formal sector. Furthermore, social inclusion was not prioritised by Néstor Kirchner's regime, reflected in the patch-work quilt of anti-poverty initiatives. Instead, welfare entitlement and inclusion within the national social pact occurred through the (formal) job creation that economic expansion facilitated – economic expansion driven by Kirchner's macroeconomic policies of fiscal discipline and an SCRER. Because these policies were driven by Kirchner himself, once again individuals rather than institutions were the driving force behind the strategy/goals. In order for these ideas to persist in Argentina, a degree of institutionalisation of *Kirchnerismo* and its policies needs to be manifested in both the Argentine government and Argentine society. This is especially true given that previous forms of state–society relation-ship in Argentina were manifested through systematic efforts to redirect the gains from growth to the working class. Therefore, institutionalisa-tion of this alternative conception of state–society relationship could be challenging given the high and persistent levels of poverty present in Argentina, poverty that will not necessarily be alleviated through economic growth and subsequent job creation as the poverty-stricken individuals do not possess the skills necessary to enter the market place, or because of the fact that the jobs have been created in the informal sector. In other words, a social pact based on formal employment could be shown to be inadequate given the high levels of informalisation present in twenty-first-century Argentina.

The failure of Néstor Kirchner to institutionalise a number of key aspects of his administration's Developmental Regime raises the sali-ence of this observation further. That Néstor Kirchner did not stand for re-election, instead endorsing his wife Cristina Fernández de Kirchner and thus facilitating her election on the crest of his popularity, was not totally expected. Given continued popular support there may be time to lay the groundwork for an institutionalisation of a *Kirchnerismo* regime. Furthermore, the fact that she (Cristina Kirchner) has by and large con-tinued his (Néstor Kirchner) policies presents an opportunity for this limitation to be further tested as Cristina will now be able to further institutionalise her husband's Developmental Regime.

Recent developments, however, perhaps suggest a less optimistic pre-diction. Contemporary Argentina is facing a number of structural chal-lenges, both in micro and macroeconomic terms. An appreciating RER vis-à-vis its major trading partners, persistent inflation, and investment levels too low to sustain the high growth of recent years are all issues which will require policy decisions. These decisions will require certain economic trade-offs. The Presidential election in October 2011 led to the re-election of Cristina, but how her government will deal with these challenges is so far unclear. Furthermore, the conjectural factors faced by the Cristina Fernández de Kirchner Presidency have been less favourable than that of the previous term of her husband. She has had to deal with serious issues such as a farmers' strike, negotiations with the Paris Club of creditors, continuing problems with inflation, falling international commodity prices, a declining fiscal surplus, and a turbulent international economy characterised by massive systemic failure in the banking sectors of OECD countries that prompted the nationalisation of the pension system in late 2008, and loss of an absolute majority in the Senate after the 2009 midterm elections. Furthermore, in November 2010 Néstor Kirchner died of a heart attack at the age of 60, casting into doubt the sustainability of the whole *Kirchnerismo* project. A number of challenges have therefore presented themselves to Cristina Kirchner, challenges that must be overcome in order to perpetuate *Kirchnerismo* in Argentina.

In Brazil there is a similar story. The challenge for Brazil in the post-crisis world is how to manage its newfound abundance effectively: ensuring greater state efficiency, managing revenues from commodity exports so that if global prices fall social programmes can be maintained, improving education and infrastructure to foster lasting productivity gains, and maintaining the macroeconomic stability that has been so vital to Brazil's development under Lula. Can all of this be achieved by the new President Dilma Rousseff? While elements of *Lulismo* have been institutionalised, there is still much scope for a new president to change the model and thus shape the developmental trajectory of Brazil. The creation of various institutions that mediate between the state, business associations, and trade unions has facilitated a form of macro neocorporatism that not only generates better policy but sees the process as an end in itself (see Chapter 7). In addition, *Bolsa Familia* is seen across a wide spectrum of literature to have been a success as a result of strong institutions guiding its implementation and bypassing traditional clientelistic structures (Kingstone, 2011: 133).

The fact that Rousseff was Lula's hand-picked successor suggests that she will continue the Lula model, and indeed she has said as much. Her actions also imply this: on 16 February 2011 she oversaw a modest increase in the minimum wage (from 510 reals a month to 545 reals), against the wishes of trade unionists, opposition politicians, and even some members of her own coalition. This parsimony was due to the impact on public-sector wages and pensions, which are linked to the minimum wage, and the subsequent effect this would have on the federal fiscal accounts (*The Economist*, 19 February 2011). In addition, rising inflation and continued loose fiscal policy in the wake of the global financial crisis are potentially facilitating an overheating economy (*The Economist*, 4 June 2011).

These examples suggest that the trajectory of Brazil and Argentina, as well as Latin America more widely, in terms of institutions is positive. Indeed, Latin America's political institutions 'probably get less credit than they deserve for functioning at least moderately well in the face of serious economic challenges and complex, fundamental policy reforms' (Kingstone, 2011: 143). Nevertheless, as with Argentina, if the Developmental Regime instilled in Brazil by Lula, and thus far seemingly continued by Rousseff, is to become a stable, long-term development strategy it must be institutionalised to the extent that it becomes the natural model of capital accumulation in Brazil for the future. While Lula certainly began this, such as the legal structure surrounding the level of primary balance on the federal accounts, or the 'development council' arrangements constructed with peak level trade union and business groups, many areas must be further brought into the mainstream for continuity to become the norm. This is a task that must be addressed by Rousseff if the Developmental Regime in Brazil is to become a multi-generational phenomenon, thus transforming the Brazilian economy into one of the drivers of the global economy.

A future research agenda

Two linked research agendas present themselves as a result of the analysis in this book. The first is concerning the next wave of presidents in Latin America. Therefore, research into the nature of Cristina Kirchner's government in Argentina and Dilma Rousseff's in Brazil will be able to further explore the potential limitations outlined in the previous section – thus facilitating a greater understanding of the long-term potential of the Developmental Regimes in those countries. Similar exercises must also be conducted for other countries that have formed part of the pink tide. Will the developmentalist project be allowed to continue, or will there be a resurgence of the right?

There are also a number of further research opportunities that present themselves, designed to test the robustness of the Developmental Regime approach. Can this model of capital accumulation help interpret other economies outside of the Latin American context? Can, for example, contemporary Malaysia be understood within this Developmental Regime framework, and if so what are the implications for Malaysia in terms of being part of the next wave of emerging markets that will break through into developed country status? This research will not only enrich the studies of the political economy of these countries and regions, but also, will help develop a model for determining future growth trajectories and thus predicting future patterns of global development. However, these are tasks for other books and publications.

Notes

1 Introduction: The Political Economy of Development and Crisis

1. South of the Tropic of Capricorn.

2 The Rise of Developmentalism in Latin America: Beyond the Washington Consensus?

1. See CEPAL (1990) Changing Production Patterns with Social Equity (Santiago, UN).

3 From Developmental States to Developmental Regimes: Lessons from Asia for Contemporary Latin America

1. Neoclassical economics broadly functions around three core assumptions: individuals have rational preferences among outcomes that can be identified and associated with a value; individuals maximise utility and firms maximise profits; people act independently on the basis of perfect information.
2. This section draws from Wylde, C. (forthcoming) 'The Developmental State is Dead, Long Live the Developmental Regime! Interpreting Néstor Kirchner's Argentina, 2003–2007, *Journal of International Relations and Development*.

4 The Economic Policies of Néstor Kirchner's Argentina 2003–7

Elements of this chapter draw from Wylde, C. (2012) 'Continuidad o cambio?: Política económica argentina posterior a la crisis y el gobierno de Néstor Kirchner, 2003–2007', *Íconos: Revista de Ciencias Sociales*, Vol. 43, May.

1. The Spanish word *corralito* is the diminutive form of *corral*, which means 'corral, animal pen, enclosure'; the diminutive is used in the sense of 'small enclosure' and also 'a child's playpen'. This expressive name alludes to the restrictions imposed by the measure.

5 Argentina, *Kirchnerismo*, and *Neodesarrollismo*: Argentine Development under Néstor Kirchner, 2003–7

1. This section draws from Wylde, C. (2011) 'State, Society, and Markets in Argentina: The Political Economy of *Neodesarrollismo* under Néstor Kirchner, 2003–2007', *Bulletin of Latin American Research*, 30(4), 436–52.

2. The dispute that Argentina has with Uruguay over the construction of paper mills on the Rio de la Plata.
3. Interview with Anonymous, 2007.
4. This section draws from Wylde, C. (forthcoming) 'The Developmental State is Dead, Long Live the Developmental Regime! Interpreting Néstor Kirchner's Argentina, 2003–2007', *Journal of International Relations and Development*.
5. See Wylde, C. (2011) 'State, Society, and Markets in Argentina: The Political Economy of *Neodesarrollismo* under Néstor Kirchner, 2003–2007', *Bulletin of Latin American Research*, 30(4), 436–52.

9   Conclusion: Continuity and Change in Post-Crisis Political Economy – The Rise of Latin America?

1. A lesson that can be drawn from the East Asian development experience more broadly (see Hira, 2007).
2. In April 2011 the BRIC countries added South Africa to their club, thus extending the acronym to BRICS.
3. Vietnam, Indonesia, South Africa, Turkey, and Argentina.
4. A second Goldman Sach's creation, which is the next 11 countries other than the BRICs who have the highest potential of becoming the world's largest economies in the twenty-first century. They are South Korea, Mexico, Turkey, Philippines, Egypt, Indonesia, Iran, Nigeria, Pakistan, Vietnam, and Bangladesh.
5. Boston Consulting Group's (BCG) publication titled *The 2008 BCG 100 New Global Challengers*.

References

Adrogué, R., Cerisola, M., and Gelos, G. (2010) 'Brazil's Long-term Growth Performance: Trying to Explain the Puzzle', *Journal of Economic Studies*, 37(4), 356–76.

Almeida, M. H. T. (2005) 'The Social Policies of Lula's Administration', *Novos Estudias*, CEBRAP, Vol. 1.

Almeida, M. H. T. (no year) 'From Cardoso to Lula: The Politics and Policies of Reform in Democratic Brazil', Unpublished paper.

Altmann, J. (1981) 'Definitiveness and Operationality of Disassociation', *Intereconomics*, 16(4), 166–70.

Amann, E. (2005) 'Structural Reforms and Economic Growth in Brazil', *World Economics*, 6(4), 149–69.

Amsden, A. H. (1989) *Asia's Next Giant: South Korea and Late Industrialisation* (New York: Oxford University Press).

Arditi, B. (2008) 'Arguments about the Left Turns in Latin America', *Latin America Research Review*, 43(3), 59–81.

Arestis, P., Paula, L. F., and Ferrari-Filho, F. (2007a) 'Inflation Targeting in Emerging Countries: The Case of Brazil', in P. Arestis and A. Saad-Filho (eds) *Political Economy of Brazil: Recent Economic Performance*, 116–40 (Basingstoke: Palgrave Macmillan).

Arestis, P., Paula, L. F., and Ferrari-Filho, F. (2007b) 'Assessing the Economic Policies of President Lula da Silva in Brazil: Has Fear Defeated Hope?' in P. Arestis and A. Saad-Filho (eds) *Political Economy of Brazil: Recent Economic Performance*, 94–115 (Basingstoke: Palgrave Macmillan).

Armijo, L. E. (2007) 'The BRICs Countries (Brazil, Russia, India, and China) as Analytical Category: Mirage or Insight?' *Asian Perspective*, 31(4), 7–42.

Azpiazu, D. and Schorr, M. (2010) 'La industria Argentina en la postconvertibilidad: reactivacióm y legados del neoliberalismo', *Problemas del Desarrollo*, 41(161), 111–39.

Baker, A. (2009) *The Market and the Masses in Latin America: Policy Reform and Consumption in Liberalising Economies* (Cambridge: Cambridge University Press).

Barrientos, A. and Santibáñez, C. (2009) 'New Forms of Social Assistance and the Evolution of Social Protection in Latin America', *Journal of Latin American Studies*, 41(1), 1–26.

Baruj, G. and Porta, F. (2005) *Politicas de Competitividad en la Argentina y su Impacto Sobre la Profundizacion del Mercosur* (Santiago de Chile: CEPAL).

BCB (2010) 'Indicadores Fiscais', *Série Perguntas mais Freqüentes*, www.bcb.gov.br. (accessed on 12 Febuary 2011).

Beccaria, L., Esquivel, V., and Maurizio, R. (2007) *Crisis y recuperación. Efectos sobre el mercado de trabajo y la distribución del ingreso* (Los Polvorines Argentina: Universidad Nacional de General Sarmiento).

Berlin, I. (2002 [1969]) 'Two Concepts of Liberty', in H. Hardy (ed.) *Liberty*, 166–217 (Oxford: Oxford University Press).

Bezchinsky, G., Dinenzon, M., Giussani, L., Caino, O., López, B., and Amiel, S. (2007) *Inversion extranjera directa en la Argentina. Crisis, reestructuración y nuevas tendencias después de la convertibilidad* (Chile: CEPAL).

Black, J. (2002) *Dictionary of Economics* (Oxford: Oxford University Press).

Blanksten, G. I. (1969) *Perón's Argentina* (New York: Russell and Russell).

Boito, Jr, A. (1994) 'The State and Trade Unionism in Brazil', *Latin American Perspectives*, 21(1), 7–23.

Boschi, R. and Gaitán, F. (2009) 'Politics and Development: Lessons from Latin America', *Brazilian Political Science Review*, 3(2), 11–29.

Branford, S. (2009) 'Brazil: Has the Dream Ended?' in G. Lievesley and S. Ludlam (eds) *Reclaiming Latin America: Experiments in Radical Social Democracy*, 153–69 (London: Zed).

Brooker, P. (2000) *Non-Democratic Regimes: Theory, Government, and Politics*, (Basingstoke, MacMillan).

Buchanan, J. (1980) *Towards a Theory of Rent-Seeking Society* (Austin Texas: A and M University Press).

Bugna, F. C., and Porta, F. (2008) 'El crecimiento reciente de la industria Argentina. Nuevo regimen sin cambio estructural', *Realidad Económica*, (233), 63–105.

Burges, S. (2009) 'Brazil: Toward a (Neo)Liberal Democracy?' in J. Grugel and P. Riggirozzi (eds) *Governance after Neoliberalism in Latin America*, 195–216 (New York: Palgrave Macmillan).

Burton, G. (2009) 'Brazil: Third Ways in the Third World', in G. Lievesley and S. Ludlam (eds) *Reclaiming Latin America: Experiments in Radical Social Democracy*, 170–82 (London: Zed).

Bustillo, I. and Velloso, H. (2009) 'The Global Financial Crisis: What Happened and What's Next', *Estudios y Perspectivas*, No. 4, February.

Cardoso, F. H. (1973) 'Associated–Dependent Development: Theoretical and Practical Implications', in A. Stephen (ed.) *Authoritarian Brazil*, 142–78 (New Haven, CT: Yale University Press).

Cardoso, F. H. (1977) 'The Consumption of Dependency Theory in the United States', *Latin American Research Review*, 12(3), 7–24.

Cardoso, F. H. (2006) 'Izquierda y Populismo en América Latina', *El Commercio*, June 18.

Cardoso, F. H. (2008) 'New Paths: Globalisation in a Historical Perspective', *International Journal of Communication*, 2, 379–95.

Cardoso, F. H. and Faletto, E. (1979) *Dependency and Development in Latin America* (Berkeley, CA: University of California Press).

Carollo, D., Bregia, Z., and Brizuela, D. (2006) 'Ley de financiamiento educativo', *Poder Ejecutivo Nacional*.

Carrera, J. (2002) 'Hard Peg and Monetary Unions. Main Lessons from the Argentine Experience', *Anales de la Asociación Argentina de economía Política*, November.

Carrera, J. (2007) Professor of Economics UBA and Deputy Head of Economic Research BCRA, 13 March, Buenos Aires.

Catao, J. (2007) 'Why Real Exchange Rates?' *Finance and Development,* www.imf.org. (accessed on 10 February 2011).

Carvalho, F. J. C. (2007) 'Lula's Government in Brazil: A New Left or the Old Populism?' in P. Arestis and A. Saad-Filho (eds) *Political Economy of Brazil: Recent Economic Performance*, 24–41 (Basingstoke: Palgrave Macmillan).

Carvalho, F. J. C. and Ferrari-Filho, F. (2007) 'The Twilight of Lula's Government: Another Failed Experiment with Left Wing Administrations?' in P. Arestis and A. Saad-Filho (eds) *Political Economy of Brazil: Recent Economic Performance*, 55–72 (Basingstoke: Palgrave Macmillan).

Castañeda, J. G. (2006) 'Latin America's Left Turn', *Foreign Affairs*, May/June, 28–43.

CEPAL (2005) *Statistical Yearbook for Latin America and the Caribbean – 2005* (Santiago, Chile: United Nations).

CEPAL (2006) *Economic Survey of Latin America and the Caribbean* (Santiago, Chile: United Nations).

CEPAL (2007a) *Economic Survey of Latin America and the Caribbean* (Santiago, Chile: United Nations).

CEPAL (2007b) *Statistical Yearbook for Latin America and the Caribbean – 2007*.

CEPAL (2008) *Economic Survey of Latin America and the Caribbean: 2007–2008* (Santiago, Chile: United Nations).

CEPAL, (2010) *Changing Production Patterns with Social Equity*, (Santiago, UN).

CEPALSTAT (2011) CEPAL Statistical Database, www.cepal.org (accessed on 12 April 2011).

Cerny, P. G. (2000) 'Structuring the Political Arena: Public Goods, States, and Governance in a Globalising World', in R. Palan (ed.) *Global Political Economy: Contemporary Theories*, 21–35 (London: Routledge).

Cerny, P. G., Soeederberg, S., and Menz, G. (2005) *Internalising Globalisation: The Rise of Neoliberalism and the Decline of National Varieties of Capitalism* (Basingstoke: Palgrave Macmillan).

Chalmers, I. and Hadiz, E. (1997) *The Politics of Economic Development in Indonesia: Competing Perspectives* (London: Routledge).

Chang, H-J. (1993) 'The Political Economy of Industrial Policy in Korea', *Cambridge Journal of Economics*, 16(2), 131–57.

Chang, H-J. (1994) *The Political Economy of Industrial Policy* (London: Macmillan).

Chang, H-J. (1995) *The Role of the State in Economic Change* (Oxford: Clarendon Press).

Chang, H-J. (1999) 'The Economic Theory of the Developmental State', in M. Woo-Cummings (ed.) *The Developmental State*, 182–99 (New York: Cornell University Press).

Chang, H-J. (2003) *Globalisation, Economic Development, and the Role of the State* (London: Zed Books).

Chang, H-J. and Rowthorn, R. (2003) 'Theories of State Intervention in Historical Perspective', in H-J. Chang (ed.) *Globalisation, Economic Development, and the Role of the State* (London: Zed Books).

Chudnovsky, D. (2007) *The Elusive Quest for Growth in Argentina* (London: Routledge).

Clarke, S. (2005) 'The Neoliberal Theory of Society', in A. Saad-Filho and D. Johnson (eds) *Neoliberalism: A Critical Reader* (London: Pluto).

Clarin (13 April 2006) 'Papeleras: el experto que firmó el estudio del BM dice que la preocupación argentina es excesiva'.

Clarin (22 July 2007) 'Para el Gobierno, la crisis energética costará 12.000 millones de pesos'.

Colás, A. (2005) 'Neoliberalism, Globalisation, and International Relations', in A. Saad-Filho and D. Johnston (eds) *Neoliberalism: A Critical Reader*, 70–80 (London: Pluto).

Cordova, A. and Selingson, M. A. (2009) 'Economic Crisis and Democracy in Latin America', *PS: Political Science & Politics*, 42(4), 673–8.

Cornia, G. A., Jolly, R., and Stewart, F. (1987) 'An Overview of the Alternative Approach', in G. A. Cornia, R. Jolly, and F. Stewart (eds), *Adjustment with a Human Face, Vol. I: Protecting the Vulnerable and Promoting Growth* (Oxford: Clarendon Press).

Cortés, R. (2009) 'Social Policy in Latin America in the Post-Neoliberal Era', in J. Grugel and P. Riggirozzi (eds) *Governance after Neoliberalism in Latin America*, 49–67 (New York: Palgrave Macmillan).

Cox, P. (2009) 'Protecting Latin America's Gains through the Current Financial Crisis', *World Affairs*, 33(2), 145–52.

Cox, R. (1996) 'Social Forces, States, and World Orders: Beyond International Relations Theory', in R. W. Cox and T. J. Sinclair (eds) *Approaches to World Order*, 85–123 (Cambridge: Cambridge University Press).

Crawford, R. M. A. (1996) *Regime Theory in the Post-Cold War World* (Aldershot: Dartmouth Publishing Co. Ltd).

Cumings, B. (1987) 'The Origins and Development of the North-East Asian Economy: Industrial Sectors, Product Cycles, and Political Consequences' in F. C. Deyo (ed.) (1987) *The Political Economy of New Asian Industrialism*, 44–83 (Ithaca: Cornell University Press).

Cumings, B. (1999) 'Webs with No Spiders, Spiders with No Webs: The Genealogy of the Developmental State', in M. Woo-Cumings (ed.) *The Developmental State*, 61–92 (New York: Cornell University Press).

D'Amato, L., Garegnani, L., and Paladino, J. M. S. (2007) 'Inflation Persistence and Changes in the Monetary Regime: The Argentine Case', Paper given at the Euro Area Seminar in Buenos Aires at the Central Bank (BCRA), August 23–4.

Damill, M., Frenkel, R., and Maurizio, R. (2007) *Macroeconomic Policy Changes in Argentina at the Turn of the Century* (Buenos Aires: CEDES).

De la Barra, X. (2010) 'Sacrificing Neoliberalism to Save Capitalism: Latin America Resists and Offers Answers to Crises', *Critical Sociology*, 36(5), 635–66.

Denison, M. (2006) 'Why do Sultanistic Regimes Arise and Persist? A Study of Government in the Republic of Turkmenistan, 1992–2006', Unpublished thesis, University of Leeds.

Deyo, F. C. (1987) *The Political Economy of New Asian Industrialism* (Ithaca: Cornell University Press).

Dinerstein, A. (2002) 'The Battle of Buenos Aires', *Historical Materialism*, 10(4), 5–38.

Di Tella, G. (1983) *Argentina under Perón: 1973–1976: The Nation's Experience with a Labour-Based Government* (Hong Kong: Macmillan Press).

Di Tella, G. and Dornbusch, R. (1989) 'Introduction: The Political Economy of Argentina 1946–83', in G. Di Tella and R. Dornbusch (eds) *The Political Economy of Argentina: 1946–83*, 6–7 (Hampshire: Macmillan).

Doctor, M. (2007a) 'Boosting Investment and Growth: The Role of Social Pacts in the Brazilian Automotive Industry', *Oxford Development Studies*, 35(1), 105–30.

Doctor, M. (2007b) 'Lula's Development Council: Neo-Corporatism and Policy Reform in Brazil', *Latin American Perspectives*, 34(5), 131–48.

Doctor, M. and Paula, L. F. (2008) 'Brazil: Mixed Impact of Financial Crises on Manufacturing and Financial Sectors', in J. Robertson (ed.) *Power and Politics after Financial Crises: Rethinking Foreign Opportunism in Emerging Markets*, 144–67 (Basingstoke: Palgrave Macmillan).

Dornbusch, R. and Edwards, S. (1991) 'The Macroeconomics of Populism', in R. Dornbusch and S. Edwards (eds) *The Macroeconomics of Populism in Latin America*, 7–14 (London: University of Chicago Press).

Dos Santos, T. (1971) 'The Structure of Dependence', *American Economic Review*, 60(2), 231–36.

Dos Santos, V. F., Vieira, W. C., and Reis, B. S. (2009) 'Effects of Alternative Policies on Income Redistribution: Evidence from Brazil', *Development Policy Review*, 27(5), 601–16.

Draibe, S. and Riesco, M. (2007) 'Introduction', in M. Riesco (ed.) *Latin America: A New Developmental State Welfare Model in the Making?* 1–20 (Basingstoke: Palgrave Macmillan/UNRISD).

Dujovne, N. (2011) Banco Galicia, 12 June, Buenos Aires.

Economist, The (20 December 2005) 'Kirchner and Lula: Different Ways to Give the Fund the Kiss Off'.

Economist, The (21 August 2008) 'Clouds Gather Again over the Pampas'.

Economist, The (23 October 2008) 'Cristina's Looking Glass World'.

Economist, The (24 June 2010) 'Special Report: Repent at Leisure'.

Economist, The (18 September 2010) 'Are We There Yet?'

Economist, The (9 October 2010) 'Special Report: How to Grow'.

Economist, The (19 February 2011) 'How Tough Will Dilma Be?'

Economist, The (9 April 2011) 'The Pacific Players go to Market'.

Economist, The (30 April 2011) 'What's Wrong With America's Economy?'

Economist, The (4 June 2011) 'Too Hot'.

Economist, The (18 June 2011) 'Sticky Patch or Meltdown?'

Economist, The (11 September 2011) 'So Near and Yet So Far: A Special Report on Latin America'.

Edwards, S. (2010) *Left Behind: Latin America and the False Promise of Populism* (Chicago: University of Chicago Press).

Eggertsson, T. (1990) *Economic Behaviour and Institutions* (Cambridge: Cambridge University Press).

EIU (2007) Country Profile: Argentina, www.eiu.com. (accessed on 12 December 2007).

Ellison, N. (2006) *The Transformation of Welfare States* (London: Routledge).

Esping-Andersen, G. (1990) *The Three Worlds of Welfare Capitalism* (London: Polity Press).

Etchemendy, S. and Collier, R. B. (2007) 'Down But Not Out: Union Resurgence and Segmented Neocorporatism in Argentina (2003–2007)', *Politics and Society*, 35(3), 363–401.

Evangelist, M. and Sathe, V. (2006) 'Brazil's 1998–1999 Currency Crisis', Unpublished manuscript.

Evans, P. (1987) 'Class, State, and Dependence in East Asia: Lessons for Latin Americanists', in F. C. Deyo (ed.) *The Political Economy of New Asian Industrialism*, 203–26 (London: Cornell University Press).

Evans, P. (1995) *Embedded Autonomy: States and Industrial Transformation* (Chichester: Princeton University Press).

Fanon, F. (1963) *The Wretched of the Earth* (New York: Grove Press).

Feldstein, M. S. (2002) 'Economic and Financial Crises in Emerging Market Economies: Overview of Prevention and Management', *NBER Working Paper No. W8837*: *National Bureau of Economic Research (NBER)*.

Fenwick, T. B. (2009) 'Avoiding Governors: The Success of Bolsa Família', *Latin American Research Review*, 44(1), 102–31.

Ferrer, A. (2005) *La economía Argentina* (Buenos Aires: Fondo).

Ffrench-Davis, R. and Reisen, H. (1998) *Capital Flows and Investment Performance: Lessons from Latin America* (Paris: ECLAC).

Filippini, M. (2002) *'La protesta social an Argentina durante diciembre del 2001'* (Buenos Aires: CELS).

Fine, B. (1997) 'State, Development and Inequality: The Curious Incident of the Developmental State in the Night-Time', Paper to Sanpad Conference, Durban, June 26–30.

Finkman, J. (2007) HSBC Chief Economist, Argentina, 9 May, Buenos Aires.

Fitzpatrick, T. (2001) *Welfare Theory* (Basingstoke: Palgrave Macmillan).

Fleming, M. J. (1962) 'Domestic Financial Policies under Fixed and Floating Exchange Rates', *IMF Staff Papers*, 9, 369–79.

Flynn, P. (2005) 'Brazil and Lula, 2005: Crisis, Corruption and Change in Political Perspective', *Third World Quarterly*, 26(8), 1221–67.

Fortes, A. (2009) 'In Search of a Post-Neoliberal Paradigm: The Brazilian Left and Lula's Government', *International Labour and Working Class History*, 75(1), 109–25.

Frank, A. (1966) 'The Development of Underdevelopment', *Monthly Review*, 18(4), 17–31.

Frankel, J. (2004) 'Experience of and Lessons from Exchange Rate Regimes in Emerging Economies', in Asian Development Bank (ed.) *Monetary and Financial Integration in East Asia: The Way Ahead*, 91–138 (New York: Palgrave Macmillan).

Frenkel, R. and Rapetti, M. (2006) 'Monetary and Exchange Rate Policies in Argentina after the Convertibility Regime Collapse', *Nuevos Documentos: CEDES*, 20.

Frenkel, R. and Rapetti, M. (2008) 'Five Years of Competitive and Stable Real Exchange Rate in Argentina 2002–2007'. *International Review of Applied Economics*, 22(2), 215–26.

Friedman, M. (1962) *Capitalism and Freedom* (Chicago: Chicago University Press).

Gamble, A. (1996) *Hayek: The Iron Cage of Liberty* (London: Polity Press).

Gamble, A. (2009) *The Spectre at the Feast: Capitalist Crisis and the Politics of Recession* (Basingstoke: Palgrave Macmillan).

Gambini, H. (2007) *Historia del Peronismo: El Poder total (1943–1951)* (Vergara: Buenos Aires).

García-Sayán, D. (2009) 'Crisis económica global: impactos económicos y politi-cos en América Latina', *Nueva Sociedad*, (223), Septiembre–Octubre.

Gerchunoff, P. and Aguirre, H. (2004) *La política economía de Kirchner en la Argentina: varios estilos, una sola agenda*, DT No. 35/200 (Madrid: Real Instituto Elcano).

Gerassi, J. (1963) *The Great Fear: The Reconquest of Latin America by Latin Americans* (New York: Macmillan).

Gereffi, G. (1992) 'New Realities of Industrial Development in East Asia and Latin America: Global, Regional, and National Trends', in R. Appelbaum and J. Henderson (eds) *States and Development in the Asia Pacific Rim*, 85–111 (London: Sage Publications).

Gerschenkron, A. (1962) *Economic Backwardness in Historical Perspective* (Chicago: University of Chicago Press).

Ghemawat, P. and Ricart, J. E. (1993) 'The Organisational Tension Between Static and Dynamic Efficiency', *Strategic Management Journal*, 14, Winter, 59–73.

Giddens, A. (1990) *The Consequences of Modernity* (Cambridge: Polity Press).

Godio, J. (2006) *El tiempo de Kirchner: El devenir de una 'revolución arriba'* (Buenos Aires: Letra Grifa).

Goldstein, A. (2007) *Multinational Companies from Emerging Economies* (London: Palgrave Macmillan).

Gough, I. and Olofsson, G. (1999) 'New Thinking on Exclusion and Integration', in I. Gough and G. Olofsson (eds) *Capitalism and Social Cohesion: Essays on Exclusion and Integration* (Basingstoke: Palgrave Macmillan).

Green, D. (2003) *Silent Revolution: The Rise and Crisis of Market Economics in Latin America* (Second edition) (London: Latin America Bureau).

Grugel, J. (2009) '"Basta de Realidades, Queremos Promesas": Democracy after the Washington Consensus', in J. Grugel and P. Riggirozzi (eds) *Governance after Neoliberalism in Latin America*, 25–49 (New York: Palgrave Macmillan).

Grugel, J. and Riggirozzi, P. (2007) 'The Return of the State in Argentina', *International Affairs*, 83(1), 87–107.

Grugel, J. and Riggirozzi, P. (2009) 'The End of the Embrace? Neoliberalism and Alternatives to Neoliberalism in Latin America', in J. Grugel and P. Riggirozzi (eds) *Governance after Neoliberalism in Latin America*, 1–24 (New York: Palgrave Macmillan).

Grugel, J., Riggirozzi, P., and Thirkell-White, B. (2008) 'Beyond the Washington Consensus? Asia and Latin America in Search of More Autonomous Development', *International Affairs*, 84(3), 499–517.

Gwynne, R. N. and Kay, C. (1999) *Latin America Transformed: Globalisation and Modernity* (New York: Oxford University Press).

Haddad, M. A. (2008) 'Bolsa Família and the Needy: Is Allocation Contributing to Equity in Brazil?' *Journal of International Development*, 20(5), 654–69.

Haggard, S. (1990) *Pathways from the Periphery: The Politics of Growth in the Newly Industrialising Countries* (London: Cornell University Press).

Haggard, S. and Kaufman, R. (1992) *The Politics of Economic Adjustment* (Princeton NJ: Princeton University Press).

Hall, A. (2006) 'From *Fome Zero* to *Bolsa Familia*: Social Policies and Poverty Alleviation under Lula', *Journal of Latin American Studies*, 38(4), 689–709.

Hall, A. (2008) 'Brazil's Bolsa Família: A Double-Edged Sword?' *Development and Change*, 39(5), 799–822.

Harlen, C. M. (1999) 'A Reappraisal of Classical Economic Nationalism and Economic Liberalism', *International Studies Quarterly*, 43(4), 733–44.

Haselip, J. and Potter, C. (2010) 'Post-Neoliberal Electricity Market "Re-Reforms" in Argentina: Diverging from Market Prescriptions?' *Energy Policy*, 38(2), 1168–76.

Hayek, F. (1944) *The Road to Serfdom* (Chicago: University of Chicago Press).

Heidrich, P. (2005) 'Argentina buscando una salida: Kirchner, el FMI y la renegociación de la deuda externa', *Chronique des Amériques*, (21), 1–8.

Heidrich, P. (2007) FLACSO, 10 April, Buenos Aires.

Heidrich, P. and Tussie, D. (2009) 'Post-Neoliberalism and the New Left in the Americas', in L. Macdonald and A. Ruckert (eds) *Post-Neoliberalism in the Americas*, 37–53 (Basingstoke: Palgrave Macmillan).

Held, D. (2000) 'Regulating Globalisation?' in D. Held and A. McGrew (eds) *The Global Transformations Reader*, 514–29, (Oxford: Blackwell).

Heymann, D. (2006) 'Buscando la tendencia: Crisis macroeconómica y recuperación en la Argentina', *Estudios y Perspectivas*, No. 31, CEPAL.

Heymann, D. (2007) CEPAL, 22 May, Buenos Aires.

Heymann, D., Galiani, S., Dabus, C., and Tohmé, F. (2006) 'Two Essays on Development Economics', *Estudios y Perspectivas*, No. 34.

Hira, A. (2007) *An East Asian Model for Latin American Success: The New Path* (Hampshire: Ashgate).

Hiroi, T. (2009) 'Exchange Rate Regime, Central Bank Independence, and Political Business Cycles in Brazil', *Studies in Comparative International Development*, 44(1), 1–22.

Hirst, P. and Thompson, G. (1999) *Globalisation in Question* (Second edition) (Cambridge: Polity Press).

Hobbes, T. (1996 [1651]) *Leviathan* (Cambridge: Cambridge University Press).

Hunter, W. and Power, T. J. (2007) 'Rewarding Lula: Executive Power, Social Policy, and the Brazilian Elections of 2006', *Latin American Politics and Society*, 49(1), 1–30.

Hunter, W. and Sugiyama, N. B. (2009) 'Democracy and Social Policy in Brazil: Advancing Basic Needs, Preserving Privileged Interests', *Latin American Politics and Society*, 51(2), 29–5.

Humphrey, J. (1979) 'Auto Workers and the Working Class in Brazil', *Latin American Perspectives*, 6(4), 71–89.

IDB (2006) *The Politics of Policies: Economic and Social Progress in Latin America – 2006 Report* (Washington, DC: ADB).

IDB (2009) 'Social and Labour Market Policies for Tumultuous Times: Confronting the Global Crisis in Latin America and the Caribbean', Paper presented at the Annual Meeting at the Board of Governors in Medellin, Colombia, March.

IMF (2010) 'World Economic Outlook: Recovery, Risk, and Rebalancing', *World Economic and Financial Surveys*, October.

IMF (2011a) 'World Economic Outlook: Tensions from the Two-Speed Recovery – Unemployment, Commodities, and Capital Flows', *World Economic and Financial Surveys*, April.

IMF (2011b) Commodities Data, www.imf.org (accessed on 16 February 2007).

INDEC (2007) *Anuario Estadístico de la Republica Argentina: 2007* (Buenos Aires: INDEC).

Interview with Carrera, J. (2007) Professor of Economics UBA and Deputy Head of Economic Research BCRA, 13 March, Buenos Aires.

Interview with Finkman HSBC Chief Economist, Argentina, 9 May, Buenos Aires.

Interview with Heidrich FLACSO, 10 April, Buenos Aires.

Interview with Heymann CEPAL, 22 May, Buenos Aires.

Interview with Mendez Bloque Desde Abajo, 2 April, Buenos Aires.

Interview with Tussie FLACSO, 15 April, Buenos Aires.

Jara, A., Moreno, R., and Tovar, C. E. (2009) 'The Global Crisis and Latin America: Financial Impact and Policy Responses', *BIS Quarterly Review*, June.

Jenkins, R. (1984) *Trans-National Companies and Industrial Transformation in Latin America* (London: Macmillan).

Jenkins, R. (1991) 'The Political Economy of Industrialisation: A Comparison of Latin American and East Asian Industrialising Countries', *Development and Change*, 22(2), 197–231.

Johnson, C. (1982) *MITI and the Japanese Miracle* (Stanford: Stanford University Press).

Johnson, C. (1987) 'Political Institutions and Economic Performance: The Government-Business Relationship', in F. C. Deyo (ed.) *The Political Economy of New Asian Industrialism*, 73–89 (Ithaca: Cornell University Press).

Karagiannis, N. and Madjd-Sadjadi, Z. (2007) *Modern State Intervention in the Era of Globalisation* (Cheltenham: Edward Elgar).

Kaufman, R. R. and Stallings, B. (1991) 'The Political Economy of Latin American Populism', in R. Dornbusch and S. Edwards (eds) *The Macroeconomics of Populism in Latin America* (London: University of Chicago Press).

Kay, C. (1989) *Latin American Theories of Development and Underdevelopment* (London: Routledge).

Kenmore, A. and Weeks, G. (2011) 'Twenty-First Century Socialism? The Elusive Search for a Post-Neoliberal Development Model in Bolivia and Ecuador', *Bulletin of Latin American Research*, 30(3), 267–81.

Keynes, J. M. (1936) *The General Theory of Employment, Interest, and Money* (London: Macmillan).

Kingstone, P. (2011) *The Political Economy of Latin America* (New York: Routledge).

Kingstone, P. and Ponce, A. (2010) 'From Cardoso to Lula: The Triumph of Pragmatism in Brazil', in K. Weyland, R. Madrid and W. Hunter (eds) *Leftist Governments in Latin America: Successes and Shortcomings*, 98–123 (Cambridge: Cambridge University Press).

Kirby, P. (2003) *Introduction to Latin America: Twenty-First Century Challenges* (London: Sage).

Kirby, P. (2010a) 'Probing the Significance of Latin America's Left Tide', *European Review of Latin American and Caribbean Studies*, 89, October. 127–34.

Kirby, P. (2010b) 'Globalisation and State–Civil Society Relationships: Lessons from Latin America', Paper presented at the ECPR Joint Session of Workshops, Muenster.

Koo, H. (1987) 'The Interplay of State, Social Class, and World System in East Asian Development: The Cases of South Korea and Taiwan', in F. C. Deyo (ed.) *The Political Economy of New Asian Industrialism*, 165–79 (Ithaca: Cornell University Press).

Kosacoff, B. (2008) 'Development of Technological Capabilities in an Extremely Volatile Economy. The Industrial Sector in Argentina', *Estudios y Perspectivas*, Vol. 40.

Kothari, U. (2005) 'A Radical History of Development Studies: Individuals, Institutions and ideologies', in U. Kothari (ed.) *A Radical History of Development Studies*, 1–14 (London: Zed Books).

Krasner, S. D. (1983) *International Regimes* (Ithaca, NY: Cornell University Press).

Krasner, S. D. (1982a) 'Structural Causes and Regime Consequences: Regimes as Intervening Variables', *International Organization*, 36(1), 185–205.

Krasner, S. D. (1982b) 'Regimes and the Limits of Realism: Regimes as Autonomous Variables', *International Organization*, 36(1), 497–510.

Krueger, A. (1974). 'The Political Economy of the Rent-Seeking Society', *American Economic Review*, 64(3), 291–303.

Krugman, P. (1996) 'What Economists can Learn from Evolutionary Theorists', Paper presented to the European Association for Evolutionary Political Economy, November.

Laclau, E. (1977) *Politics and Ideology in Marxist Theory: Capitalism, Fascism, and Populism* (Thetford: Lowe and Brydone).

Lapavitsas, C. (2005) 'Mainstream Economics in the Neoliberal Era', in A. Saad-Filho and D. Johnston (eds) *Neoliberalism: A Critical Reader*, 30–40 (London: Pluto).

Leiva, F. I. (2008) 'Towards a Critique of Latin American Neostructuralism', *Latin American Politics and Society*, 50(4), 1–25.

Levy, M. L. (2004) *We are Millions: Neo-Liberalism and New Forms of Political Action in Argentina* (London: Latin American Bureau).

Lievesley, G. and Ludlam, S. (2009a) 'Introduction: A "Pink Tide"?', in G. Lievesley and S. Ludlam (eds) *Reclaiming Latin America: Experiments in Radical Social Democracy*, 1–18 (London: Zed).

Lievesley, G. and Ludlam, S. (2009b) 'Conclusion: *Nuestra América* – The Spectre Haunting Washington', in G. Lievesley and S. Ludlam (eds) *Reclaiming Latin America: Experiments in Radical Social Democracy*, 217–29 (London: Zed).

Linz, J. J. (1973) 'Opposition In and Under an Authoritarian Regime: The Case of Spain', in R. A. Dahl (ed.) *Regimes and Oppositions,* 171–259 (New Haven, CT.: Yale University Press).

Linz, J. J. (2000) *Totalitarian and Authoritarian Regimes* (Second edition) (Boulder, CO: Lynne Reinner).

List, F. (1983 [1841]) *The National System of Political Economy*, W. O. Henderson (trans. and ed.) (London: Cass).

Llaudes, R., Salman, F. and Chivakul, M. (2010) 'The Impact of the Great Recession on Emerging Markets', IMF Working Paper WP10/237.

Lora, E. and Pagés, C. (2011) 'Face-to-Face with Productivity', *Finance and Development*, March.

Lowenthal, A. (2007) 'Argentina: Weak Institutions Keep a Good Country Down', *New Perspectives Quarterly*, 23(4), 42–56.

Luckham, R. (2002) 'Are there Alternatives to Liberal Democracy?' in M. Robinson and G. White (eds) *The Democratic Developmental State: Politics and Institutional Design*, 306–342 (Oxford: Oxford University Press).

Lynch, N. (2007) 'What the "Left" Means in Latin America Now', *Constellations*, 14(3), 373–83.

MacDonald, L. and Ruckert, A. (2009) 'Post-Neoliberalism in the Americas: An Introduction', in L. MacDonald and A. Ruckert (eds) *Post-Neoliberalism in the Americas*, 1–20 (Basingstoke: Palgrave Macmillan).

MacGregor, S. (2005) 'The Welfare State and Neoliberalism', in A. Saad-Filho and D. Johnstone (eds) *Neoliberalism: A Critical Reader*, 142–8 (London: Pluto).

MacIntyre, A., Pempel, T. J., and Ravenhill, J. (2008) 'East Asia in the Wake of the Financial Crisis', in A. MacIntyre, T. J. Pempel, and J. Ravenhill (eds) *Crisis as Catalyst: Asia's Dynamic Political Economy*, 1–25 (Cornell: Cornell University Press).

Madrid, R., Hunter, W., and Weyland, K. (2010) 'The Policies and Performance of the Contestatory and Moderate Left', in K. Weyland, R. Madrid, and W. Hunter (eds) *Leftist Governments in Latin America: Successes and Shortcomings*, 140–80 (Cambridge: Cambridge University Press).

Marx, K. (1967 [1848]) *The Communist Manifesto* (London: Penguin).

McPherson, M. S. (1984) 'Limits of Self-Seeking: The Role of Morality in Economic Life', in D. Colander (ed.) *Neoclassical Political Economy*, 71–85 (Cambridge, MA: Ballinger Publishing).

Meltzer, A. H. (2000) 'International Financial Institution Advisory Commission', *Report of the International Financial Institution Advisory Commission* (Washington, DC: No publisher specified).

Mendez, A. (2007) Bloque Desde Abajo, 2 April, Buenos Aires.

Menezes, H. Z. (2011) 'Again, Industrial Policy as an International Issue: The Brazilian Experience under Lula's Government', Paper presented at the ISA Annual Convention, Montreal, 16–19 March.

Mercado, P. R. (2007) 'The Argentine Recovery: Some Features and Challenges', *VRP Working Paper: LLILAS*.

Ministry of Economy and Production (2009) *Argentine Economic Indicators*, http://www.mecon.gov.ar (accessed on 12 November 2009).

Mollo, M. L. R. and Saad-Filho, A. (2006) 'Neoliberal Economic Policies in Brazil (1994–2005): Cardoso, Lula and the Need for a Democratic Alternative', *New Political Economy*, 11(1), 99–123.

Montero, A. P. (2005) *Brazilian Politics* (Cambridge: Polity).

Morais, L. and Saad-Filho, A. (2003) 'Snatching Defeat from the Jaws of Victory? Lula, the "Losers Alliance", and the Prospects for Change in Brazil', *Capital and Class*, Issue 81, 17–23.

Munck, R. (2003) *Contemporary Latin America* (Basingstoke: Palgrave Macmillan).

Munck, R. (2005) 'Neoliberalism and Politics, and the Politics of Neoliberalism', in A. Saad-Filho and D. Johnstone (eds) *Neoliberalism: A Critical Reader,* 60–69 (London: Pluto).

Munck, R. (2009) 'Democracy and Development in a Globalised World: Thinking About Latin America from Within', *Studies in Comparative International Development*, 44(4), 337–58.

Neto, A. F. C. and Vernengo, M. (2007) 'Lula's Social Policies: New Wine in Old Bottles?' in P. Arestis and A. Saad-Filho (eds) *Political Economy of Brazil: Recent Economic Performance*, 73–93 (Basingstoke: Palgrave Macmillan).

North, D. (1981) *Structure and Change in Economic History* (New York: W. W. Norton and Company, Inc.).

Nun, J. (1969) 'Superpoblación relativa, ejercito industrial de reserva y masa marginal', *Revista Latinoamericana de Sociologia*, 5(2), 178–236.

Ocampo, J. A. (2009a) Latin America and the Global Financial Crisis, *Cambridge Journal of Economics*, 33(4), 703–24.

Ocampo, J. A. (2009b) Impactos de la crisis financeria mundial, *Revista CEPAL*, 97, April, 9–32.

Obstfeld, M. and Rogoff, K. (1995) 'Mirage of Fixed Exchange Rates', *Journal of Economic Perspectives*, 9, Fall, 73–96.

O'Donnell, G. (1973) *Modernisation and Bureaucratic Authoritarianism* (Berkeley: Institute of International Studies).

Ohmae, K. (1995) *The End of the Nation State* (London: HarperCollins).

Ortiz, R. and Schorr, M. (2009) 'Crisis internacional y alternativas de reindustrialización en la Argentina', Documentos de Investigación Social, *IDAES*, Número 7.

Ougaard, M. and Higgott, R. (2002) *Towards a Global Polity* (London: Routledge).

Öniş, Z. (1991) 'Review: The Logic of the Developmental State', *Comparative Politics*, 24(1), 109–26.

PAC (2010) 'Crescimento do País', www.brasil.gov.br/pac (accessed on 9 Febuary 2010).

Palan, R. (2000) 'New Trends in Global Political Economy', in R. Palan (ed.) *Global Political Economy: Contemporary Theories*, 1–18 (London: Routledge).

Palley, T. I. (2005) 'From Keynesian to Neoliberalism: Shifting Paradigms in Economics', in A. Saad-Filho and D. Johnstone (eds) *Neoliberalism: A Critical Reader*, 20–9 (London: Pluto).

Paulani, L. M. (2007) 'The Real Meaning of the Economic Policy of Lula's Government', in P. Arestis and A. Saad-Filho (eds) *Political Economy of Brazil: Recent Economic Performance*, 42–54 (Basingstoke: Palgrave Macmillan).

Paus, E. (2009) 'The Rise of China: Implications for Latin American Development', *Development Policy Review*, 27(4), 419–56.

Panizza, F. (2005) 'Unarmed Utopia Revisited: The Resurgence of Left-of-Centre Politics in Latin America', *Political Studies*, 53(4), 716–34.

Panizza, F. (2009) *Contemporary Latin America: Development and Democracy beyond the Washington Consensus* (London: Zed).

Pearson, R. (1985) 'Technology Transfer and Technological Dependency: A Case Study of the Argentine Cement Industry 1875–1975', *Monographs in Development Studies – UEA*, No. 12.

Pempel, T. J. (1998) *Regime Shift: Comparative Dynamics of the Japanese Political Economy* (London: Cornell University Press).

Pempel, T. J. (1999) 'The Developmental Regime in a Changing World Economy', in M. Woo-Cumings (ed.) *The Developmental State*, 137–81 (New York: Cornell Paperbacks).

Pereira, L. C. B. (2010) *Globalisation and Competition: Why Some Emergent Countries Succeed While Others Fall Behind* (Cambridge: Cambridge University Press).

Perry, G. and Serven, L. (2003) 'The Anatomy of a Multiple Crisis: Why Was Argentina Special and What Can We Learn From it?' *World Bank Policy Research Working Paper*, 3081.

Petras, J. (2006) 'Centre–Left Regimes in Latin America: History Repeating Itself as Farce?' *Journal of Peasant Studies*, 33(2), 278–303.

Petras, J. (2007) 'Latin America: Four Competing Blocs of Power', James Petras Website, www.countercurrents.org. (accessed on 10 Febuary 2010).

Petras, J. (2009) 'Crisis in Latin America', *Latin American Perspectives*, 26(4), 192–213.

Petras, J. and Veltmeyer, H. (2009) *What's Left in Latin America? Regime Change in New Times* (Surrey: Ashgate).

Pieterse, J. N. (2000) 'Trends in Development Theory', in R. Palan (ed.) *Global Political Economy: Contemporary Theories*, 197–214 (London: Routledge).

Polanyi, K. (1944) *The Great Transformation* (Boston: Beacon Press).

Porta, F. (2005) 'Especialización productiva e inserción internacional. Evidencias y reflexiones sobre el caso argentine', *PNUD*, Project FO/ARG/05/012.

Portantiero, J. C. (1989) 'Political and Economic Crisis in Argentina', in G. Di Tella and R. Dornbusch (eds) *The Political Economy of Argentina, 1946–83*, 16–31 (Hampshire: Macmillan).

Porzecanski, A. (2010) 'Should Argentina be Welcomed Back?' Paper presented at a special EMTA Seminar on 'Argentina: Pros and Cons', held at EMTA's New York offices on 5 November.

Porzecanski, A. C. (2009) 'Latin America: the Missing Financial Crisis', *Estudios y Perspectivas*, No. 6, October.

Prebisch, R. (1950) *The Economic Development of Latin America and its Principal Problems* (New York: Columbia University Press).

Quijano, A. (1973) 'Redefinición de la dependencia y proceso de marginalización en America Latina', in F. Weffort and A. Quijano (eds) *Populismo, Marginalización y Dependencia,* 171–329 (San Jose, Costa Rica: Editorial Universitaria Centroamericana).

Radice, H. (2008) 'The Developmental State Under Global Neoliberalism, *Third World Quarterly,* 29(6), 1153–74.

Radice, H. (2011) 'Confronting the Crisis: A Class Analysis', *Socialist Register,* 47, 21–43.

Rapley, J. (2008) *Understanding Development: Theory and Practice in the Third World* (London: Lynne Rienner Publishers).

Rawlings, L. (2004) *A New Approach to Social Assistance: Latin America's Experience with Conditional Cash Transfer Programs* (Washington, DC: World Bank).

Redrado, M. (19 March 2008) 'On Argentina's Monetary Policy', *Letter to the Economist.*

Richardson, G. B. (1972) 'The Organisation of Industry', *Economic Journal,* 82(3), 883–96.

Riggirozzi, P. (2008) 'Argentina: State Capacity and Leverage in External Negotiations', in J. Robertson (ed.) *Power and Politics after Financial Crises: Rethinking Foreign Opportunism in Emerging Markets,* 125–43 (Basingstoke: Palgrave Macmillan).

Riggirozzi, P. (2009) 'After Neoliberalism in Argentina: Reasserting Nationalism in an Open Economy', in J. Grugel and P. Riggirozzi (eds) *Governance after Neoliberalism in Latin America,* 89–113 (New York: Palgrave Macmillan).

Riesco, M. (2009) 'Latin America: A New Developmental Welfare State Model in the Making?' *International Journal of Social Welfare,* 18(1), 22–36.

Roberts, K. (2007) 'Latin America's Populist Revival', *SAIS Review,* 27(1), 3–15.

Robertson, J. (2008a) 'Introduction: Key Theoretical Divides and Directions', in J. Robertson (ed.) *Power and Politics after Financial Crises: Rethinking Foreign Opportunism in Emerging Markets,* 1–30 (Basingstoke: Palgrave Macmillan).

Robertson, J. (2008b) 'Conclusion: Contesting the Return to State-Led Economies', in J. Robertson (ed.) *Power and Politics after Financial Crises: Rethinking Foreign Opportunism in Emerging Markets,* 252–60 (Basingstoke: Palgrave Macmillan).

Robinson, L. (1932) *Essay on the Nature and Significance of Economic Science* (London: Macmillan and Co.).

Robinson, W. (2004) 'Global Crisis and Latin America', *Bulletin of Latin American Research,* 23(2), 135–53.

Robinson, M. and White, G. (2002) *The Democratic Developmental State* (Oxford: Oxford University Press).

Rock, D. (2002) 'Arruinar Argentina', *New Left Review,* 17, September/October, 53–85.

Roxborough, I. (1992) 'Inflation and Social Pacts in Brazil and Mexico', *Journal of Latin American Studies,* 24(3), 639–64.

Rupert, M. (1993) 'Alienation, Capitalism, and the Inter-State System: Towards a Marxian/Gramscian Critique', in S. Gill (ed.), *Gramsci, Historical Materialism and International Relations,* 67–92 (Cambridge: Cambridge University Press).

Saad-Filho, A. (2005) 'The Political Economy of Neoliberalism in Latin America', in A. Saad-Filho and D. Johnstone (eds) *Neoliberalism: A Critical Reader*, 222–9 (London: Pluto).

Saad-Filho, A. (2007) 'Neoliberalism, Democracy and Economic Policy in Brazil', in P. Arestis and A. Saad-Filho (eds) *Political Economy of Brazil: Recent Economic Performance*, 7–23 (Basingstoke: Palgrave Macmillan).

Saad-Filho, A., Iamini, F., and Molinari, E. J. (2007) 'Neoliberalism, Democracy, and Economic Policy in Latin America', in P. Arestis and M. Sawyer (eds) *Political Economy of Latin America: Recent Economic Performance*, 1–35 (Basingstoke: Palgrave Macmillan).

Santarcángelo, J. E., Fal, J., and Pinazo, G. (2011) 'Los motores del crecimiento economic en la Argentina: rupturas y continuidades', *Investigación económica*, LXX(275), 93–114.

Santiso, J. (2006) *Latin America's Political Economy of the Possible: Beyond Good Revolutionaries and Free Marketeers* (Cambridge, MS and London: MIT Press).

Schumpeter, J. (1942) *Capitalism, Socialism, and Democracy* (New York: Harper and Bros).

Schweinheim, G. F. F. (2003) '¿Podria una institucionalidad administrativa republicana contribuir a la transción politica después de una crisis? Lecciones de la República Argentina', *Reforma y Democratica: Revista del CLAD*, 27.

Segura-Ubiergo, A. (2007) *The Political Economy of the Welfare State in Latin America: Globalisation, Democracy, and Development* (Washington, DC: IMF).

Senghaas, D. (1979) 'Dissociation as a Development Strategy', *Security Dialogue*, 10(2), 192–6.

Shaikh, A. (2005) 'The Economic Mythology of Neoliberalism', in A. Saad-Filho and D. Johnstone (eds) *Neoliberalism: A Critical Reader*, 41–9 (London: Pluto).

Simon, H. A. (1983) *Reason in Human Affairs* (Oxford: Basil Blackwell).

Sklar, R. L. (1996) 'Towards a Theory of Developmental Democracy', in A. Leftwich (ed.) *Democracy and Development: Theory and Practice*, 25–44 (Cambridge: Polity Press).

Skocpol, T. (1985) 'Bringing the State Back In: Strategies of Analysis in Current Research', in P. Evans, D. Ruescheneyer, and T. Skocpol (eds) *Bringing the State Back In*, 3–43 (Cambridge: Cambridge University Press).

Smith, A. (1974 [1776]) *The Wealth of Nations* (Books I–IV), A. Smith (ed.) (Harmondsworth: Penguin Books).

Smith, W. C. (1991) 'State, Market, and Neoliberalism in Post-Transition Argentina: The Menem Experiment', *Journal of InterAmerican Studies and World Affairs*, 33(4), 45–82.

So, A. Y. (1990) *Social Change and Development: Modernisation, Dependency, and World-System Theories* (London: Sage).

Sobreira, R. and Gaya, P. (2005) 'Fixed Income Debt Management and Uncertainty in the Lula Administration, 2002–2005', in P. Arestis and A. Saad-Filho (eds) *Political Economy of Brazil: Recent Economic Performance*, 194–216 (Basingstoke: Palgrave Macmillan).

Soederberg, S. (2005) 'The Rise of Neoliberalism in Mexico: From a Developmental to a Competition State', in S. Soedeberg, G. Menz, and P. G. Cerny (eds) *Internalising Globalisation: The Rise of Neoliberalism and the Decline of National Varieties of Capitalism*, 167–82 (Basingstoke: Palgrave Macmillan).

Sola, L. (2008) 'Politics, Markets, and Society in Lula's Brazil', *Journal of Democracy*, 19(2), 31–45.

Sørensen, G. (1991) *Democracy, Dictatorship, and Development: Development in Selected Regimes in the Third World* (London: Macmillan).

Sotero, P. (2010) 'Brazil's Rising Ambition in a Shifting Global Balance of Power', *Politics*, 30(1), 71–81.

Sotero, P. and Armijo, E. (2007) 'Brazil: To Be Or Not To Be A BRIC', *Asian Perspective*, 31(4), 43–70.

Stigler, G. (1971) 'The Theory of Economic Regulation', *Bell Journal of Economics*, 2(1), 3–21.

Stiglitz, J. (1988) *Principal and Agent* (Princeton NJ: Princeton University Press).

Stiglitz, J. (2002) *Globalisation and its Discontents* (London: Penguin Books).

Stokes, S. C. (2001) *Mandates and Democracy: Neoliberalism by Surprise in Latin America* (Cambridge: Cambridge University Press).

Sunkel, O. (1973) 'Transnational Capitalism and National Disintegration in Latin America', *Social and Economic Studies*, 22(1), 132–76.

Svampa, M. (2008) 'The End of Kirchnerism', *New Left Review*, 53 (September–October), 79–95.

Tavolaro, S. B. F. and Tavolaro, G. M. (2007) 'Accounting for Lula's Second-Term Electoral Victory: "Leftism" Without a Leftist Project?' *Constellations*, 14(3), 426–44.

Tedesco, L. (2002) 'Argentina's Turmoil: The Politics of Informality and the Roots of Economic Meltdown', *Cambridge Review of International Affairs*, 15(3), 469–81.

Teixeira, A. (2007) 'An Industrial Policy for Brazil', ABDI, www.abdi.com.br (accessed on 15 Febuary 2010).

Thirlwall, A. P. (2008) *Growth and Development* (Eighth edition) (London: Palgrave Macmillan).

Thomas, A. (2004) 'The Study of Development', Paper presented for session on the Concept of Development Studies, Development Studies Association Conference, London.

Torre, J. C. and Riz, L. (1991) 'Argentina since 1946', in L. Bethell (ed.) *The Cambridge History of Latin America Vol. VIII*, 73–195 (Cambridge: Cambridge University Press).

Tresca, G. (2005) *El collapso de la convertibilidad y el Nuevo modelo de desarrollo argentino* (Buenos Aires: Ateneo).

Tussie, D. (2007) FLACSO, 15 April, Buenos Aires.

Tussie, D. (2009) 'Economic Governance after Neoliberalism', in J. Grugel and P. Riggirozzi (eds) *Governance after Neoliberalism in Latin America*, 67–89 (New York: Palgrave Macmillan).

UNDP (2002) *HDR – Deepening Democracy in a Fragmented World*, http://hdr.undp.org (accessed on 20 February 2010).

UNDP (2005) *HDR – International Cooperation at a Crossroads: Aid, Trade and Security in an Unequal World*, http://hdr.undp.org (accessed on 20 February 2010).

UNDP (2006) *HDR – Beyond Scarcity: Power, Poverty, and the Global Water Crisis*, http://hdr.undp.org (accessed on 20 February 2010).

UNDP (2007–8) *HDR – Fighting Climate Change: Human Solidarity in a Divided World*, http://hdr.undp.org (accessed on 20 February 2010).

Valadão, M. A. P. and Gico, I. T. Jr (2009) 'The (Not So) Great Depression of the 21st Century and Its Impact on Brazil', Universidade Católica de Brasília, Working Paper No. 0002/09.

Vellacott, C. (2006) 'Institutions and Economic Stabilisations in Argentina and Spain 1958–59: The Political Economy of Reform in Crony Capitalist Systems', Paper presented at Economic History Society Annual Conference, University of Reading.

Vidotto, C. and Sicsú, J. (2007) 'The Interest Rate During the Lula Government: A Research Agenda', in P. Arestis and A. Saad-Filho (eds) *Political Economy of Brazil: Recent Economic Performance*, 180–93 (Basingstoke: Palgrave Macmillan).

Vogel, S. K. and Barma, N. H. (2008) *The Political Economy Reader* (New York: Routledge).

Wade, R. (1990) *Governing the Market: Economic Theory and the Role of Government in East Asian Industrialisation* (Princeton: Princeton University Press).

Wallerstein, I. (1983) *Historical Capitalism* (London: Verso).

Weiss, L. and Hobson, J. M. (1995) *States and Economic Development: A Comparative Historical Analysis* (Cambridge: Polity Press).

Weiss, L. (2003) *States in the Global Economy: Bringing Domestic Institutions Back In* (Cambridge: Cambridge University Press).

Weyland, K. (1999) 'Neoliberal Populism in Latin America and Eastern Europe', *Comparative Politics*, 31(4), 379–401.

Weyland, K. (2010) 'The Performance of Leftist Governments in Latin America: Conceptual and Theoretical Issues', in K. Weyland, R. Madrid, and W. Hunter (eds) *Leftist Governments in Latin America: Successes and Shortcomings*, 1–28 (Cambridge: Cambridge University Press).

White, G. (1995) 'Towards a Democratic Developmental State', *IDS Bulletin*, 26(2), 27–36.

White, G. (2002) 'Constructing a Democratic Developmental State', in M. Robinson and G. White (eds) *The Democratic Developmental State*, (Oxford: Oxford University Press).

Williams, C. C. (2005) *A Commodified World? Mapping the Limits of Capitalism* (London: Zed Books).

Williamson, J. (1990) *Latin American Adjustment: How Much Has Happened?* (Washington, DC: Institute for International Economics).

Williamson, J. (2004) 'The Years of Emerging Market Crises: A Review of Feldstein', *Journal of Economic Literature*, 42(3), 822–37.

Willett, T. D. (2007) 'Why the Middle is Unstable: The Political Economy of Exchange Rate Regimes and Currency Crises', *The World Economy*, 5(5), 709–32.

Wilson, G. (2003) *Business and Politics: A comparative introduction* (New York: Palgrave).

Wilson, D. and Purushothaman, R. (2003) 'Dreaming with BRICs: The Path to 2050', *Global Economics Paper No. 99, Goldman Sachs*.

Wolff, J. (2005) 'Ambivalent Consequences of Social Exclusion for Real-Existing Democracy in Latin America: The Example of the Argentine Crisis', *Journal of International Relations and Development*, 8(1), 58–87.

World Bank (2001) *WDR 2000/01 – Attacking Poverty: Opportunity, Empowerment, and Security* (Oxford: World Bank).

World Bank (2004) *Global Development Finance: Harnessing Cyclical Gains for Development* (New York: World Bank).

World Bank (2009) *World Development Indicators,* www.worldank.org (accessed on 27 February 2010).

World Bank (2010a) 'Implementation Completion and Results Report: *Bolsa Familia*, IBRD-72340', *Report No. ICR00001486.*

World Bank (2010b) *WDR – Development and Climate Change* (Oxford: World Bank).

Wu, Y. (2008) 'The Role of Institutional Quality in a Currency Crisis Model', *IMF Working Paper*, WP/08/5.

Wylde, C. (2011) 'State, Society, and Markets in Argentina: The Political Economy of *Neodesarrollismo* under Néstor Kirchner, 2003–2007', *Bulletin of Latin American Research*, 30(4), 436–52.

Index